Capilano University Library

PARADISE LOST AT SEA

PARADISE LOST AT SEA

Rethinking Cruise Vacations

Ross A. Klein

Fernwood Publishing • Halifax • Winnipeg

.b Z319044
.0 1279993
70 112612

Editing and text design: Brenda Conroy
Cover design: John van der Woude
Printed and bound in Canada by Hignell Book Printing
Printed on paper containing 100% post-consumer fibre.

Published in Canada by Fernwood Publishing
Site 2A, Box 5, 32 Oceanvista Lane
Black Point, Nova Scotia, B0J 1B0
and #8 - 222 Osborne Street, Winnipeg, Manitoba, R3L 1Z3
www.fernwoodpublishing.ca

Fernwood Publishing Company Limited gratefully acknowledges the financial support
of the Government of Canada through the Book Publishing Industry Development
Program (BPDIP), the Canada Council for the Arts and the Nova Scotia
Department of Tourism and Culture for our publishing program.

Library and Archives Canada Cataloguing in Publication

Klein, Ross A.
Paradise lost at sea: rethinking cruise vacations / Ross Klein.

Includes bibliographical references and index.
ISBN 978-1-55266-276-2

1. Cruise lines--Political aspects. 2. Cruise lines--Economic aspects.
3. Cruise lines--Environmental aspects. I. Title.

G550.K645 2008   387.5'42   C2008-903356-6

Contents

Chapter 1

Cruising in the Twenty-First Century

The idea of a cruise vacation is almost mythic. Our perception of cruises is often based on idyllic images we've seen in movies and on television. Such images usually depict classic ocean liners, which are quite unlike the ships commonly used today. As well as being significantly larger, today's ships are no longer designed primarily for travel but rather are large-scale, water-based resorts.

Despite these significant changes in cruising and the cruise industry over the past fifty years, glamorous images of opulence and "class" have remained relatively intact. These elements frequently underlie the motivation for choosing a cruise vacation. Consumers are buying an image of what they believe a cruise will be—an image more informed by what cruising used to be. Most consumers, for example, still assume a cruise is all inclusive. This is no longer true, and most cruise lines have dropped claims of all inclusiveness from their advertising and brochures. But this may not be obvious to consumers because cruise advertising is purposely abstract and scarce on concrete statements about the cruise or ship itself. Cruise advertising is full of "feel good" messages. Examples include Royal Caribbean's "Get out there" commercials, which highlight activity and adventure, and Carnival's dancing palm trees. These abstract ads leave viewers to focus on whatever is most appealing to them about a cruise vacation.

The cruise industry enjoys an image that is more positive than deserved. This is in part a product of collectively spending more than a billion dollars a year on advertising and public relations. As well as advertising in newspapers, magazines and television, the cruise industry benefits from friendly media coverage of cruise ship events. The industry also spends millions of dollars on lobbying federal and state/provincial governments and on political campaigns at all levels, including local port commissions (see Klein 2005a: 58–85). It effectively promotes itself and its interests and is efficient at countering messages it views as threatening to its clean and responsible image.

This book explores five areas in which industry claims differ from the reality on board cruise ships. We will see how the industry projects messages and images to reassure passengers of the positives of a cruise while displacing or refocusing any problems. Chapter two focuses on the industry's mantra that a cruise vacation is the safest form of transportation. While the cruise industry frequently reinforces the idea that one is safer on a cruise than practically anywhere else, it is faced with problematic rates of sexual assault, has come under scrutiny for passengers missing under suspicious circumstances and has been called to appear four times in three years before a U.S. Congressional subcommittee looking into crimes against U.S. citizens on cruise ships. A careful review of the hearings gives insight into the nature and breadth of the problem. The hearings demonstrate that those planning a cruise need to think realistically about safety and personal security, be forewarned about the limits to their rights on a cruise ship and be aware of the cruise line's limited liability (as stated in the cruise contract, which the passenger accepts by embarking the ship).

Cruise industry environmental practices, explored in chapter three, is the second area explored. The cruise industry actively promotes itself as environmentally responsible and often touts itself as a leader in embracing environmental initiatives. This contrasts starkly with cruise line history, with the industry's current practices and with the results of a study by the U.S. Environmental Protection Agency (EPA), which found that cruise ships routinely discharge effluent that significantly exceed national recommended water quality criteria (EPA 2007).

Recent technological innovations such as advanced wastewater treatment systems (also known as advanced wastewater purification systems) are better than traditional marine sanitation devices, but they have problems. First introduced on cruise ships in 2001, advanced systems have been installed on roughly 40 percent of ships operated by major U.S. cruise lines (at the start of 2008, all thirteen of Norwegian Cruise Line's ships, seven of Royal Caribbean's nineteen ships, and one of Carnival Cruise Lines' twenty two ships). The EPA's 2007 report reinforces previous research and many of the concerns raised by environmentalists about traditional as well as advanced systems. The chapter takes a close look at the industry's environmental impact, at sources for concern and at initiatives undertaken by the industry's environmental critics.

The third area explored is illness and health care. As regards illness, particularly norovirus, at issue is not the illness so much as the industry's claim that passengers bring it with them. By deflecting focus on the cruise ship and its workers as a source of infectious illnesses, the cruise line effectively places blame elsewhere. It isn't their fault, so the cruise line avoids liability when an outbreak occurs. This strategy means that cruise ships are not as effective as they might be at controlling outbreaks. Quarantine of ill crewmembers is often for inadequate periods of time, and quarantine itself has become a disincentive to reporting illness by crew and passengers.

Onboard health care services are also a source of concern. It is commonly assumed that a cruise ship has a full complement of medical facilities—that a ship is prepared to deal with almost any medical eventuality. Most passengers are surprised to learn that a shipboard infirmary is more akin to a neighbourhood clinic than to a hospital emergency room. It is adequate but has obvious limitations given space and other issues. However, of greater concern for passengers who require medical care is that cruise lines, per the passenger cruise contract, assume no liability for the care given by their own medical professionals. Medical services are offered for the convenience of the passenger, and any dispute is between the physician (frequently from a far away place) and the patient.

Chapter five turns attention to economic issues and industry claims that cruise ships leave millions of dollars behind in the ports they visit. There are two sides to understanding the credibility of the claim. One is the structure of the cruise ship and onboard life. Revenue from onboard profit centres has ballooned over the past decade such that today a cruise ship often earns less from ticket sales than it does from onboard spending by passengers. In addition, the cruise line generates revenue from activities and spending in port. This poses a problem to most ports: money spent on board means less money to spend in port, and even if the port captures more spending it kicks back a significant portion to the cruise line. It is a difficult situation for ports that is made worse by onboard shops promising not to be undersold.

Ports also find themselves in competition with one another for cruise ship visits. This competition is not only encouraged by cruise lines but is exploited. Cruise lines gravitate to the port offering the best deal, and, because ships are mobile, ports become interchangeable from one year to the next. A port that tries to increase local revenue from cruise ship visits may find the cruise ship going elsewhere in future, unless the ship is also increasing its revenue. What most ports fail to recognize is that land-based tourism yields much greater economic benefit than does cruise tourism. A study done in 2007 in Belize, where cruise passengers increased fourteen fold from 2000 to 2005 and then significantly declined, found that stay-over guests spent more than twice as much per day as cruise visitors ($44 versus $96 per day) and were responsible for 90 percent of the employment in the tourism industry (CESD 2006). Ports need to have a realistic view of cruise tourism so they can make fully informed decisions about whether to pursue cruise tourism, to what degree and at what cost.

The dynamic is further complicated by recent acquisitions and construction of cruise terminals by cruise corporations. Carnival Corporation's terminal on Grand Turk, for example, welcomed 367,000 passengers (173 ship calls) in 2007, the port's second year of operation. These passengers would have visited other islands in 2005 and before—meaning fewer calls at other Caribbean ports. The number of corporate-owned terminals is increasing worldwide, creating even greater competition between ports operating their own terminals. Cruise lines maintain a buyer's market and do everything possible to keep ports from recognizing that the best way to increase their income is to cooperate with one another and work as a united front.

The final area discussed relates to labour issues. Chapter six is framed by a commonly heard statement: "Our international crew is here to serve you." It implies that diversity among onboard crewmembers is there by design. This shifts attention away from the main reason why cruise ships attract an international crew: they draw workers who are willing to work eleven to fourteen hours a day for ten to twelve months without a day off and at wages that are low by developed world standards. A galley worker works more than 330 hours per month and may earn a guaranteed salary of $400 to $500 a month. Many crewmembers earn twice or three times as much, but there are also many who scrape by on $500 a month or less. And they do this in an environment with ethnic and racial tensions, in living conditions that are for many marginal at best and in a culture that in varying degrees is blind to sexual harassment and abuse. Passengers and the public generally need to be aware of the living and working conditions of those who serve them so they can make informed judgements about cruising and the cruise industry.

The book concludes with a chapter that rethinks the idea of cruise tourism. It discusses salient issues for consumers considering a cruise vacation, important considerations for ports choosing to embrace cruise tourism and concerns for potential employees of a cruise line. The chapter raises issues that need to be addressed if the ports and cruise ship workers are to get a fair share of the money made by cruise ships and their corporate owners. It also discusses moral issues that are relevant for passengers to consider.

Before exploring these five areas it is helpful first to look at the development of the cruise industry. This context is important for understanding the issues as they have developed and as they appear today.

Cruising into 2010

The cruise industry has grown phenomenally since the emergence some forty years ago of leisure cruising. Princess Cruises, established in 1965 by Stanley B. McDonald, was the first of today's modern cruise lines to focus on the leisure travel market. McDonald began the cruise line by chartering Canadian Pacific's 6,000 ton *Princess Patricia* during the off season of its cruises from Vancouver to Alaska's Inside Passage and offered cruises to Mexico's west coast. After two years with demand exceeding capacity, Princess Cruises added a second ship and in November 1968 added a third.

On December 19, 1966, a year after Princess Cruises initiated cruises from Los Angeles, Norwegian Caribbean Line (NCL) began sailing from Miami. The cruise line was a marriage of convenience between Ted Arison and Knut Kloster. Arison had passengers lined up for cruises and no ships after those he had chartered were repossessed by the Israeli Government when the ships' owner went bankrupt. Kloster in contrast had a brand new ship, *Sunward*, but no passengers after he had to cancel his planned cruises to Gibraltar for political reasons. Arison approached Kloster and suggested that if Kloster would send *Sunward* to Miami they could both make some money. Thus began NCL. A second ship, *Starward*, was added in 1968, followed by *Skyward* in 1969 and *Southward* in 1971. With four ships, NCL had more than 3,000 berths to fill every week.

The partnership between Kloster and Arison ended in December 1971. Three months later, with financial support from an old friend (Meshulam Riklis, a successful entrepreneur and master at corporate takeovers, often involving leveraged buyouts), Arison launched Carnival Cruise Lines. Its first ship, *Mardi Gras*, set sail March 7, 1972. The company lost money its first two years, which led Riklis to sever his association with Carnival. He signed over the *Mardi Gras* (and its $5 million mortgage) to Arison for one dollar. Arison slashed prices, opened casinos and discos onboard and devised new ways to generate onboard revenue. The company finally turned a profit in 1975. According to Micky Arison, this was the beginning of the "Fun Ship" concept. It wasn't so much a grand plan as an immediate strategy to generate enough income to meet the weekly payroll (Kessel 2000).

With his profit, Arison bought the *Empress of Britain* and renamed it *Carnivale*. The ship entered service on February 7, 1976, and turned a profit its first year. In 1977, Arison bought his third ship, sight unseen. The S.A. *Vaal* entered the Carnival fleet in 1978 as *Festivale*. Carnival Cruise Lines introduced its first purpose-built cruise ship, *Tropicale*, in 1982. At the end of 2007 Carnival Cruise Lines had twenty-two ships.

The other major player in the cruise industry today, Royal Caribbean, also had its start in the late 1960s. The idea for the company germinated in 1967, and in 1970 the first of three purpose-built ships for leisure cruising, *Song of Norway*, was introduced. *Nordic Prince* began sailing in 1971, followed by *Sun Viking* in 1972. The cruise line was profitable from the start and used its profits to expand. It first stretched (inserted a middle section to the existing ship and added 300 additional beds) *Song of Norway* in 1978 and in 1980 did the same to *Viking Sun*. Then in 1982 Royal Caribbean introduced its fourth ship, *Song of America*. The company had grown to nineteen ships by the end of 2007.

The number of North Americans taking a cruise increased exponentially as these companies grew. Passenger numbers more than doubled between 1970 and 1980: from 600,000 to 1.4 million. They then increased five-fold in the twenty-year period to 2000, to close to 7 million. Passenger numbers grew another 80 percent, to 12.6 million, between 2000 and 2007. Worldwide the number of passengers grew a more modest 37 percent between 2000 and 2007, from 12 million to 16.4 million.

This pattern of growth is expected to continue. More than 26,000 berths are added by ten new ships built in 2008—on an annual basis this adds more than one million passengers. Nine new ships will be delivered in 2009, contributing more than 23,000 berths, twelve more with 33,000 berths will be delivered in 2010, and in 2011 at least seven new ships are planned, with 16,000 berths. Taken together, the new construction in these four years will add thirty-eight new ships with more than 100,000 berths (approximately five million additional passengers annually). Introduction of new ships is a continuing phenomenon. Between 2002 and 2007 the cruise industry added fifty new ships with just over 100,000 berths. Thus, between 2002 and 2011, the industry will have introduced eighty-eight newly constructed ships containing more than 200,000 berths. The scale of growth is put into vivid perspective when considering that the North American cruise industry had 41,000 berths in 1981; it had a total of 264,000 berths at the end of 2007.

Also, between 2002 and 2007, the size of ships increased by approximately 30 percent: from an average of 2,000 berths to an average of 2,600. New ships, mainly built for the North American and European markets, have grown the cruise industry worldwide by using fewer ships that accommodate many more passengers. Many new ships replace older and smaller ships that are redeployed to new markets or sold to small cruise lines or niche operators. Cruise tourism in Asia and Australia, two newly expanding markets, rely heavily on older ships. Older ships have historically been used in the Mediterranean and Europe.

From Cruise Ship to Resort with Lifeboats

In contrast to the early ships used by Norwegian Cruise Line, Royal Caribbean, Carnival Cruise Lines and Princess Cruises, which could accommodate 750 to 1,000 passengers, new purpose-built cruise ships took on increasingly larger numbers. Competition emerged for the largest ship. In 1985 Carnival unveiled the 46,000 ton *Holiday* and touted it as the largest ship ever built for vacation cruises. Its capacity was 1,500 passengers. Three years later, Royal Caribbean welcomed *Sovereign of the Seas* and branded it "the world's largest cruise ship." Built at a cost of $185 million, and at a weight of 73,192 tons, the ship carried as many as 2,852 passengers. As each new ship appeared, the celebratory hoopla became more colourful and grand.

A building frenzy during the 1990s produced a continual flow of newer and bigger ships. In November 1991 Royal Caribbean's *Monarch of the Seas*, at 73,941 tons and with a passenger capacity of 2,744, became the newest cruise ship to claim the largest passenger capacity. In July 1992, the ship embarked 2,655 passengers—the most to embark on a single voyage on a modern cruise ship. Royal Caribbean announced it had submitted the necessary documentation to the *Guinness Book of World Records*. So began another element in the competitive race.

Competition for the biggest renewed in 1995 when Princess Cruises came out with *Sun Princess*—the largest cruise ship ever built at 77,000 tons, but with a passenger capacity of only 1,950. Competition reached new heights in November 1996 with the entry to the cruise market of a new wave of mega ships. Carnival began with the $400 million, 101,000 ton *Carnival Destiny* which has a maximum passenger capacity of 3,400. It entered the *Guinness Book of World Records* for carrying 3,269 passengers on December 22, 1996, and 3,315 on March 29, 1997; its sister ship, *Carnival Triumph*, took the honour on August 22, 1999, with 3,413 passengers.

Princess Cruises re-entered the competition for the largest ship in May 1998 with the *Grand Princess*. The 2,600-passenger ship cost $400 million and weighed 109,000 tons. A year and a half later, Royal Caribbean reclaimed the title with *Voyager of the Seas*. Costing $500 million, it was the largest in both weight (142,000 tons) and passenger capacity (3,840 passengers). *Voyager of the Seas* quickly claimed the title for most passengers on a single voyage, exceeding 3,600 passengers on a single cruise in June 2000.

Cunard's *Queen Mary 2* rekindled competition for biggest and best in 2003. As reported in the press worldwide, the *Queen Mary 2* was the largest (151,400 tons), longest (1,132 feet), tallest (236 feet), widest (135 feet) and most expensive ($800 million) passenger vessel ever built. But it was soon eclipsed by Royal Caribbean's *Freedom of the Seas* (and sisters *Liberty of the Seas* and *Independence of the Seas*), which is both larger and has an unprecedented passenger capacity of 4,370 (over 5,700 people including crew). At 160,000 tons, the $720 million *Freedom of the Seas* is roughly 15 percent larger than the Voyager class ships.

Competition is likely to end in the short term after Royal Caribbean introduces its first Genesis class vessel in fall 2009. Each of two ships are a whopping 220,000 tons, have accommodations for more than 6,000 passengers and carry a complement of close to 2,000 crewmembers. It is staggering to compare this to the ships Royal Caribbean and Carnival started with—*Song of Norway* at 18,000 tons and 724 passengers and *Mardi Gras* at 27,300 tons and 1,024 passengers.

As ships grew they also changed. Classic ocean liners and many of the early purpose-built vessels had a considerable amount of open deck space from which to view the ocean. Passengers could sit and relax away from other people and enjoy being at sea. New cruise ships have converted much of this space—prime for ocean-view and balcony cabins—into revenue generation and have reduced the "outdoors" mainly to a central area, often two or three decks in height, around the pools and other activity centres. Some ships have installed giant screens above the main pool area for showing movies, rock concerts and other forms of entertainment day and night. Princess Cruises describes its system as a Times Square-style LED screen. This monstrous 300 square foot screen features a 69,000 watt sound system. This is not an area for cruising peacefully and nodding off for a nap.

Larger ships have also changed the nature of cruising. It is common to find ten or more restaurants onboard cruise ships built in the past decade. Many of these restaurants charge a fee, something that when introduced on cruise ships in the early 1990s was withdrawn because passengers wouldn't pay—today's passengers appear more than willing to pay. Traditional elements of cruises such as formal nights and midnight buffets have also been discarded. As well, the sheer number of people affects the general dynamic among passengers and the nature of the experience. When ships were first introduced with 2,000 and more berths, a cruise line executive observed, "Cruising on a mega ship compared to a small ship is like going to a cocktail party with 2,000 people compared to going to a party at someone's house. In the first instance, chances are that you will only remember the meatballs, in the second instance, you will remember the people you meet" (CINQ 1998: 104). It is difficult to imagine what he would say with ships three times larger.

With size, a cruise ship has increasingly become more like a land-based resort/amusement park and less akin to the traditional image of cruising. Part of this change is because larger ships make it possible, and part is because the industry increasingly relies on generating onboard revenue to maintain profitability. Some activities may be provided without cost, but many have fees that quickly add up for both the passenger and the cruise ship's bottom line. A new ship is likely to have a rock climbing wall, ice skating rink, golf simulator, virtual reality and video games, different enrichment classes, casino, art auctions, full agenda of entertainment and much more. It will also have shopping—lots of shopping. Royal Caribbean's Voyager class ships have a four-storey-tall shopping mall (the "Royal Promenade") deep in the bowels, running a considerable length of the ship. One writer says of the range of activity and shopping options on Voyager of the Seas: "The idea is to grab a larger slice of the vacation market by offering so many things to do and places to explore onboard—so that even people who don't particularly care for sea cruises may want to go because the experience may not seem like they're on a ship" (Blake 2003).

The Corporate Landscape

The cruise industry has been marked by periods of growth and consolidation. The industry today is dominated by just three corporations, which together control 95 percent of the North American market: Carnival Corporation, Royal Caribbean Cruises Limited and Star Cruises, which owns Norwegian Cruise Line (GAO 2004).

Carnival Corporation, controlling 53 percent of the market, is the largest. It was formed in 1987 with Carnival Cruise Lines' initial public offering of

23.6 million common shares. The proceeds were used to pay debt incurred in construction of the company's two newest ships and to finance forays into non-cruise business such as the Crystal Palace Resort and Casino in Nassau and Carnival Air Line. While Carnival had consistently done well with its cruise line, it didn't have the same luck with businesses outside this core. The hotel was sold for $80 million in 1994 after racking up hundreds of millions of dollars in losses; Carnival Air Line terminated operations in April 1998 after merging with Pan Am, which filed for bankruptcy protection in February 1998. Carnival's expansion in the cruise industry was much more successful.

Carnival began a pattern of expansion through acquisition in 1989, when it paid $615 million for the travel and tourism businesses of Holland America Line. The acquisition boosted Carnival's number of berths by 50 percent (Holland America Line had four ships, and its tall ship subsidiary Windstar Cruises had three) and included Westours, which was the oldest and largest cruise and tour operator in Alaska and the Yukon. Carnival reached agreement in 1991 to further expand by buying Premier Cruises, which had three ships and was at the time the official carrier to Disney World, but the deal fell through seven weeks before it was to conclude. A key factor was disagreement over future earnings in the wake of the first Gulf War.

Carnival took a 25 percent equity interest in Seabourn Cruises in February 1992 in return for providing sales and marketing support. (It increased its stake to 50 percent in December 1995 by converting a $10 million loan to equity and in April 1998 bought the remaining 50 percent.) Carnival's next target was the Greek-owned Epirotiki Line. In September 1993 Carnival traded its original ship, *Mardi Gras*, for a 16.6 percent equity interest in the company. Epirotiki was an ideal platform for the company to expand into Europe at relatively low cost. Carnival increased its stake to 43 percent in March 1994 when it transferred *Carnivale* to Epirotiki, and to 49 percent in February 1995 as part of a restructuring agreement with Epirotiki's owners, George and Andreas Kotsoufis. The partnership collapsed two months later and the Kotsoufis' paid Carnival $25 million for its equity in the company.

Carnival's next expansion targets were again international in nature and intended to penetrate regional markets. In April 1996, the corporation acquired a 29.5 percent equity interest in British Airtours, which owned 770 retail travel agency locations in the U.K. and Scandinavia, a charter air fleet of thirty-two planes, forty-one hotels in the Mediterranean and two cruise ships, marketed as Sun Cruises. Less than six months later Carnival entered into an agreement with Hyundai Merchant Marine to form a fifty-fifty joint venture to target the Asian vacation market. The joint venture purchased Carnival's *Tropicale*, but it failed to get off the ground because of irreconcilable differences between the partners. According to Howard Frank, Carnival's vice chair, Carnival didn't share the same view as Hyundai of the Asian cruise market, and the two "had very different views as to how the joint venture should be managed and the strategic direction it should take" (CND 1997).

Carnival continued to expand in Europe. In June 1997 it acquired, in partnership with Airtours, Italy-based Costa Cruises. Costa was seeking an infusion of capital (the Carnival-Airtours partnership paid $300 million for the cruise line) in order to retain its market share (70 percent of the Italian market, 55 percent of the French market and 20 percent of the Spanish market). Carnival became the sole owner of Costa Cruises when it purchased Airtour's share in September 2000. In April 1998, Carnival partnered with a group of Norwegian investors led by Christiana Markets to acquire U.K.-based Cunard Line; Carnival bought its partners' share in October 1999.

Carnival's most recent and largest acquisition was its merger with P&O Princess in April 2003. The merger combined Carnival Corporation's six brand names (Carnival Cruise Line, Holland America Line, Windstar Cruises, Seabourn Cruises, Cunard Line and Costa Cruises) with seven brands operated by P&O Princess (U.S.-based Princess Cruises; U.K.-based P&O Cruises, Ocean Village and Swan Hellenic Line; Germany-based Aida and A'Rosa; and Australia-based P&O Australia). Carnival has since divested of A'Rosa, Windstar and Swan Hellenic. It further strengthened its position in Europe in September 2007 by entering a joint venture agreement with Orizonia Corporation, Spain's largest travel company, to form Spain-based Ibero Cruises. At the end of 2007 Carnival Corporation had eighty-five ships with a total of 158,352 berths.

The second largest cruise corporation, controlling 33.4 percent of the North American market, is Royal Caribbean Cruises Limited. It has also expanded through acquisition and joint ventures, though its effort to take over Costa Cruises in early 1996 failed, as did its planned merger with Princess Cruises in 2002—Carnival successfully snatched those cruise lines. However, Carnival was not able to interfere with Royal Caribbean's acquisition in July 1997 of Celebrity Cruises. Celebrity, founded in 1990 by a partnership between John Chandris and Overseas Shipping Group, had grown into a viable and popular premium cruise line that competed effectively with Carnival's premium brands. It operated five ships with 7,800 berths. Under Royal Caribbean's leadership the cruise line doubled in size (nine ships with 15,600 berths) by the end of 2002. In 2004, Celebrity entered the expedition/adventure travel niche with Celebrity Xpeditions, a single-ship cruise line focused on the Galapagos Islands and side tours to Ecuador's Machu Picchu. It also expanded into the premium cruise market with establishment in 2007 of Azamara Cruises, formed with deployment of two 700-passenger ships.

Royal Caribbean has also expanded into Europe, but not at the same pace as Carnival. In 2002, it entered into a joint venture with First Choice Holidays to establish U.K.-based Island Cruises. The company's first ship, *Island Escape*, was Royal Caribbean's 1971-built *Viking Serenade*; in 2006 Royal Caribbean transferred Celebrity Cruises' oldest ship, the 1990-built *Horizon*, which was renamed *Island Star*. Also in 2006, Royal Caribbean acquired Madrid-based cruise and tour operator Pullmantur S.A. It transferred Pullmantur's newest ships, two 2000-built vessels formerly operated by Renaissance Cruises, to Azamara (the *Azamara Quest* and *Azamara Journey*) and transferred to Pullmantur Celebrity Cruises' 1991-built *Zenith* and Royal Caribbean's 1988-built *Sovereign of the Seas*. Both ships were the oldest vessels in their respective fleets. At the end of 2007, Royal Caribbean Cruises operated thirty-five ships with a total of 71,150 berths.

In December 2007, Royal Caribbean announced further expansion in Europe through a joint venture with Germany-based TUI. The joint venture will establish TUI Cruises and focus on the German cruise market. TUI is already involved in the U.K. cruise industry through its ownership of Thomson Holidays (operator of Thomson Cruises) and its merger in 2007 with First Choice Holidays. TUI Cruises will begin service with one ship in early 2009 (most likely a ship already in Royal Caribbean's fleet) and grow quickly with two new ships planned for 2011 and 2012.

The third major player in the industry is Malaysia-based Star Cruises. Its Norwegian Cruise Line (NCL) controls 9 percent of the North American market. Established in 1993 with a focus on Asia and the Pacific, Star expanded into North America and Europe in 2000, when it prevailed in a bidding war with Carnival Corporation and acquired NCL. Star refocused plans for expansion in Asia and instead invested considerably in building and expanding NCL (which itself had bought Majesty Cruise Line in 1997 and Orient Line in 1998). It added three new ships to the NCL fleet within the first two years after acquiring the cruise line.

In 2002 Star Cruises made a bold move when it announced plans for a U.S.-flagged cruise line, NCL America. The cruise line was started in 2004 with the 1999-built *Norwegian Sky*, renamed *Pride of Aloha*. Two additional ships were added, in 2005 and 2006, but weak demand led the company in 2008 to redeploy two of those ships, leaving only one ship under the NCL America brand. At the end of 2007, Star Cruises had twenty-one ships (thirteen in the NCL fleet) with 32,300 berths.

NCL's relationship to Star Cruises changed in January 2008, when it was spun off as an independent company, which is now jointly owned by Star Cruises and Apollo Management LP, a private equity group that invested one billion dollars for 50 percent of NCL. Apollo had previously acquired Oceania Cruises (operator of three ships with 2052 berths) and Regent Seven Seas Cruises (operator of five ships with 2,620 berths).

The remainder of the North American market, comprising less than 4 percent of the total, consists of small cruise lines operating two or three ships (e.g., Crystal Cruises, Disney Cruise Line), niche operators such as ultra luxury Silversea Cruises and tall-shipped Windstar Cruises, and companies deploying small ships on "pocket cruises" (e.g., Cruise West, American Cruise Lines, Majestic America Cruises). Though there are a variety of brands and options, the vast majority of the cruise market is controlled and dominated by "the big three" corporations. They in effect set the standards in the industry (for both the product and corporate behaviour) and define the nature of relationships between the industry and ports, the industry and labour, and the industry's orientation toward environmental issues and passenger safety.

Chapter 2

A Cruise Ship is the Safest Form of Commercial Transportation

The cruise industry not only promotes itself as safe but says it is the safest form of commercial transportation. That is a grand claim. It is one that most passengers take at face value and believe. But that may not be wise.

The Morgans (a pseudonym) took a cruise in 2005, never thinking twice about it being unsafe for their eight-year-old middle daughter to go back to the family's cabin on her own. Along the way the youngster became confused and asked a crewmember in uniform for assistance. Instead of helping, the male (wearing a cruise line name plate) allegedly took the girl to the dark end of a corridor where he masturbated in front of her. There were few passengers around at the time given that the ship was in port in the Bahamas. It was subsequently learned that the crewmember had previously worked for a different cruise line, which had "do not rehire" marked on his personnel file. But he passed background checks and was hired by the current cruise line. It seems the cruise line also failed to notice that the name under which the man had applied for employment was different than the name on his passport.

Laurie Dishman also believed a cruise was safe. She and her best friend chose a cruise to the Mexican Riviera in February 2006 to celebrate thirty years of friendship and to celebrate Laurie's birthday. But things quickly turned from good to bad when Laurie was raped by a security guard on day two of the cruise. The security guard she learned later was actually a janitor filling in for security in lounges to check IDs because there was not enough security personnel onboard.

The cruise industry would prefer these experiences not be broadcast; when they are made public they are characterized as isolated exceptions or as statistically insignificant. But sexual assaults have been recognized as an ongoing problem on cruise ships for decades.

Sexual Assaults

Sexual assaults on cruise ships gained the national media's interest in 1999. One peak was in July 1999, when Carnival Cruise Lines disclosed in the discovery phase of a lawsuit involving an alleged rape that it had received 108 complaints of sexual assaults involving crewmembers in the five-year period ending August 1998. Royal Caribbean said it had had fifty-eight reported sexual assaults on its ships during the same five-year period.

Several months earlier an investigative journalist with the *New York Times*, Douglas Frantz, published an article entitled "On Cruise Ships, Silence Shrouds Crimes," where he describes an alarming range of passenger claims of sexual assault and discusses how they were handled by the cruise lines. Based on examination of court records and on interviews with cruise line employees, law enforcement officials and passengers and their lawyers, Frantz describes

> a pattern of cover-ups that often began as soon as the crime was reported at sea, in international waters where the only police are the ship's security officers. Accused crewmembers are sometimes put ashore at the next port with airfare to their home country. Industry lawyers are flown to the ship to question the accusers; and aboard ships flowing with liquor, counterclaims of consensual sex are common. The cruise lines aggressively contest lawsuits and insist on secrecy as a condition of settling. (Frantz 1998)

He cites a former chief of security for Carnival Cruise Lines as saying:

> "You don't notify the FBI. You don't notify anybody. You start giving the victims bribes, upgrading their cabins, giving them champagne and trying to ease them off the ship until the legal department can take over. Even when I knew there was a crime, I was supposed to go in there and do everything in the world to get Carnival to look innocent." (Frantz 1998)

Once a crime is reported, there are problems with preserving evidence. Passenger cabins are routinely cleaned twice a day so much evidence is destroyed very quickly, and there is often a delay between an attack and landing at a U.S. port. Rape experts suggest that cases reported within seventy-two hours provide the best forensic evidence but this time frame is often impossible for victims attacked on a cruise ship. In addition, many victims likely delay making a report as long as they are aboard a ship because of fear of reprisal and because there is no independent investigator or rape treatment centre. Sadly, rapes on cruise ships may often not be reported until it is too late for criminal investigation.

In those cases where a sexual assault is reported in a timely manner, victims and prosecutors were traditionally faced with a common practice among cruise lines to immediately send the accused back home, purportedly because they have violated company policies that prohibit fraternizing between passengers and crew. Reporters for the *Miami New Times* found that in each of five lawsuits against Carnival Cruise Lines they reviewed the employee was sent out of the country immediately after the ship arrived in port. In one case the employee was later rehired by the company and was subsequently served with a summons while the ship was at the dock in Los Angeles. However, Carnival's lawyers successfully argued the Indian citizen couldn't be sued in U.S. courts because U.S. laws did not apply to him: not only is he a foreigner but the alleged crime took place in Barbados on a ship registered in Panama. The passenger's suit against Carnival Cruise Lines was settled out of court (Korten 2000).

The Victims

"Cruise ships are as safe an environment as you can find," was what a Carnival Cruise Lines spokesperson said during a court case involving a fourteen-year-old child who was raped in 1989 on Carnival's *Carnivale*. Rape, he said, "happens in houses, offices, hotels, and parking lots" (Adams 1990: 1).

In this child's case, the rape occurred onboard in a cleaning closet. As the ship was returning to Miami from the Bahamas she went to the family's cabin (while other family members remained on deck) at 5:30 a.m. to check on a suitcase. While in the elevator, a male crewmember—a cleaner onboard the ship—kissed and fondled her. He then dragged her from the elevator to a cleaning closet and raped her on the floor. The girl picked the thirty-two-year-old crewman, a Colombian national and father of two, out of a line-up. In February 1990, he was found guilty of the charges and sentenced to thirty years in prison. The case received considerable attention because it was the first time a crewmember on a foreign-flagged cruise ship had been successfully prosecuted. The assault had occurred while the ship was within U.S. territorial waters (Adams 1990: 1).

There were other cases involving children in the 1990s. In 1991 a twelve-year-old girl was fondled in the elevator of Carnival Cruise Line's *Jubilee*. The perpetrator was never found. In 1992 a fifteen-year-old girl was raped on Windjammer Cruises' *Fantome*. None of the cabins had doors that locked at the time so the crewman easily gained entry. In 1994 a crewman on Dolphin Cruises' *Seabreeze* molested a thirteen-year-old boy. And in 1995 a crewman broke into a cabin and raped two girls under the age of ten. The offender in both the latter cases was identified, but it is unknown whether he was prosecuted (Klein 2002).

Between 1995 and 2000, the media reported at least eight additional cases involving children: a sixteen-year-old girl celebrating her birthday was raped on Royal Caribbean Cruise Line's *Monarch of the Seas* after striking up a conversation with a bartender who later was her attacker (Frantz 1998); a fourteen- and a sixteen-year-old girl were raped in separate incidents several weeks apart in 1996 by the same crewman aboard Carnival Cruise Line's *Fascination*—the latter case came to light because of publicity from the first

Laurie Dishman, sexual assault victim, 2006

In February 2006, thirty-six-year-old Laurie Dishman and her best friend, Michelle, decided to celebrate their thirty-year friendship by embarking on Royal Caribbean's *Vision of the Seas* for a cruise to the Mexican Riviera. However, instead of seven days of fun in the sun, the trip quickly turned into a nightmare when an employee of the cruise line allegedly raped Laurie in her cabin.

According to Laurie's public statement posted at the International Cruise Victims Association website:

Michelle and I were in the Viking Crown Lounge, when we were approached by a crewmember, whose badge indicated that he was a "security guard." He demanded to see our IDs and asked whether we were old enough to be drinking in the bar. He asked for our cabin number.

As the night continued, Michelle and I talked and danced with other passengers. When I decided to go up and request a song, that same crewmember approached me and held my wrist and kissed me, while trying to whisper something in my ear. I said, "No, get away." Then, I headed back to be with Michelle and get away from this man. I was upset, so Michelle brought me back to my cabin and waited for me to fall asleep, before she headed back to the lounge.

Later there was a knock at the door. It was dark. Thinking it was Michelle I opened the door halfway [the door had no peep holes or chain locks] but it was him! He forced his way into my cabin and pushed me onto the bed. I struggled and tried to resist but he raped me. He left me passed out on the bed with ligature marks around my neck.

When I woke up I didn't know who to call because my rapist was supposedly "security." I told Michelle what had happened and we decided to call the Purser's desk, which prompted two officers to come to our cabin. Instead of securing the cabin they sat on the bed where the rape occurred. Eventually I was permitted to go to the ship's doctor but he told Michelle and I to go back to our cabin and collect the sheets & clothing from the incident and to place then in plastic bags which they had provided. I also wrote a demanded statement and gave it to the officers on the ship. The entire process was so humiliating! That same day [after identifying my assailant] I told the Captain that I was frightened and just wanted to go home. (Dishman 2007)

Laurie subsequently learned that her case would not be pursued by the Department of Justice because it was one of "he said/she said." The crewmember apparently denied having been in her room. She also learned that the crewmember was a janitor who had been filling in as a security guard.

Laurie was dissatisfied with how Royal Caribbean handled her case. Aside from having to collect her own evidence and not being provided sensitive support onboard, she says the cruise line delayed notifying the FBI and delayed sealing her cabin; her medical treatment was delayed until after she completed statements demanded by security and after she went back to the cabin to gather evidence; and delayed release of information that had been requested (e.g., medical records, statements and the assailant's personnel file).

She says, "The only thing I received from the cruise line, following this incident, was a promotional letter from the President of RCCL which stated, 'Thank you for sailing with us and giving us the opportunity to send you home with an experience to remember.' He even included a discount coupon!"

(Frantz 1998); a thirteen-year-old child was the victim of an attempted sexual assault by a thirty-year-old passenger in 1997 aboard Premier Cruises' *Atlantica*; a fifteen-year-old boy was molested in 1998 by a bartender on a Royal Caribbean Cruise Line ship after he was served more than a dozen glasses of champagne and then taken to an empty cabin where he was stripped and sexually assaulted (Oliphant 1999); and in 1999 a thirteen-year-old girl was assaulted by a waiter aboard Celebrity Cruises' *Galaxy*, and a twelve-year-old boy was molested by a kitchen steward aboard a ship belonging to Norwegian Cruise Lines. In October 2000 a thirty-year-old youth coordinator on Norwegian Cruise Line's *Norway* was arrested and charged with sexually assaulting a twelve-year-old girl who had come with him to his cabin. In this last case, the parents are suing Norwegian Cruise Line for not properly screening their employees: the youth coordinator had an arrest record that included indecent exposure (*Travel Weekly Crossroads Daily e-letter*, June 28, 2001).

Sexual assaults are not limited to children. Though short of sexual assault, one dimension of the problem is reflected in a 1991 *Los Angeles Times* letter to the editor (Richards 1991: L-22). Written by a forty-year-old woman who had recently returned from a cruise with her mother, she warns single women about what is in store for them on a cruise. She describes being propositioned by her cabin steward and being relentlessly pursued by a dining room waiter who wouldn't take "no" for an answer. Enjoyment of her cruise was compromised and she was forced to remain in the company of others for protection. Other women experience more than harassment.

In 1990 a passenger with Carnival Cruise Lines accused her cabin steward of entering her cabin while she was asleep. He climbed on top her and fondled her but was scared away when the woman and her roommate both began screaming. The woman reported the incident to the safety officer but nothing happened. In 1992 a thirty-one-year-old woman travelling on Carnival Cruise Lines' *Festivale* claimed that a waiter had snuck into her cabin while she was getting dressed in the bathroom. She filed a report with the

Barbados police, but nothing happened. Neither the woman nor Carnival contacted the FBI. The woman settled her case against Carnival Cruise Lines out of court (Frantz 1998). And in 1993 a sixty-two-year-old woman on Seawind Cruise Line's *Seawind Crown* was strangled to death following a failed rape attempt when she was using a public toilet at 9:00 a.m. The two crewmen were caught because they were seen throwing the body overboard as the ship left the harbour in Aruba. They were detained and prosecuted in Aruba (Glass 1993: 3).

In June 1997 a thirty-five-year-old woman aboard Royal Caribbean Cruise Line's *Majesty of the Seas* said she was raped after returning at 4:00 a.m. from the nightclub where she had consumed only non-alcoholic beverages. She said she was attacked by a member of the cleaning crew and picked him out of a line-up conducted by the ship's security officers. Questioned by the ship's security officer and a company lawyer who had flown in, the worker denied being anywhere near a passenger. He said he had been washing decks at 4:00 in the morning. He attributed the scratches on his body to minor work accidents. He was indicted and as his trial approached DNA evidence linked him to the assault. He switched his story and his lawyers argued that the woman had consented to sex. Because the woman had filed for bankruptcy just before going on the cruise the lawyers suggested the suit against Royal Caribbean had been planned. A jury acquitted the alleged attacker after four hours of deliberation. In court papers, Royal Caribbean "said it was not responsible for a crewmember's actions outside his official duties" (Frantz 1998).

There were two cases reported against Carnival Cruise Lines in 1998. In one a woman on a Caribbean cruise with her husband accused a waiter of drugging their dinner drinks and later raping her in their cabin as her husband lay unconscious. The couple complained to cruise officials who responded in part by moving them to a better cabin for the remainder of the cruise. The case was settled just before it was set to go to trial (Frantz 1998). In another case a woman travelling with her mother claimed a room steward had raped her. "She asserts... [he] pushed her down on one of the beds and raped her. She reported the incident immediately to ship personnel who questioned [the steward]. He denied the charge" (Korten 2000). The disposition of the case is not known.

Also in 1998, a fifty-four-year-old woman who worked at the ship's gift shop on *Crystal Harmony* initiated a lawsuit claiming she was forced to engage in sex with the captain for fear that if she refused she would lose her job. She characterized the cruise ship as a more blatant sexually promiscuous environment than she had ever seen, where the officers and captain think they can take liberty with anyone, and nobody wants to complain because they would lose their job (*SF Gate News* 1998).

Jane Doe, sexual assault victim, 2007

In testimony before the House of Representatives Subcommittee on Coast Guard and Maritime Transportation in March 2007 Laurie Dishman identified herself as the "the next Janet Kelly," relating her story to that of another sexual assault victim who had previously testified before Congress. Six months later, the Committee heard testimony from William M. Sullivan, Jr., a lawyer representing a woman who, he stated, was "the next Laurie Dishman." Referred to as "Jane Doe," his client went on what she perceived to be a safe vacation but instead "was brutally raped by her Royal Caribbean cabin steward, who entered her cabin with his Royal Caribbean-issued passkey, after hours, to rape Jane while she slept" (Sullivan 2007).

Jane was a twenty-year-old college student who went on a March 2007 cruise with some of her female friends. One evening midway through the cruise an off-duty crewmember imposed himself on Jane and her friends. He brought alcohol and encouraged them to drink with him.

> During this time, the crewmember watched and lingered as Jane and one of her friends fell sound asleep. Jane's friends escorted him out of the cabin and closed and locked the door behind them before going to their own cabin. Shortly thereafter the crewmember used his… [passkey to enter Jane's cabin] and forcibly raped her.
>
> Jane awoke as a result of the rape. She struggled to push the rapist off her. She fled the room to seek help. The cabin steward pursued her into the hallway, telling her that nobody would hear her cries for help. She then fled back to the room and slammed the door on him. While Jane and her friend cowered in the cabin, there was a persistent knocking on the door. Because Royal Caribbean's door did not have a peephole, there was no way for Jane and her friend to see who it was. (Sullivan 2007)

There were unfortunately no security tapes in the hallway because Royal Caribbean limits the use of such equipment to other areas such as stairwells and lounges.

Jane's companions reported the crime, which was initially not taken seriously, to the ship's emergency phone number. She was taken to the infirmary but instead of being examined and receiving medical treatment and emotional support she was injected with a sedative, Lorazepam. After the drug took effect Jane was asked to complete a Royal Caribbean statement form. She wasn't told the information was not for medical use but instead was to be turned over to Royal Caribbean's risk management personnel and lawyers. Jane remained sedated in the infirmary and says she did not receive treatment. She and her friends had their requests to call their parents for help and guidance refused by the ship's physician. They were told they would have to wait until the ship sailed from port.

Jane and a friend disembarked the ship, leaving their friends behind. With apparently inadequate help and support from Royal Caribbean she sought medical care and began her trek back to the United States. The crime scene (her cabin) reportedly had not been properly secured. One of her friend's expressed feeling of being unsafe onboard the ship was not only dismissed, but she was pressured be a senior ship's officer to retract her statement to that effect to her father back home.

According to Jane's lawyer, Royal Caribbean betrayed its duty to her when

it gave a rapist unrestricted access to her and her cabin, when it injected her with a dangerous drug to inhibit her ability to report her attack, and when it failed to provide the medication she needed to prevent HIV infection, and it continues to betray her as it fails to support her efforts to see the rapist brought to justice. (Sullivan 2007)

And then in July 1999, in the midst of considerable media interest and attention, Carnival Cruise Lines and Royal Caribbean disclosed together they had received 166 sexual assault complaints from 1993 to 1998. The disclosure was made in discovery in a lawsuit brought by a woman who had worked as a nurse onboard a cruise ship for three years. She said she had been raped and sodomized in August 1998 by the ship's engineer, allegedly an experienced sexual predator, while working on Carnival Cruise Lines' *Imagination*. She had immediately reported the incident and the engineer was promptly fired; not because of the rape but because he had been drinking within six hours of going on duty and for being tardy. The case was settled out of court in December 1999, less than two weeks before trial (Senes 1999: 40).

Cruise Lines Pledge Zero Tolerance on Crime

In the midst of the heightened media coverage and interest, four cruise corporations (Carnival Corporation, Royal Caribbean Cruises Limited, Crystal Cruises and Princess Cruises) representing more than 75 percent of the industry signed a letter of commitment in July 1999. Issued under the auspices of the International Council of Cruise Lines, they pledged a "zero tolerance policy" for crimes committed onboard ships and established an industry standard requiring allegations of onboard crime be reported to the appropriate law enforcement authorities. For vessels calling on U.S. ports or crime involving U.S. citizens this meant the Federal Bureau of Investigation (FBI).

Interestingly, cruise lines were already expected to report to the U.S. Coast Guard all crimes involving U.S. citizens on cruise ships but it isn't clear that the information was being reported or sought. U.S. authority in these cases extends from the special maritime and territorial jurisdiction of the United States (USC 18 CFR). Under U.S. Code, the government can exert authority over U.S. territorial seas, any place outside the jurisdiction of a nation with respect to an offence against a U.S. national and a foreign-flag vessel during a voyage to or from the U.S. where an offence is committed against a U.S. national.

The cruise industry announced its zero tolerance for crime policy with a press release. It reassured passengers of background checks on prospective employees, that crewmembers violating rules against fraternization with guests would be dismissed, that there were highly trained security personnel on every vessel and that there were established procedures to investigate, report and refer incidents of onboard crime to appropriate law enforcement authorities. The press release told U.S. passengers that they were protected by U.S. laws, that cruise lines were subject to civil liabilities in U.S. courts and that they were safer on a cruise ship than in urban or rural America. The industry said the number of reported shoreside aggravated sexual assaults was at least twenty to fifty times greater than the total number of all reported shipboard assaults of any type, a claim that was never measured against actual rates on and off ship.

Some cruise lines (if not all) undertook initiatives to address the problem of sexual assaults and other crimes, though this was mostly done out of the public's sight. Royal Caribbean, for one, received reports in May/ June 1999 from two consultants charged with making recommendations for preventing sexual harassment and assault. The problem was obvious. As one report stated, "Improper activity occurs frequently aboard cruise ships, but goes unreported and/or unpunished" (Krohne 1999: 2). The other report acknowledged that "crewmembers generally understand that if they commit an offence and are caught they are most likely going to lose their job and be returned home, but not spend time in jail" (Greenwood 1999: 4).

The reports make a range of recommendations. These include increased video surveillance of high risk areas (including the disco bar and dance area, main service corridors on crew decks, key intersections on passenger decks and youth activity areas); cameras already in place be monitored periodically, at least on a random basis, and be recorded at all times; an increase in the number of security staff by two per ship; and increased training and education of staff and crewmembers. In addition they recommended that response to sexual harassment and assault be standardized across brands and ships, that training for medical personnel include an interview protocol for sexual assault incidents, that a staff member be identified and assigned responsibility to serve as an advocate for the target of sexual harassment or assault, that a shoreside hotline be established to receive telephone reports of wrongdoing and that investigations be consistent and evenly handled.

> ## Janet Kelly, sexual assault victim, 2000
>
> In February 2000 after the sudden loss of her eighteen-year-old daughter, fol-
> lowed six months later by her husband's heart attack and open heart surgery,
> Janet went on a "healing" four-day cruise with some neighbours. It started out
> being everything she expected; the end was anything but. On the last night
> of the cruise, in between a show and dinner, the ship's bartender mixed and
> served Janet a drug-laced drink. As the drug took effect the bartender led her
> to a "crewmembers only" location and raped her.
>
> Janet reported the crime to local authorities who told her the FBI had ju-
> risdiction over crimes at sea. It took the FBI many months to investigate and
> to interview the assailant, and in the end they decided there was not enough
> evidence for prosecution. This is despite having Janet's clothing, a rape kit, the
> assailant's identity and the victim's statement.
>
> On top of the apparent failure of the justice system, Janet was left with
> the fear of having been exposed to HIV. It was only after she filed a civil suit
> against the cruise line and the assailant that the cruise line conceded to have
> the crewmember tested for HIV. They then fired him and sent him back to
> Jamaica. Not too long later Janet discovered that her rapist had been employed
> by another cruise line. Her lawyer notified the cruise line of the worker's past
> and he was fired.

Given their assumption that cruise passengers were unaware of the prohibi-
tion between crew and guest social interactions (and that passengers often,
unintentionally, put a crewmember in an uncomfortable position by engaging
him or her socially), they also recommended better educating passengers and
better signage onboard demarcating areas that are "off limits" to passengers.
The recommendations are great, but the degree to which they have been
embraced and implemented is questionable.

The consultants also identified cultural challenges to reducing sexual
harassment and assault. For example, senior officers and management need
to break from the traditionally hierarchical and militaristic structure of a
ship and instead treat their crew and staff members fairly and respectfully.
They need to reinforce the need for staff and crewmembers to treat each
other and passengers respectfully. If they wish to prevent sexual harassment
and abuse then they must have zero tolerance for both no matter the rank
or position of the offender.

Diverse cultural perceptions of sexual harassment and conduct among
a ship's crew present another challenge. There is a diverse population drawn
from around the world and in many of these cultures women, women's
rights and sexuality are seen quite differently than they are by most North
Americans. These differences need to be addressed through better training
and more effective oversight and supervision.

Cruise Lines in the News and in Congress

The issue of sexual assaults on cruise ships re-emerged in the media in late 2005 and was kept alive with the establishment in 2006 of the International Cruise Victims Association (ICV), an organization devoted to promoting concern for and representing the rights of victims of crime on cruise ships. This was the first time in a decade that an organization or group had looked out for the interests of crime victims on cruise ships. The time previous was in 1995 when Congress approved a tort reform measure attached to the Coast Guard Reauthorization bill. The amendment, for the most part written by the International Council of Cruise Lines, was introduced by Representative Don Young of Alaska, who referred to it as a "noncontroversial manager's amendment" (Glass 1996: 1). It passed the House by a vote of 406 to 12. Only afterwards did people read the final print.

One provision directed at mounting claims from injuries and sexual assaults on cruise ships raised considerable concern. It sought to limit cruise line liability to passengers and crew for "infliction of emotional distress, mental suffering or psychological injury" unless negligence or an intentional act could be proven. The American Trial Lawyers Association characterized the amendments as "dangerous legislation" that "jeopardized the safety of women on cruise ships." Opposition also came from the Women's Defense Fund, the National Organization for Women's Legal Defense Fund, the Maritime Committee of the AFL-CIO, and rape treatment centers (Fox and Fox 1995: E4).

The amendment languished for more than a year waiting to go to a House-Senate conference, where lawmakers would resolve the House and Senate versions of the Coast Guard Reauthorization Bill. The cruise industry lobbied hard for the amendments but it wasn't entirely successful. In the end, ship owners were prohibited from limiting their liability in cases involving sexual harassment, sexual misbehaviour, assault or rape in cases where the victim is physically injured. Limitations were allowed in all other situations (i.e., where there is no physical injury).

Other than this single occasion, the rights and concerns of sexual assault victims on cruise ships had not been championed by any national group or organization until the founding of the ICV. A voluntary organization, the ICV is made up of victims and victim's families; it operates without staff and without funding. The organization is concerned with sexual assaults and other crimes onboard cruise ships, as well as with broader issues of safety and security. In fact its genesis was in cases where cruise passengers had disappeared or gone overboard in mysterious or unclear circumstances.

Passengers Gone Overboard

The International Cruise Victims Association was founded in January 2006 by Bree Smith and Ken Carver; each had lost a family member overboard from a cruise ship. They first met December 2005 at Congressional hearings that focused on safety, security and crime on cruise ships. The hearings were spurred by two sets of events. One was an attack on November 5, 2005, of Seabourn Cruise Line's *Seabourn Spirit* by two pirate speedboats 115 kilometres off the coast of Somalia. None of the 151 passengers was injured from machine gun shots and rocket propelled grenades fired at the vessel, including an unexploded grenade wedged in the wall of a cabin, though there were injuries among the crew. The pirates were eventually repelled with a long range acoustic device that sent a powerful sonic wave and the cruise ship escaped.

The other set of events leading to the hearings was a cluster of cases where a passenger disappeared from a cruise ship. The issue was raised in June 2005 in a *Business Journal of Jacksonville* article written by Mary Moewe. She found that since 2000 at least twelve cruise ship passengers had gone overboard or disappeared in eleven incidents involving cruise ships that frequent U.S. ports. Two of the passengers were rescued, two were confirmed dead and the eight remaining missing passengers are still a mystery (Moewe 2005).

Unbeknownst to Moewe the numbers were actually much higher. Because none of the cruise lines kept track of persons going overboard and no federal agency had responsibility for monitoring these events she was left to rely on information that was readily available. The most comprehensive list of persons going overboard from cruise ships at the time was online at Cruise Junkie dot Com (see <www.cruisejunkie.com/Overboard.html>). The site reports forty-seven incidents during the same time period covered by Moewe's article; in nine cases the person was rescued alive. Some cases were clearly suicide, some were accidents and many remain mysterious. Alcohol was a factor in a fair number of suicides and accidents, large gambling losses were a factor in at least three cases, and an argument with a spouse or travelling companion preceded four incidents (three men, one woman—in two of these cases the passenger was rescued alive). There was a single case where one passenger was observed throwing another overboard. In September 2001 Myrtha Vogt, a sixty-nine-year-old woman from New Mexico, was pushed overboard, as her husband watched, by a fellow passenger who was a former mental patient. They were on the third day of an eleven-day cruise of Norway's fjords.

Some of the unexplained disappearances include Cris Allen Swartzbaugh, a thirty-nine-year-old man who disappeared between Tahiti and Raiatea in the South Pacific the first night of a cruise aboard the *Paul Gauguin* in April

2000; Manuelita Pierce, a thirty-nine-year-old woman who disappeared without a trace at the end of her week-long Caribbean cruise aboard Royal Caribbean's *Enchantment of the Seas* in October 2000; Randall Gary, a fifty-year-old psychotherapist who in May 2003 disappeared from Holland America Line's *Veendam* somewhere between Vancouver and Alaska; Merrian Carver, a forty-year-old woman who in May 2004 disappeared from an Alaska cruise aboard Celebrity Cruises' *Mercury*; Annette Mizener, a thirty-seven-year-old woman who disappeared from a nine-day Mexican Riviera cruise aboard *Carnival Pride* in December 2004—in her case the surveillance camera viewing the deck area from where she seems to have disappeared following a struggle was obscured by a map of the ship; and in May 2005 Hue Pham (age seventy-one) and his wife of forty-nine years, Hue Tran (age sixty-seven), disappeared in the Caribbean between the islands of Barbados and Aruba from *Carnival Destiny*. What started out as a Mother's Day gift—a seven-night Caribbean cruise with their daughter and granddaughter—turned into a tragic and mysterious disappearance. There were common patterns in these cases: search for the missing passenger was either not undertaken or was inordinately delayed; there appeared to be an absence of investigation; and in some cases law enforcement authorities were not initially notified.

While these cases suggest a problem, the disappearance of George Allen Smith IV, a twenty-six-year-old on his honeymoon aboard the *Brilliance of the Seas* in the Mediterranean in July 2005 captured the world's attention and catapulted passenger disappearances into the public eye. The newlyweds had been drinking heavily and gambling at the ship's casino before his disappearance. The story that emerged was that while George's wife, Jennifer Hegel-Smith, lay passed out on a floor far from the couple's cabin (and with no recollection of events) George was taken back to his cabin by some drinking buddies who claim they put him to bed. The next morning a youngster in a nearby cabin reported seeing blood on a canopy above a life boat under the Smith cabin and an investigation determined that at least one of the Smiths was missing. Jennifer was located that morning in the gym unaware that anything had happened.

George's disappearance was reported to Turkish authorities who came aboard to investigate. To this day, the investigation remains open and conclusions have yet to be drawn. There is some indication of foul play and some believe they know who was involved but no one has been formally identified or charged.

In late June 2006 Jennifer reached a settlement with the cruise line over her husband's disappearance. George's parents the same day filed suit against the cruise line claiming the cruise line deliberately and intentionally portrayed the incident as an accident and hampered a full blown, appropriate investigation into the facts and circumstances of George's death. Specifically

Merrian Carver, disappeared, 2004

On August 27, 2004, Merrian Carver boarded Celebrity Cruises' *Mercury* for a one-week cruise of Alaska's Inside Passage. The forty-year-old from Cambridge, Massachusetts, left on the cruise from Seattle while her thirteen-year-old daughter stayed with her ex-husband in England. She was last seen on August 29, 2004.

Merrian's disappearance became known after her father, Ken, received a frantic call from his granddaughter, who was unable to reach her mother. Ken also tried to reach his daughter without success. After several days he asked Cambridge police to check her apartment but they found no clue to her whereabouts. A week later he filed a missing person report. Within several days the detective assigned to the case accessed Merrian's bank records and told Ken she had booked the cruise.

Ken immediately called the cruise line to find out whether his daughter had in fact been a passenger on the cruise. Three days later he heard back from Celebrity Cruises' Risk Management Department, which confirmed that Merrian had embarked the ship but she had stopped using her cabin after the second night of the cruise and they could not confirm whether she left the ship in Vancouver. The room steward collected and packed up all of her personal belongings at the end of the cruise: her clothes and other items (including a gold wristwatch) were given to charity; her purse which contained papers, keys and computer disks were put into storage. Although the room steward had notified his supervisor of Merrian's disappearance there had been no notification to shoreside authorities or to Merrian's family. Ken learned that videotapes from the cruise had already been erased (three weeks after the cruise) and later found out the cruise line reported to the FBI that there had been no "Oscar, Oscar, Oscar emergency on that voyage" (person overboard) (Carver 2007: 3).

The Carvers were at a loss. The Cambridge police couldn't help, the FBI was out of the loop because it hadn't been notified of the disappearance and the RCMP in Vancouver (where the ship disembarked) also had not been notified. With no other recourse they hired a private investigator who met with cruise officials and toured the ship in November. While the investigator was permitted to view a cabin that was identical to the one Merrian occupied, his time on the ship was severely limited. He found the company less than cooperative: it refused to name a cabin steward who had contact with Merrian during the cruise, it refused to allow the security guard in charge of video surveillance to be interviewed, and the hotel manager who had worked Merrian's cruise was on vacation and could not be interviewed.

In January 2005, the room steward and hotel manager were deposed after Carver's lawyers in Florida and Massachusetts obtained court ordered subpoenas for their appearance. The room steward said he had reported

Merrian's disappearance but was told by his supervisor to just do his job and that the supervisor would take care of the matter. The hotel manager said that although they had not acted on Merrian's disappearance the company began its own internal investigation at the end of September after being contacted by Cambridge police. He also said the room steward's supervisor had been fired for failing to report Merrian's absence. The Carvers interpreted this as the company "cleaning house" and continuing in what they perceived to be a cover-up.

Their perception was reinforced when they were given in February a copy of the security report about Merrian's disappearance. The report noted that company regulations had been violated—the ship's captain, bridge and security office should have been notified as soon as Merrian disappeared and her personal belongings should not have been removed or her cabin disturbed until outside investigators arrived onboard. The more Ken learned the more he felt he wasn't being given all of the information. He also had the impression from documents he did receive that the company was covering up something. A year after Merrian's disappearance the Carvers sued the cruise line in a Miami court. Celebrity Cruises subsequently issued a statement stating that "Mrs. Carver had severe emotional problems, had attempted suicide before and appears to have committed suicide on our ship.... The death of Merrian Carver is a horrible tragedy, but, regrettably there is very little a cruise line, a resort, or a hotel can do to prevent someone from committing suicide" (Anglen 2005). Ken's response: how can they conclude Merrian committed suicide without an investigation and without facts? There is a range of other less attractive possibilities for the cruise line that are supported by fact, but by closing discussion with a definitive conclusion such as suicide these possibilities remain unexplored.

they claim the cruise line delayed reporting the incident to the FBI, deciding instead to report the case to Turkish authorities. When Royal Caribbean did contact the FBI, the suit claims the cruise line failed to tell authorities about loud noises and arguing in Smith's cabin and the discovery of blood inside and outside the cabin. As well, the family accuses Royal Caribbean of contaminating a possible crime scene by sending crewmembers into the cabin to investigate and take photographs and by cleaning blood from the canopy above a life boat.

The Smith case dominated news media in the United States for months and was the focus of stories in both print and television magazines. It particularly caught the attention of Smith's member of Congress, Christopher Shays, who was aware of some of the other cases involving disappearances from cruise ships and who pushed for and who chaired the first two Congressional hearings.

Congressional Hearings, Round 1

On December 13, 2005, joint hearings were convened by two subcommittees of the House of Representatives Committee on Government Reform: the Subcommittee on National Security, Emerging Threats and International Relations, chaired by Christopher Shays, and the Subcommittee on Criminal Justice, Drug Policy and Human Resources, chaired by Mark Souder. The hearings had a twofold purpose. First, given the attack of the *Seabourn Spirit* by pirates, they sought to determine the decision-making procedures and processes that were in place to determine the extent to which the U.S. Government responds to a ship being attacked by terrorists or pirates. In addition to the attack on the Seabourn ship, there was the hijacking of the *Achille Lauro* in the Mediterranean on October 7, 1985; the attack of the USS *Cole* in Aden, Yemen, on October 12, 2000; the attack of a French oil tanker on October 6, 2002, as it headed into a Yemeni port; and in 2004 some 330 acts of piracy directed against maritime vessels reported to the International Maritime Organization.

The second purpose of the hearings was to determine jurisdictional conflicts that occur when U.S. citizens traveling on a foreign-flagged vessel are involved in a criminal incident. These incidents included sexual assaults, physical assaults, robbery and missing persons. In addition to the disappearance of George Smith, the Committee acknowledged the disappearance of Hue Pham and Hue Tran from the *Carnival Destiny* in May 2005 and of James Scavone, a twenty-two-year-old man who disappeared from the *Carnival Destiny* on July 5, 1999, between San Juan and Miami. Just three days before the hearings opened another passenger, fifty-nine-year-old Canadian Jill Begora, disappeared from Royal Caribbean's *Jewel of the Seas* on its way to Nassau in the Bahamas.

The hearing received testimony from government officials, including the Department of Defense, the Coast Guard and the FBI, and from cruise industry representatives from the International Council of Cruise Lines, Royal Caribbean Cruises Limited and Carnival Corporation. It also received written testimony from family members of passengers who had disappeared. The cruise industry used the hearings, and surrounding media attention, as an opportunity to promote the safety and security of a cruise ship. This contrasts starkly with the briefing memo provided to members of the subcommittee conducting the hearings:

> Certain issues about cruise line travel should be highlighted to passengers. American passengers should be aware that even though they board a ship in a U.S. port it does not necessarily mean they are fully protected by the United States justice system. Most ships are registered outside the United States and travel in territorial waters where U.S. laws might not apply. Additionally, the cruise

industry does not report crime data consistently. The governing law, the International Maritime Law, is not as well developed as U.S. law. And finally, reporting a crime on board a cruise ship does not mean anything will be done or that a crime will be investigated. Passengers should be made aware of these issues. (Palarino and DeQuattro 2005: 12)

The hearings concluded with an assurance they would reconvene in March in order to hear directly from victims. In the meantime families of those victimized on cruise ships who met at the hearings launched the International Cruise Victims Association. The group's purpose was to provide support to the victims of crimes that occur on cruise ships, to advocate for legislative reform which would protect passengers from cruise crimes and to increase the rights of cruise crime victims.

Hearings reconvened March 7, 2006. The cruise industry was challenged to provide committee members with an understanding of their onboard security systems. It was also asked to present honest statistics about the incidence of crime on cruise ships. For the latter the industry hired James Alan Fox, a sociologist at Northeastern University in Boston, to compare incidents of sexual assault on cruise ships with incidence in the U.S. generally. This is a difficult task given that the U.S. does not keep track of sexual assaults; its crime statistics are limited to reports of rape. So Fox compared reports of sexual assault (defined as involving sexual contact or a sexual act) on cruise ships with the rate of forcible rape in the U.S.

In his testimony, Fox concluded that passengers were far safer onboard a cruise ship than in their home communities. He determined, based on data provided by the cruise lines, that the rate of sexual assault on cruise lines is—at worst—half the U.S. rate of forcible rate and said the low levels of rape "makes reasonable sense in view of the confined and highly secured environments offered on major cruise ships" (Fox 2006). Fox suggested a person is more likely to get struck by lightening than sexually assaulted on a cruise and that the odds of disappearing from a ship are less than one in a million. Committee Chair Shays expressed scepticism about the accuracy of the statistics. The scepticism was echoed by maritime attorney Brett Rivkind, who called attention to the fact that each of the major cruise corporations had previously altered reports and had lied to hide illegal dumping of waste and other environmental violations.

The hearings also heard from six witnesses who were either victims or related to victims. They heard the story of Lindsay O'Brien, a fifteen-year-old girl from Ireland who disappeared January 5, 2006, from *Costa Magica* as the ship sailed toward Cozumel—she had apparently been served more than ten alcoholic drinks within a short time frame and was so intoxicated that she fell overboard while vomiting over a balcony railing; of Janet Kelly, a forty-nine-year-old real estate agent from Arizona who was raped by a cruise ship employee in February 2000 after drinking two alcoholic beverages that she suspects were laced with drugs; of Merrian Carver, whose disappearance from Celebrity Cruise's *Mercury* in August 2003 had not been reported to authorities or her family; of Ira Leonard, who claimed that $6,700 worth of jewellery had been stolen during a cruise because employees had unauthorized access to his cabin—the cruise line said it would not report the theft to the FBI because the loss was less than $10,000; of Deborah Shaffer's fifteen-year-old daughter, who had been raped on *Carnival Legend* in April 2003; and of a couple that escaped from Vietnam in 1975, Hue Pham and Hue Tran, who disappeared from *Carnival Destiny* in May 2005. While the cruise line would prefer to view Mr. And Mrs. Pham's disappearance as a suicide, their son doubts that that was the case given they were looking forward after the cruise to a planned return to their native country for the first time in thirty years.

The Committee heard a number of recommendations from the ICV, many of which addressed known gaps and problems identified through victim experiences:

- better background checks of crewmembers and officers (including creation of a main database for reporting all terminated employees to ensure they are not rehired by another cruise line);
- placement of an independent police force or U.S. Marshals on cruise ships and public reporting of all crimes;
- security enhancements and better training of security personnel (including development of check lists for the handling of crimes and crime scenes);
- structural enhancements to make it more difficult for a passenger to go overboard;
- an upgrade to existing surveillance systems, an increase in the number of cameras and that cameras be monitored 24/7;
- use of access or security bracelets that include microchips so a passenger who is missing or falls overboard can be located;
- a ship be required to turn around and initiate a search immediately after a passenger is identified as missing;
- rape kits required to be available on all ships, that doctors be available 24/7, that no request or case be taken lightly and that written documentation be provided, signed and issued to the patient;
- that a cruise line be held accountable for the safety of its passengers on excursions it sells; and
- that cruise lines be accountable for the safety of their guests while onboard the ship.

The cruise industry was less than enthusiastic about the ICV's recommendations. Royal Caribbean's senior vice president for marine operations, Captain Bill Wright, claimed after the hearings that a majority of the recommendations were already being done and that others might be problematic under international law. He also suggested the requirement that "everyone wear microchips would raise civil liberty concerns... while U.S. marshals would not be practical given the size and complexity of a ship and the fact they would have jurisdiction over only U.S. citizens." He stated: "We have security officers and we have the ability to arrest and investigate" (Seatrade Insider 2006).

Subsequent to the hearing Representative Shays introduced on June 28, 2006, HR 5707, the *Cruise Line Accurate Safety Statistics Act*. The bill was straightforward. It required cruise ships that call at a port in the United States to report all crimes occurring on the ship in which a U.S. citizen is involved. It also required this information to be made available to the public on the Internet. The cruise industry didn't embrace the legislation and the legislation died in committee.

A Coroner's Inquest in Australia

As the hearings wound down in Washington, DC, a similar inquiry began in Australia. A coroner's inquest was convened to look into the death of Dianne Brimble, a forty-two-year-old woman from Brisbane who was given a date rape drug by a fellow passenger and found naked and dead on the floor of that passenger's cabin. As the inquest worked to untangle what happened to Dianne it heard accounts about cruise ship practices that had parallels with stories told about ships sailing from North American ports. The ship on which Dianne Brimble died was operated by P&O Australia, a subsidiary of U.S.-based Carnival Corporation.

The inquest heard that nudity, streaking and sex in public were common practices on the cruise ship and had been for at least ten years. According to the ship's night manager, such behaviour was so frequent that it would take up all their time to record the incidents. She also confided that she had once observed someone pour something into a drink that he was buying for a young lady. She had previously told a newspaper reporter that the ship's management had ignored requests that the cabin where Dianne died be treated as a crime scene (ABC Radio News 2006).

The day following these disclosures the cruise line released a new behaviour policy saying that passengers caught on nude romps or having sex in public would automatically be kicked off the ship at the next port of call. The cruise line also announced onboard bars would close for six hours from 4:00 a.m. (previously they operated around the clock), the number of security staff would be doubled from ten to twenty, surveillance cameras would be

Dianne Brimble, died from date rape drug, 2002

Dianne Brimble, a forty-two-year-old mother of three, worked in a furniture store in Brisbane. She had saved $2,100 for her and her twelve-year-old daughter to take a ten-day cruise aboard P&O Australia's *Pacific Sky*. She regretted that she couldn't afford to also take her two sons, aged fifteen and eighteen.

Dianne embarked the ship on September 23, 2002. She went to the disco with a friend that evening and later was seen dancing with a group of eight men. The next morning she was found dead on the floor of a cabin shared by four of the men. Lawyers assisting a coronial inquiry in Sydney alleged: "The normally prudish woman was given a fatal dose of the drug gamma hydroxybutyrate, known as GBH or fantasy.... Brimble was unable to refuse sexual advances from the men and she had sexual intercourse with one of them and performed oral sex on another before she died" (King 2006). One of the men told a group of other passengers that they'd considered throwing the body overboard, but there was too much traffic onboard the ship.

Much of what the inquiry initially learned was from women in a nearby cabin who had been pursued by three of the men while Dianne lay unconscious in their room. The women said:

> One of the men was running up and down the corridors, naked except for a life jacket. His friends said he had just "fucked a fat chick," and the women said they were shown pictures to prove it. Another member of the group passed out; the others stripped him, and started to play with his genitals, photographing him for posterity. (Topham 2006: 70)

Other passengers onboard also told of being approached and harassed by the men. Most felt intimidated and stayed out of the men's way.

Dianne's death was reported the morning of September 24—some reports suggest she had already been dead for up to three and a half hours. Australian police were notified and met the ship two days later in Noumea. But the investigation was already flawed. The cabin where Dianne was found had not been sealed as a crime scene. In fact, the men who would become persons of interest in her death had been allowed back into the cabin by staff to collect their belongings and then moved to a new cabin. Perversely, Dianne's daughter was kept locked out of her cabin, in which Dianne had not slept.

In addition, the investigation was hampered because interview of key witnesses had been delayed by up to four days. And only by good fortune was a key piece of evidence, a digital chip from one of the men's camera, not lost. It had been found by a child passenger and turned into lost and found. But then it was removed from lost and found by a junior assistant purser who thought the memory chip would fit his camera. After an unidentified passenger came looking for the memory chip, the junior purser was contacted by his supervisor,

> who suspected he had taken it. He confessed to having lifted the item but he also brought the supervisor's attention to information on the chip that might be of interest to police.
>
> The coronial inquest ran from March 2006 to July 2007. In the end, the New South Wales deputy coroner, Jacqueline Milledge, concluded there was evidence capable of satisfying a jury that "known persons" had committed indictable offences. She specifically recommended that two of the eight men of interest in the coronial inquiry be charged over Dianne Brimble's death.

installed and bartenders would receive training in the responsible service of alcohol (Carter 2006). It subsequently also eliminated commissions paid to bar staff for their volume of sales. A couple of months earlier the company announced it would begin using sniffer dogs to check for drugs being brought onboard by passengers. And it acknowledged that a 2003 advertising campaign was in poor taste. The campaign used a postcard that on the front had "a prostrate row of four tanned women, like so many sausages on a spit, with the line: 'Seamen wanted.'... Along with a photograph of the *Pacific Sky*, P&O's ad featured the slogan: 'More girls. More sun. More fun. There's nothing else a guy needs to know'" (Devine 2006: 15).

The inquest also heard that the crime scene had not been secured—the men whose cabin in which Dianne's body lay (while there were attempts to revive her) were allowed to enter the room to retrieve their belongings (including pills and bottles). And it heard from a passenger who, before Dianne even met the men, complained to the service desk about the men implicated in her death after they behaved inappropriately toward the woman's teenaged daughters, but the complaint yielded no apparent response; and from an onboard entertainer who said he was told by security and by the cruise director to keep his mouth shut when he attempted to provide information about Brimble. He testified that he was told not to talk to anyone about this and said he'd been told, "This has gone straight to head office and if the media gets hold of this they will have a field day" (Davies 2006).

While the inquest was ongoing, the cruise line finally apologized in February 2007, four and a half years after Dianne's death, for the grief suffered by her family and it offered financial compensation. The apology was incorporated in a press conference where Peter Radcliffe, CEO of the Princess/P&O division of Carnival Corporation spoke. In addition to pointing out changes that have been initiated since after the inquest began he acknowledged he had met with Dianne's ex-husband, Mark Brimble, who headed the International Cruise Victims Association in Australia and who was lobbying both the cruise line and the Australia government for substantive changes such as those being advocated in the United States.

Congressional Hearings, Round 2

Shays' *Cruise Line Accurate Safety Statistics Act* died in Committee when the Congressional session ended December 2006. The issue of crime on cruise ships could have ended with the shift in Congress from a Republican to a Democrat majority. But two things appear to have stemmed that possibility.

First, the *Los Angeles Times* published an article on January 20, 2007, which based on internal documents from Royal Caribbean said sex related onboard incidents was a larger problem than the cruise industry suggested in March 2006. The documents revealed 273 reported incidents within a period of thirty-two months, including ninety-nine cases of sexual harassment, eighty-one of sexual assault, fifty-two of inappropriate touching, twenty-eight of sexual battery and thirteen cases that fit into other categories (Yoshino 2007). When the company-specific numbers were subjected to the same statistical analysis as done with industry-wide data for James Fox's 2006 testimony before Congress, the rate of sexual assault was not half the average rate for rape in the U.S. but 50 percent greater than the U.S. rate (see Klein 2007b). In contrast to 17.6 cases per 100,000 people shown in the industry's analysis the Royal Caribbean data yielded a rate of 48.1.

One explanation offered by the cruise industry for the discrepancy between their presentation in 2006 and the testimony in 2007 was that the data presented to Congress in 2006 did not include passengers who were groped, were subjected to indecent exposure or had crewmembers enter their rooms without permission to proposition them. To a large degree most of these types of incidents had also been excluded from the analysis of the Royal Caribbean data so the explanation doesn't work. At the same time, it is difficult to know precisely what was included and excluded from the industry's analysis without the raw data being made public and available for independent analysis.

The second factor that pushed for a new round of hearings was that Representative Doris Matsui from California had a constituent, Laurie Dishman, appeal to her for help. Matsui was not only concerned about the way Laurie had been treated and her case handled but also with discrepancies in crime statistics. She told the *Los Angeles Times* that she planned to co-sponsor a new version of Shays' *Cruise Line Accurate Safety Statistics Act*. From her position on the House Transportation and Infrastructure Committee she pushed for a new round of hearings to be held March 27, 2007, before the Subcommittee on Coast Guard and Maritime Transportation. The purpose of the hearing was to examine the incidents of crime that occur on cruise ships and the extent to which federal agencies have the information, legal authorities pertaining to these crimes and resources necessary to investigate and prosecute crimes that may occur on these ships.

The first witnesses before the Subcommittee were from the Coast Guard and the FBI. They opened by announcing an agreement that had just been reached with the cruise industry whereby cruise line members of the Cruise Line International Association (CLIA) agreed to report to the FBI (either a field office in the U.S. or the FBI Legal Attaché at an embassy or consulate closest to the vessel's location at the time of the incident) all crimes against U.S. citizens on their ships. To many the timing of the announcement was suspicious. As well, the agreement appeared to be a rehash of the "zero tolerance" policy announced by the International Council of Cruise Lines in 1999 and it was redundant to reporting requirements already in place. The key difference was a standardized form for reporting crimes to the FBI, for use in establishing a data set from which reports could be drawn for Congress and other government authorities. The data would not to be available to the public.

The second set of witnesses presented concerns of victims. Ken Carver again testified about Merrian's disappearance and presented recommendations and concerns in his role as President of ICV. Laurie Dishman, in heart wrenching testimony, told her story of being raped on Royal Caribbean's *Vision of the Seas* in February 2006. At one point she asked whether the cruise industry had forgotten about their pledge in hearings held four weeks after she was raped, where they said they would cooperate with victims and provide them information. Her experience was that the promise was not being fulfilled. The other two witnesses for ICV were myself, a sociologist and professor of social work at Memorial University of Newfoundland, and James Hickey, a maritime lawyer in Miami who had earlier in his career represented Royal Caribbean. As already mentioned, my testimony (based on the data presented in the article in the *Los Angeles Times* two months earlier) was that the rate of sexual assault on cruise ships is 50 percent greater than the rate for forcible rape in the U.S. generally.

The final witnesses were representatives of the cruise industry. As in earlier hearings, they used the forum to talk about their commitment to passenger safety, to re-emphasize that cruising is safe and to discuss recent initiatives. One industry representative, Gary Bald, senior vice president of global security for Royal Caribbean Cruises, specifically outlined initiatives undertaken since his arrival with the cruise corporation in June 2006. Prior to his employment with Royal Caribbean he served as director of the National Security Branch of the FBI and as leader of the counterterrorism division. A month after the hearings, Royal Caribbean hired another FBI employee. Eleni Pryles Kalisch, the FBI's assistant director of congressional affairs, was hired to serve as Royal Caribbean's vice president of congressional affairs. It appears Royal Caribbean is doing with the FBI what the industry has generally done with retired members of the Coast Guard—they are hired to work for the cruise line and to interface with their former colleagues and associates who remain with the government agency.

At the end of the hearings the subcommittee chair, Elijah Cummings, called on the CLIA and ICV to get together and to attempt to find some common ground and solutions. He said he'd prefer a solution that did not require legislation but also said that legislation was always an option. He gave the two sides six months and said the hearings would reconvene in September.

Following from Cumming's request the ICV made several efforts to have a meeting that included a small group of its members and supporters and a similar sized group from the CLIA. The meeting finally took place late July. It allowed for a sharing of views and perspectives but did not resolve with any firm agreement or direction. To the contrary, progress was limited given that, while the CLIA was dragging its feet in agreeing to meet with the ICV, it was working to convene a meeting of cruise victims with a view toward establishing a survivor's working group. Ironically, the CLIA expected the ICV to cooperate in establishing this group by inviting its members to attend even though the advisory group would overlap the ICV's mission and would likely be used to marginalize and usurp the ICV's role in the process.

The industry convened its meeting of survivors on August 14, 2007. It was facilitated by Carolyn Coarsey from the Family Assistance Foundation. According to its website, the Family Assistance Foundation was formed initially in response to airplane disasters. It is an independent nonprofit foundation established for the purpose of empowering people following tragedy. Its mission is to support and improve business and industry responses to emergencies and disasters. In this case it was contracted by the cruise industry to assist in dealing with the problem of cruise victims. To members of the ICV it appeared perverse that an organization claiming a commitment to empowering people following tragedy would allow itself to be used by the cruise industry to disempower an existing group of several hundred people who had experienced tragedy at the hands of the cruise industry.

Attendance at the CLIA convened meeting of victims was light with a total of thirteen victim families. Eleven families were members of the ICV; the other two were invited by Carnival and were qualitatively different than victims represented by the ICV—each had experienced a family member dying from natural causes while on a cruise.

The meeting concluded with the CLIA president, Terry Dale, announcing plans to establish a survivor working group. The group's purpose would be to facilitate a continued and structured dialogue among survivors of incidents on cruise ships and representatives of CLIA member cruise lines and CLIA management. Issues of common concern include how cruise lines respond to allegations of crime or tragedies involving the safety, health and welfare of cruise passengers. Among the topics to be addressed are enhancement of cruise ship security and safety, prevention measures, vetting of shore excursions, training of staff, timely reporting of incidents to law enforcement, preservation of evidence, appropriate communications and care and assistance to those in need. These are issues on which the ICV had been working for almost two years but the CLIA appeared to prefer a hand picked group under its control to an independent body representing a grassroots constituency such as ICV.

Hearings Reconvened

The day before the Congressional subcommittee reconvened on September 19, 2007, Representatives Matsui and Shays with twenty-three co-sponsors introduced a House Resolution to call attention to the growing level of crime on cruise ships and the lack of federal regulations overseeing the cruise industry. In a press release announcing the resolution, Matsui stated:

> It is simply unacceptable that American citizens are susceptible to such nefarious crimes on cruise ships. Victims continue to have little or no recourse when they have been assaulted. Awareness is a key part of prevention, and this legislation will educate the public about the possibility for crime to occur on cruise ships. Congress needs to provide the oversight and leadership to ensure that vacationers and families are safe and understand their risks. This resolution is a strong first step in establishing this priority. (Matsui 2007)

The purpose of the reconvened hearings was to receive an update on the status of discussions between the ICV and CLIA and to examine whether the security practices and procedures aboard cruise ships are adequate to ensure the safety of all passengers. As before it received testimony from the FBI and Coast Guard, which discussed the implementation of the reporting framework announced at the previous hearings; from the ICV and several of its members; and from the cruise industry.

Not surprisingly the cruise industry painted a picture that said everything was under control, that it is working diligently to improve situations raised as sources of concern by its critics and that cruises continue to be safe (see Dale 2007). The claim of safety was based in large part on the FBI receiving from cruise ships only forty-one reports of sexual assault and twenty-eight cases of sexual contact between April 1 and August 23, 2007. Together, these numbers give an annualized rate for sexual abuse on CLIA member cruise lines of 172 incidents; a rate of 56.9 per 100,000 passengers. The industry also used the hearings to announce formation of its survivor working group,

The Committee also heard from several victims or survivors. These included the parents of Daniel DiPiero. Daniel, aged twenty-one, disappeared from Royal Caribbean's *Mariner of the Seas* in the early morning hours of May 15, 2005. The story that unfolded was that Daniel had left the disco at

Richard Liffridge, died of smoke inhalation, 2006

On March 23, 2006, at approximately 3 a.m. a fire broke out in an exterior stateroom balcony of the *Star Princess*, on its passage from Grand Cayman to Montego Bay, Jamaica. A subsequent investigation suggests the fire was caused by a discarded cigarette end heating combustible materials on a balcony on Deck 10. The fire smouldered for about twenty minutes before flames developed, but once established, the fire spread quickly. Within six minutes it had spread up to decks 11 and 12 and into staterooms as the heat shattered the glass in stateroom doors. Fortunately it was contained by the fire smothering system and the restricted combustibility of the room's contents (MAIB 2006).

Richard and Victoria Liffridge were onboard and awoke to the short, faint sound of an alarm followed by static on the ship's intercom. Victoria opened their cabin door and observed a crewmember knocking on the door across the hall but he said nothing to her. As she began to close the door she heard a friend yelling, "The ship is on fire! Everyone get out!" Victoria turned to Richard and repeated the words. She says in her statement on the International Cruise Victims Association website that he sat there in shock for a few seconds. She then called to him to get up and get dressed! As they began exiting their cabin the only light shining in the hallway was from their room.

They crawled through thick, black smoke barely able to see their hands in front of them, Victoria holding Richard's shirt tail so they wouldn't become separated. But the ship suddenly shifted and she lost her grip.

I was unable to speak or call out to Richard, because the smoke had gotten into my lungs. As I moved to the right side of the hallway, the ship shifted again, ramming my right shoulder into the corner of the wall. As a result, I was no longer able to extend my arm out in reach of Richard. My shoulder felt as though someone had stabbed me, but when I was finally able to extend it, I heard Richard say, "Vicky, don't let me die!" I kept trying to find him in the darkness.

The sprinklers never came on, and there were no lights or fire extinguishers or smoke detectors in the hallway. Moments later, I heard a door close and I assumed Richard had made it to the emergency exit.

I started crawling as fast as I could, but just before reaching the emergency door, I heard a woman call out, "Someone help me, please. I don't know which way to go." I felt her in front of me. As hard as I could, I tugged on her clothing, pulling her in my direction.

I felt myself getting weak, as though I was going to pass out, but I finally reached the emergency door and pushed it open. (Liffridge 2007)

Victoria was taken to the auditorium, which was being used as a muster station. She asked a staff person about her husband and was told forty-five minutes later that everyone had been located and they were safe in Muster Station B. Not long after she was transported to the infirmary and learned that Richard had died. Initial reports from the cruise line were that he died of a heart attack. An autopsy indicated he died from smoke inhalation.

Victoria notified one of Richard's children of his death, who then notified his siblings. Richard's daughter Lynette was reached at work. When she told work associates what had happened she learned that a few had heard about the fire and even printed an article that was on the Internet. The article included her father's name even though next of kin had not yet been notified. One article had a toll free number for family members to call for more information and Lynette immediately called. She was told they were not able to release any information to her. After several calls she became irate; then there was an effort to help. She was given the phone number for the local hospital where Victoria was being treated. When Lynette called, Victoria thought she had been contacted by Princess Cruises because Lynette was listed as the person to contact in an emergency. But that sadly was not the case.

While Princess Cruises offered passengers on the ill-fated cruises a 25 percent discount on a future cruise and provided transportation back home, the cruise line would not commit to paying the cost of bringing Lynette's father home. The cruise line also continued to report the cause of Richard's death as a heart attack. In Lynette's words:

> Five months later, we still have no answers. What we do know is that my father died needlessly from smoke inhalation trying to escape a death trap. The death trap was caused by no emergency lighting, no fire extinguishers in the corridors and no sprinklers. We do know that the fire originated on an external stateroom balcony sited on deck 10 on the vessel's port side. We know that the ship was a Bermuda registered cruise ship and was not required to have fire extinguishers, sprinklers or smoke detectors on the external areas of the ship. We also know that it took one to one and a half hours to fight the fire due to the construction and partitioning of the balcony areas. We know that highly combustible materials were used on the balconies and the balcony partitions were of a polycarbonate material that produced large amounts of dense black smoke. It should be noted that we still have not received a note, phone call or sympathy card from Princess Cruise Line. It is as if this never happened. (Hudson 2007)

Eighteen months after his death the family established The Richard Liffridge Foundation, which has as its mission the enhancement of fire safety regulations and safety in general on cruise ships and to influence substantive changes to the *Death on the High Seas Act* (DOHSA).

around midnight after one of the bartenders stopped serving him; he and his friends went to another bar where they obtained additional drinks. A bit later Daniel left his friends and went out onto the deck of the vessel and fell asleep on a deck chair. At 2:15 a.m. a surveillance video camera observed Daniel awakening, walking over to the railing, apparently vomiting and then sliding over the rail into the sea. His parents later learned that the cruise line never monitored its surveillance videotapes and it hadn't reviewed surveillance videotapes promptly when they learned that Daniel was missing. As a result they assert there was a significant delay in notifying the authorities that Daniel was missing and that rescue efforts took place many hours after he went overboard.

Another survivor witness was Angela Orlich. Angela is a college student who took a cruise with a group of friends in January 2003 on Royal Caribbean's *Nordic Empress*. Onboard she purchased a shore excursion in Cozumel that included scuba diving. She went on the tour and was molested by the dive instructor while she was 60 feet under water (see Orlich 2007). Angela reported the incident to the cruise line and to the U.S. consulate in Mexico. The cruise line's position was that they had no liability for the actions of concessionaires and service providers not directly employed by Royal Caribbean and they had no obligation or intent to report the attack to the FBI.

Two other victims' stories were told. One was told by the lawyer for Jane Doe, the twenty-year-old woman who was raped in March 2007 by a crewmember onboard a Royal Caribbean ship. The other was told by Lynette Hudson, whose father died of smoke inhalation on Princess Cruises' *Star Princess* in March 2006. The fire, likely caused by a discarded cigarette, broke out in the early morning hours when the ship was between Grand Cayman and Montego Bay, Jamaica. It was extinguished within about ninety minutes. Seventy-nine cabins were destroyed. Lynette's father, Richard Liffridge, was the sole casualty. Eleven other passengers were seriously injured.

An investigation of the fire by U.K.'s Marine Accident Investigation Branch complimented the ship's initial response to the fire, but also raised significant concerns. According to the report,

> It was fortunate the fire was contained and extinguished by the crew. Had external assistance been required, the time lost by not sending [the urgency] PAN PAN message could have been significant. (MAIB 2006: 44)

The report also raised concern that the probability that passengers were trapped in the rooms only became apparent when the staff engineer recovered two passengers from their stateroom, and that one couple trapped in their room by smoke found they were unable to alert the crew that they needed help by calling 911 from their stateroom telephone because the customer service desk was not staffed after the crew alert of the fire was signalled. The fire instigated a wave of smoking bans subsequently introduced by a number of cruise lines (Sloan 2007).

The *Star Princess* fire also rekindled concern about the cruise industry's response to recommendations from the National Transportation Safety Board (NTSB). The industry had initially opposed a NTSB recommendation that locally sounding fire alarms be placed in passenger cabins, a recommendation that followed from three cruise ship fires in 1996, one of which was the *Universe Explorer*, in which five crewmembers died and sixty-seven crew and two passengers were injured (see NTSB 1998). The cruise industry dropped its opposition in 2000 and issued a press release stating a commitment to install locally sounding alarms but it did not give a timetable or deadline. It isn't clear whether the *Star Princess* had locally sounding alarms but it did lack emergency call systems from rooms, something recommended by the NTSB following the fire on Carnival Cruise Lines' *Ecstasy* in 1998 (MAIB 2006: 43).

Less than a week after the hearings the House Committee on Homeland Security approved by voice vote inclusion of language in the *Coast Guard Authorization Act* requiring cruise lines to notify the Department of Homeland Security Secretary of security related incidents involving U.S. persons when it advises its next port of call of its arrival. Incidents required to be reported under the legislation include any act that results in death, serious bodily injury, sexual assault, a missing person or that poses a significant threat to the cruise ship, any cruise ship passenger, any port facility or any person in or near the port. Unlike Representative Shays' *Cruise Line Accurate Safety Statistics Act* the reports would not be made public.

At the same time there was a move involving Senator John Kerry and Representatives Matsui, Shays and Maloney to write legislation that would require cruise ships to immediately notify the FBI about crimes, suicides and disappearances. The legislation would also provide protocols for collecting evidence. The legislation in many ways is like the agreement announced in March 2007 between the CLIA and the FBI but it would be mandatory. A key requirement of any legislation or regulation, if it is to be useful to the public, is public disclosure—it is unclear whether this will be achieved. At issue is that passengers should know the history of problems and incidents on a cruise ship, much the same as they can view reports of sanitation inspections conducted on cruise ships by the Centres for Disease Control.

Is There a Pattern to Sexual Assault?

One is left to wonder whether there are discernible patterns given the number of sexual assaults on cruise ships. Is it possible to gain insight into why incidents appear to be increasing rather than decreasing despite industry efforts

Table 2.1: RCI Reported Sex Related Incidents by Ship, 2003–2005

Ship	Inappropriate Touch	Sexual Harassment (SH)	Sexual Assault (SA)	Total Incidents of SH + SA
Empress of the Seas	2	7	8	15
Annualized rate per 100,000		97.22	111.11	208.33
Monarch of the Seas	6	5	15	20
Annualized rate per 100,000		47.62	142.86	190.48
Voyager of the Seas	2	11	14	25
Annualized rate per 100,000		79.71	101.45	181.16
Explorer of the Seas	2	13	11	24
Annualized rate per 100,000		94.20	79.71	173.91
Majesty of the Seas	1	10	7	17
Annualized rate per 100,000		95.24	66.67	161.91
Brilliance of the Seas	2	6	7	13
Annualized rate per 100,000		64.52	75.27	139.79
Sovereign of the Seas	1	5	7	12
Annualized rate per 100,000		49.02	65.63	114.65
Rhapsody of the Seas	0	3	7	10
Annualized rate per 100,000		33.33	77.77	111.10
Radiance of the Seas	4	7	3	10
Annualized rate per 100,000		75.27	32.26	107.53
Navigator of the Seas	3	6	8	14
Annualized rate per 100,000		43.48	57.97	101.45
Enchantment of the Seas	1	4	4	8
Annualized rate per 100,000		45.97	45.97	91.94
Vision of the Seas	7	4	4	8
Annualized rate per 100,000		44.44	44.44	88.88
Serenade of the Seas	0	5	2	7
Annualized rate per 100,000		53.76	21.51	75.27
Legend of the Seas	2	2	4	6
Annualized rate per 100,000		24.69	49.38	74.07
Mariner of the Seas	0	6	4	10
Annualized rate per 100,000		43.48	28.99	72.47
Adventure of the Seas	0	3	5	8
Annualized rate per 100,000		21.74	36.23	57.97

Ship	Inappropriate Touch	Sexual Harassment (SH)	Sexual Assault (SA)	Total Incidents of SH + SA
Grandeur of the Seas	1	2	3	5
Annualized rate per 100,000		22.99	34.48	57.47
Splendour of the Seas	1	2	0	2
Annualized rate per 100,000		24.69	0.0	24.69
Jewel of the Seas	1	1	0	1
Annualized rate per 100,000		10.75	0.0	10.75
Totals	36	102	113	215
Annualized rate per 100,000		53.12	58.85	111.97

Source: Cruise Junkie dot Com

to deal with the problem?

Some interesting insights can be derived from analysis of data of sex related incidents disclosed by Royal Caribbean in discovery in a lawsuit. The data set combines the previously discussed data reported by the *Los Angeles Times* in January 2007 and cases reported to Congress in March 2006. While the data focuses on a single cruise line it is safe to assume it reflects an industry-wide pattern. The rate of sexual assault using this data (2003 to 2005) is not significantly different from the rate found in 2007 for all CLIA members (58.85 vs. 56.9 incidents per 100,000 passengers).

Table 2.1 shows a breakdown by ship of sex related incidents on Royal Caribbean ships. Adopting the labels used by the cruise line as much as possible (and resolving competing labels on different lists) the table distinguishes between incidents of inappropriate touching, sexual harassment (often with a physical component or including non-consensual contact of a sexual nature) and sexual assault.

The Royal Caribbean data also revealed that 67 percent of the incidents involve a crewmember and passenger, 22 percent involve two passengers and almost 11 percent involve two crewmembers. This last category is likely under represented because the subpoena leading to discovery focused on assaults of passengers. All crew-on-crew assaults may not have been included and many may have been classified as personnel issues rather than assault.

As can be seen there is a wide variation between ships. Some, such as *Jewel of the Seas*, have relatively few incidents. Others, such as *Monarch of the Seas*, *Empress of the Seas* and *Voyager of the Seas*, have many. The obvious question is what can be extrapolated from these differences. That question was posed to several Royal Caribbean onboard staff members. Their responses touched on several issues.

One factor is that incidents vary by cruise length and itinerary. Shorter cruises (three or four days in length) often attract a different type of passenger than cruises lasting a week or more. Those on an over-weekend mini-cruise may drink more and take greater part in the nightlife, sometimes to excess. They risk becoming more vulnerable to crewmembers or other passengers. There are also special interest cruises (including partial charters or large affinity groups) that attract passengers who are different than the norm depicted in advertising (e.g., swingers, bikers, hard rockers, etc). While it is difficult to assign a degree of increased risk there is reason to believe that passengers are at greater risk on some cruises than on others simply because of the itinerary, the nature of other cruise passengers or the cruise length.

A large factor in risk to passengers and to crew is the onboard culture set by management. Some ship captains maintain higher expectations and low tolerance for misbehaviour by crewmembers than others. Others, however, may be less respectful to their crew (acting authoritarian and being unfair in decision-making, such as an officer denying promotions to subordinates involved with female crewmembers he liked) and create an environment that is less healthy for staff and potentially higher risk for passengers. This difference in management styles was cited by some workers as a key factor in the rate of incidence of sexual assault and harassment. Some officers provide better role models than others through their own behaviour, both in terms of alcohol consumption and treatment of women crew and passengers. A womanizing captain, or a captain who allows senior staff to sexually exploit staff/crew and passengers, sets a tone and gives permission to others to behave the same.

Shipboard culture overlaps with the culture from which crewmembers come. Many locations in the world have different attitudes than those commonly held in North America about women's rights and about the nature of relationships between men and women. Specific cultural views of what constitutes sexual harassment and unwanted attention are a possible risk factor. As Greenwood states, "It was the subjective opinion stated by many officers and crewmembers that the cultural inclination toward aggressive sexual behaviour, general low regard for the status of women and the attractiveness and charming personalities of these nationals [(referring to one cultural/ethnic group)] is a risk factor to be considered" (1999: 3–4). The problem is that a crewmember may behave in ways that are acceptable in his or her home culture but that are inappropriate or abusive in North American culture.

There is no simple solution to the problem but the ship-by-ship comparison suggests that some ships and ship management are doing things better than others. There are likely things to be learned by focusing on those ships where sex related incidents are relatively few and comparing them to those where incidents are many. The differences may provide insight and direction for positive change. But this type of analysis is not being done. As the industry stated in 2007, they lack the metrics for doing this. While the goal of each cruise line should be consistency across the ships in its brand, it is something that is not being achieved (Krohne 1999).

Michael Eriksen, a lawyer who represents victims of crime on cruise ships has another perspective. He says some forms of crew misconduct derive from the cruise industry's business models and hiring practices.

> Crew members live and work in confined quarters, are away from home for extended periods, and work long hours with little downtime, even during port calls. The crew's alienation from normal home and family activities leaves many vulnerable to social entanglements with passengers. (Eriksen 2006: 48)

Eriksen posits that many if not most crewmembers alleged to have committed sexual offences against passengers aboard cruise ships have been cabin stewards, bartenders, dinner waiters or others whose jobs involve daily passenger contact. He suggests:

> To deter such misbehaviour, a cruise line must do more than write up a "zero tolerance" policy and pay lip service to it. Criminals aboard cruise ships, like those elsewhere, commit crimes because they perceive a minimal risk of detection and prosecution. Some cruise lines fail to install sufficient surveillance cameras in public areas to identify and deter potential perpetrators. Other carriers fail to hire enough supervisors and security guards to adequately keep tabs on the rest of the crew. Some carriers fail to make it clear to crewmembers that zero tolerance also applies to crew-passenger contact ashore. Carriers also generally do not warn passengers to be wary of crewmember misconduct. (Eriksen 2006: 49)

The Complexion of Risk

There are, as well, other risks to going on a cruise ship, though most pale in comparison to those already discussed. Ships have accidents—running aground or colliding with an object or another ship—and some have sunk. While these incidents attract broad media attention, most passengers needn't be more concerned about these than they are about the likelihood of the plane in which they are flying crashing or having some other major accident. After all, accidents happen.

While many accidents such as fires (rarely totally disabling) and propulsion problems appear to be randomly distributed across the industry, others appear to have greater likelihood on some ships. For example, ships that have sunk in the past decade with few exceptions have been older ships owned by small companies (see <www.cruisejunkie.com/Sunk.html> for a list of ships that have sunk since 1979). Two cruise ships sank in 2007: Louis Cruises' *Sea Diamond* sunk after running aground off Santorini in April (two passengers perished) and GAP Adventures' *Explorer* sunk off Antarctica near the South Shetland Islands after hitting ice and was evacuated in the middle of the night without loss of life. Both incidents underlined the importance of safety equipment and procedures. Evacuation of *Sea Diamond* was reportedly disorganized and not well facilitated by officers or staff. Abandoning *Explorer* was hampered by lifeboats that didn't easily deploy and engines on lifeboats that wouldn't start, which could have been catastrophic had weather and ice conditions been bad.

This shouldn't be taken as an indication to not travel on an old ship or on a ship operated by a niche player or foreign corporation. Relatively new ships have had their share of problems. Princess Cruises' *Crown Princess* had been in service about a month when scores of passengers were injured when the ship listed as much as twenty-four degrees. The second officer, the senior watch officer on the bridge, had disengaged the automatic steering mode of the vessel's integrated navigation system and taken manual control of the steering (NTSB 2008). And Hurtigruten's (Norwegian Coastal Voyages) *Fram* was less than a year old when on December 27, 2007, it lost power for about two hours while near Brown Bluff on the northern tip of the Antarctic Peninsula and drifted straight toward a towering wall of ice. The collision with the glacier bent the railing and a lifeboat was completely crushed. The engine was restarted and the ship headed for King George Island, where it was inspected for damage. The cruise was cancelled so repairs could be made.

The fact that all ships have accidents and problems (for details see <www.cruisejunkie.com/events.html>) is a reminder that passengers need to be prepared regardless of the ship. This means being familiar with safety procedures, escape routes and taking seriously the lifeboat drill held at the start of most if not all cruises. Too few passengers take these seriously and as a result risk not knowing what to do if an accident happens.

Before You Embark

It is tempting to believe that cruise ships are safe. But this is not justified, even if the only consideration is recent testimony before the U.S. Congress. Some perils, such as ship accidents and fires, are well beyond a passenger's control, which means one must be prepared to endure the inconvenience when something happens. In most cases a cruise line responds to these things as quickly and fairly as possible (though not always). But they are in business to make money so expectations for compensation need to be modest (especially given international conventions that govern liability). For example, after Louis Cruises' *Sea Diamond* sank off the coast of Santorini in April 2007 with the loss of two passengers' lives, those evacuated received 1,400 euros (approximately US$1,896) in compensation. This included 1,000 euros for lost luggage, the maximum amount payable under the International Maritime Organization's Athens Convention (relating to damage or loss suffered by passengers on seagoing vessels) and 400 euros for the missed port call at Santorini. Each passenger was also given 200 euros after evacuation for immediate expenses. Losses exceeding these limits were either absorbed by the passenger or claimed on their household insurance, if they had appropriate coverage.

There are other things about which cruise passengers should be aware. For example, they should know there is no guarantee that anything will happen even though a crime against them has been reported to the FBI (which has jurisdiction over crimes against Americans but not necessarily over crimes against other against nationals—the FBI does not receive reports of crimes against non-U.S. citizens). At the very least, robberies normally must exceed $10,000 in value for the FBI to investigate. Sexual assaults similarly must reach a threshold of severity for action to be taken. "He said/she said" cases aren't pursued. This means criminal prosecution is unlikely in many situations. A passenger's only recourse may be a civil case.

If a passenger does plan to initiate civil action then they must take responsibility for collecting evidence and for securing the names and contact information of witnesses and perpetrators. They should also ensure that a crime is reported to authorities off the ship by contacting the FBI directly or a law enforcement agency in a port and/or their home country.

Cruise ship passengers should also know they are treated differently than airline passengers under the *Death on the High Seas Act*. The Act, originally passed in 1920, presently does not allow non-pecuniary and punitive damages to families of someone who has died while at sea on a cruise ship. These limits were deemed to be unfair in the context of aviation cases and were removed but they were not changed for passenger ships. House Resolution 2989, introduced by Representative Doggett on July 11, 2007, intends to correct this inconsistency but to date it has not been approved. This means that for now a cruise line's liability is limited in the case of a marine disaster. It cannot be punished for its role in a death on the high seas and family members are not entitled to compensation for the loss of care, comfort and companionship from the loss of a loved one.

Perhaps the best preparation before going on a cruise is to read two documents. One, "The Cruise Passenger's Rights and Remedies," is written and regularly updated by New York Supreme Court Justice Thomas A. Dickerson; it is available online. It gives a comprehensive accounting of legal cases involving cruise lines and passengers and is a sobering reminder of the rights, or limited rights, a passenger has. The other document, which is more accessible and relevant for most people, is the cruise ticket contract issued with a passenger's cruise documents before boarding and which may be found (not necessarily easily) on the website of most cruise lines.

The cruise contract is important because passengers are deemed to have accepted its terms and conditions when they embark a cruise. The contract defines where disputes must be settled (usually in the city and state where the cruise line is centred, even if one is not a U.S. resident), the time frame within which notification must be given of a claim (usually six months) and the means by which claims are resolved (some lines require binding arbitration, except in claims involving personal injury, illness or death). It also limits the cruise line's liability such that it is not held responsible for the behaviour or actions of the ship's physician, nurse, onboard concessions (e.g., the gift shop, spa, beauty salon, fitness centre, golf and art programs, video and snorkel concessions) or for shore excursions sold onboard. And it is not liable for intentional or negligent acts of its employees committed while off duty or outside the scope of their employment. This last point, often challenged in lawsuits, suggests there are few instances in which a cruise line is liable for a sexual assault given that the assault occurs outside the scope of the person's employment and they are presumably off-duty.

Not surprisingly the cruise contract is biased toward the cruise line's interest. This is most obvious in provisions that give the cruise line free and exclusive rights to use pictures and videos of its guests in its advertising or in other promotional material, but passengers are limited to only private use of their photographs and videos taken onboard; they are strictly prohibited (without the cruise line's written consent) from distributing or broadcasting any images of themselves, other passengers or the ship. One company states this last point as a condition to being permitted onboard the vessel.

For those who choose to cruise, it is important to take responsibility and caution. The risk for sexual assault and accidents demands it. Children should be supervised and if allowed to explore the ship should be accompanied by an adult or an older child. In any case, they should be advised on how to protect and defend themselves and be told what to do should they find themselves in a situation that doesn't feel right. Adults, particularly women, also need to take precautions. Try not to wander the ship alone, especially late at night when others aren't around. Also, both men and women should control alcohol use in order to maintain their senses and defences should a threat be present. It isn't just the risk of assault, but the number of mysterious disappearances from ships that suggests the need for caution.

It is important not to assume safety. Treat a ship like one would a hotel in a major city. If there is no peephole in the door to see who is knocking then don't answer the door. Unlike hotels few cruise ship rooms have peepholes and none have secondary locks in the form of chains or deadbolts. There are deadbolts on the door handles but these give a false sense of security given that on some cruise lines the room steward's passkey can override the lock and on all ships there is a key that can be used for override. It isn't a matter of living in fear on a ship but of taking precautions to ensure safety. The main thing is to not believe cruise industry claims about safety. Treat a cruise ship like any other vacation destination that is unfamiliar and populated mainly by unknown strangers.

If something does happen, do not assume the same law enforcement involvement or investigative processes as would be found at home. A cruise ship is self contained and the cruise line has its own interests at play. Admitting to the problem of sexual assault and allowing incidents to become public is not in their interest. As a result, incidents may not always be reported and, when reported, may not be investigated or prosecuted because of lack of usable evidence. It is unfortunately incumbent upon a victim to take responsibility for building a case that may be used by shoreside authorities and/or in a civil suit should an attack or other crime take place. Just as the cruise line often sends its lawyers or risk management team to a ship when an attack occurs, the victim must take similar precautions and actions. They need to consult a legal professional who can provide advice and if necessary look out for and protect their interests.

Chapter 3

We Visit Some of the
Most Pristine Areas of the World

" We visit some of the most pristine areas of the world and our income depends on them staying that way, so why would we pollute?" That's a common cruise industry response to those who challenge its environmental practices. Their question is disarming at first. But it can be turned back on the industry. Why aren't they more conscientious in their environmental practices, especially given the increasing presence of cruise ships in environmentally delicate areas such as the Amazon, Antarctica, the Galapagos Islands and areas of the Indian Ocean such as Seychelles? A *London Times* reporter observes: "The more isolated the destination, the more the marketing people seem to love to send their vessels there" (Elliot 2007). But it isn't just remote areas that warrant concern. This chapter looks at the waste streams produced by cruise ships and at other environmental issues. It discusses developments in environmental regulation of cruise ships and organizations that are promoting stronger environmental policies.

Cruise Ship Waste Streams

Cruise ship discharges into the marine environment include black water (sewage), grey water, hazardous wastes, oily bilge water, ballast water, solid waste and air emissions from incinerators and engines. If not properly treated and disposed of these wastes can be a significant source of pathogens, nutrients and toxic substances that are potentially harmful to human health and sea life (Copeland 2007). The air emissions are significant—a cruise ship on average discharges three times more carbon emissions than aircraft, trains and passenger ferries.

> Carnival, which comprises 11 cruise lines, said in its annual environmental report that its ships, on average, release 712 kg of CO^2 per kilometer.... This means that 401g of CO^2 is emitted per passenger per kilometre, even when the boat is entirely full. This is thirty-six times greater than the carbon footprint of a Eurostar passenger train and more than three times that of someone travelling on a standard Boeing 747 or a passenger ferry. (Starmer-Smith 2008)

The cruise industry frequently claims that it is only a small part of the problem given the proportionately larger number of other ocean going vessels and that these vessels too produce waste. While this may be true for some waste streams, it is not the case with others. With its large number of passengers and crew, wastes such as black water, grey water, solid waste and air emissions are greater on cruise ships than on other ships. In addition, because cruise ship operations tend to concentrate in the same geographic locations and along the same sea routes, their cumulative impact on local areas can be significant. Add to this the potential for and reality of accidental discharges and the environmental impacts are a serious concern.

Black Water

Black water is the waste from toilets and medical facilities. A cruise ship produces as much as thirty litres per day per person. The amount per day for a ship such as Royal Caribbean's *Freedom of the Seas* is as much as 180,000 litres, or about 1.25 million litres on a one-week cruise. These wastes contain harmful bacteria, pathogens, disease, viruses, intestinal parasites and harmful nutrients. If not adequately treated they can cause bacterial and viral contamination of fisheries and shellfish beds. In addition, nutrients in sewage such as nitrogen and phosphorous promote algal growth. Algae consume oxygen in the water, which can be detrimental or lethal to fish and other aquatic life.

Black water from cruise ships has traditionally been treated by a type II or type III marine sanitation device (MSD). Type III MSDs, not commonly used by large cruise ships, store wastes and do not treat them. The waste is landed ashore for treatment or, depending on the jurisdiction, is held until the ship is beyond three miles from shore where it can be discharged legally.

A type II MSD treats waste chemically or biologically and is supposed to produce effluent containing no more than 200 fecal coliform per 100 millilitres and no more 150 milligrams per litre of suspended solids. Whether MSDs reach that standard was called into question in 1999 when the state of Alaska found that seventy-nine of eighty samples taken from cruise ships were out of compliance—by as much as 100,000 times higher than allowed (Klein 2002: 105). According to the Juneau port commander for the Coast Guard, the results were so extreme that it might be necessary to consider possible design flaws and capacity issues with the Coast Guard-approved treatment systems (McAllister 2000). The problems identified then with MSDs continue today (see EPA 2007).

Treated waste from type II MSDs is unregulated under U.S. law because ships are exempt from requirements of the National Pollution Discharge Elimination System (NPDES) under the U.S. *Clean Water Act*. As a result, wastewater discharges from land-based sources are regulated through permits and inspections, but discharge of the same waste in coastal waters from a mobile source are not. U.S. law permits a ship to discharge untreated sewage beyond three miles from shore (treated sewage may be discharged within three miles). Jurisdictions that have ratified Article IV of the International Convention for Prevention of Pollution from Ships (MARPOL) have a four mile limit.

About the time that Alaska was calling attention to the inadequacy of MSDs the cruise industry began installing advanced wastewater treatment systems (later referred to as advanced wastewater purification systems) on its ships. State legislation in 2001 banning discharge in Alaska state waters of wastewater not meeting Alaska water quality standards was a strong incentive. A ship with an advanced wastewater treatment systems (AWTS) avoided the need to travel outside Alaska state waters to discharge treated sewage. Installation of AWTSs for ships visiting areas other than Alaska has been at a much slower pace. For example, Carnival Corporation had AWTSs installed on slightly more than one third of its fleet at the end of 2007. However only one of Carnival Cruise Lines' twenty-two ships had an AWTS. Carnival Cruise Lines only sends one ship to Alaska per season. The corporation's spokesperson says they try to make sure AWTSs are included on ships that go to Alaska and to other sensitive areas. By contrast, all of Norwegian Cruise Line's thirteen ships, seven of Royal Caribbean International's nineteen vessels and six of Celebrity Cruises' eight ships had an AWTS at the end of 2007 (Brannigan 2008).

The advanced systems are a vast improvement—yielding what the industry refers to as drinking-water quality effluent. However the term must be treated with caution. The water cannot be recycled for onboard human consumption, nor can it be used in the laundry because sheets and towels apparently turn grey. A key problem is that the AWTS doesn't adequately address nutrient loading, which means it poses similar problems as MSDs with regard to nitrogen and phosphorous. In addition, tests in Alaska have shown levels of copper, nickel, zinc and ammonia that are higher than the state's water quality standards (Alaska DEC 2004: 29).

Most AWTSs filter solids from sewage as part of treatment. This yields on average thirty-five tons of sewage sludge per day. In sum, it is estimated that 4.2 million gallons of sewage sludge are produced every year by ships as they pass through Washington State waters on their way to Alaska (King County Wastewater Treatment Division 2007). This is small compared to what cruise ships generate outside Washington state waters. In some cases (about one in sixteen ships) sewage sludge is dewatered and then incinerated. In other cases the sludge is dumped at sea. Some jurisdictions permit this to be done beyond three miles of shore; in others the ship must go beyond twelve miles. In either case, these bio-solids have a high oxygen demand and are detrimental to sea life. Sewage sludge poses the same problem as sewage but in a more concentrated form.

Grey Water

Grey water is wastewater from sinks, showers, galleys, laundry and cleaning activities aboard a ship. It is the largest source of liquid waste from a cruise ship: as much as 350 litres per day per person; over 2 million litres per day for a ship such as *Freedom of the Seas*. Like sewage, grey water can contain a variety of pollutants. These include fecal coliform bacteria, detergents, oil and grease, metals, organics, petroleum hydrocarbons, nutrients, food waste and medical and dental waste (Copeland 2007). The greatest threat posed by grey water is from nutrients and other oxygen-demanding materials. The cruise industry characterizes grey water as innocuous, at worst. A report from the EPA in 2007 said:

> Untreated ship graywater concentrations exceeded EPA standards for discharges from Type II MSDs (for fecal coliform and total suspended solids). In addition, untreated graywater concentrations exceeded all wastewater discharge standards under Title XIV for continuous discharge from cruise ships in Alaska, and secondary treatment discharge standards from land-based sewage treatment plants. (EPA 2007: 3: 19)

Except for the Great Lakes and Alaska, grey water is largely unregulated. As recently as the 1980s ships were designed with pipes that directly discharged grey water overboard no matter where the ship was. Today grey water is more commonly collected in a holding tank and discharged through a screen that filters out plastics when a ship is one mile from shore. Vessels with an AWTS may mix grey water with black water and treat them together, but this isn't always possible. Grey water lacks sufficient nutrients for a bioreactor system to properly function, so ships using this design release their grey water with limited or no treatment.

Many of the advances that have occurred in treatment of grey and black water have been motivated by Alaska's requirement that all discharges in its waters meet or exceed state water quality standards with regard to fecal coliform and suspended solids. Alaska has demonstrated that legislation is effective in achieving environmental protection.

Hazardous Waste

A ship produces a wide range of hazardous waste. These include photo processing chemicals, dry cleaning waste, used paint, solvents, heavy metals, expired chemicals and pharmaceuticals, waste from the print ship, hydrocarbons and chlorinated hydrocarbons, used fluorescent and mercury vapour light bulbs and batteries (U.S. Bureau of Transportation Statistics 2002). Although the volume produced by a ship may be relatively small (less than 1,000 litres in a typical week), the toxicity of these wastes makes them a serious concern. They need to be carefully managed in order to avoid their contaminating other waste streams (e.g., grey water, solid waste, bilge water, etc).

Following a dismal record in the 1990s cruise lines today appear to be fairly responsible in their hazardous waste handling. Norwegian Cruise Line (NCL) and Royal Caribbean had each pleaded guilty to a charge of discharging hazardous waste (and oily bilge water) from their ships: Royal Caribbean paid fines and restitution of $18 million in 1999 and another $3.5 million in 2000; NCL paid a fine and restitution of $1.5 million in 2002 (see Klein 2002 and Klein 2005a). Each was on probation for five years and required to file compliance reports every six months.

Cruise industry compliance in the U.S. must be seen in the context of confusion over what regulations apply. The *Resource Conservation and Recovery Act* (RCRA) is the primary federal law governing hazardous waste but it is not entirely clear what elements apply to cruise ships. RCRA rules that cover small-quantity generators (those that generate more than 100 kilograms but less than 1,000 kilograms of hazardous waste per month) are less stringent than those for large-quantity generators (generating more than 1,000 kilograms per month), and it is not clear whether cruise ships are classified as large or small generators of hazardous waste. Further, it is unclear whether these limits are applied for each ship individually or whether they apply to a company's full complement of ships. Some cruise companies say they generate less than 100 kilograms per month and therefore should be classified in a third RCRA category, as conditionally exempt small generators, a category that allows for less rigorous notification and recordkeeping requirements (Schmidt 2000). The confusion leads to inconsistencies in practice and some would argue to less stringent recordkeeping than should be required (especially of cruise ships with regular trans-boundary itineraries).

Oily Bilge Water

A typical large cruise ship will generate an average eight metric tons of oily bilge water for each twenty-four hours of operation (National Research Council 1995: 38–39). According to Royal Caribbean's 1998 Environmental Report its ships produce an average of 25,000 gallons of oily bilge water on a one-week voyage. This water collects in the bottom of a vessel's hull from condensation, water lubricated shaft seals, propulsion system cooling and other engine room sources. It contains fuel, oil and wastewater from engines and other machinery, and it may also include solid wastes such as rags, metal shavings, paint, glass and cleaning agents.

The risks posed to fish and other marine organisms by oil and other elements in bilge water are great. Even in minute concentrations, oil can kill fish or have numerous sub-lethal effects such as changes in heart and respiratory rates, enlarged livers, reduced growth, fin erosion and biochemical and cellular changes. Research also finds that by-products from the biological breakdown of petroleum products can harm fish and wildlife and pose threats to human health if these fish and wildlife are ingested.

Oily bilge water in U.S. waters is regulated by the *Clean Water Act*. The Act prohibits the discharge of oil or hazardous substances in such quantities as may be harmful within 200 miles of the coast. It permits discharge of oil within twelve miles of shore when it is passed through a fifteen parts per million (ppm) oily water separator and does not cause a visible sheen. Beyond twelve miles, oil or oily mixtures can be discharged while proceeding en route and if the oil content of the effluent without dilution is less than 100 ppm. The oil extracted by the separator can be reused, incinerated and/or offloaded in port. Vessels are required to maintain an oil record book that documents disposal of oily residues and discharges overboard or disposal of bilge water.

Each of the three major cruise corporations in the world have been caught and fined for illegal discharge of oily bilge. Royal Caribbean pleaded guilty to falsifying oil record books in order to conceal its practice of bypassing the oily water separator so that waste could be discharged directly into the sea. Investigators found that seafarers had discharged oil-contaminated bilge water directly overboard on a regular and routine basis. In 2002, Norwegian Cruise Line pleaded guilty to the same practices on its ships. Also in 2002, Carnival Corporation pleaded guilty to violations committed by Carnival Cruise Lines. One condition of the guilty plea was that other brands in Carnival Corporation family would not be investigated. Carnival Corporation's Holland America Line pleaded guilty in 1998 to bypassing the oily water separator on one of its ships and couldn't afford a second felony conviction.

Collectively from 1998 through 2002 the three corporations (Royal Caribbean Cruise Line, Norwegian Cruise Line, and Carnival Corporation) paid fines and restitution of $50 million for discharging (or falsifying records to conceal discharging) oily bilge water and hazardous waste. The practice of using bypass pipes appears to have ceased on cruise ships but continues to be found on other types of ships.

The obvious question is why a cruise ship would adopt such a practice. A key incentive was the monetary savings associated with not using the oily water separator. The membranes for the separator could cost as much as $80,000 per year. In addition it could cost another $300,000 per year to dispose ashore the waste oil derived from the separator. Not only did the company save money but a ship's officers could receive larger end-of-the-year bonuses for staying under budget (Frantz 1999a).

Solid Waste

A cruise ship produces a large volume of non-hazardous solid waste. This includes huge volumes of plastic, paper, wood, cardboard, food waste, cans and glass. It was estimated in the 1990s that each passenger accounted for 3.5 kilograms of solid waste per day (Herz and Davis 2002: 11). With better attention to waste reduction this volume in recent years has been reduced, maybe by as much as half. But the amount is still significant—more than eight tons in a week from a moderate sized ship. Twenty-four percent of the solid waste produced by vessels worldwide comes from cruise ships (Copeland 2007: 5).

Much of a cruise ship's garbage is discharged at sea. Food and other waste not easily incinerated is ground, or macerated, and discharged overboard. Solid waste and some plastics are incinerated on board and the ash then goes into the ocean. By-products left in the ash of incinerated plastics can be harmful to sea life and the environment. As well, incinerator air emissions can contain carcinogens such as furans and dioxins. Glass and aluminum are increasingly held onboard and landed ashore for recycling when the itinerary includes a port with reception facilities.

Under MARPOL (and U.S. and Canadian law) no garbage can be discharged within three miles of shore. Between three and twelve miles garbage can be discharged if ground and capable of passing through a twenty-five millimetre screen. Most food waste and other garbage can be discharged at sea when a ship is more than twelve miles from shore. Throwing of plastic into the ocean is strictly prohibited everywhere. It poses an immediate risk to sea life that might ingest it. It also has a long term risk. As plastic degrades over time it breaks down into smaller and smaller pieces but retains its original molecular composition. The result is a great amount of fine plastic sand that resembles food to many creatures. Unfortunately, the plastic cannot be digested so sea birds or fish can eventually starve to death with a stomach full of plastic (Reid 2007).

Ballast Water

Cruise ships like other ocean going vessels use a tremendous amount of ballast water to stabilize the vessel during transport. This water is often taken on in one location after a ship discharges wastewater or unloads cargo and then discharged at the next port of call. Ballast water typically contains a variety of biological materials, including plants, animals, viruses and bacteria. It can also include non-native, nuisance, exotic species that can cause extensive ecological and economic damage to aquatic ecosystems. Ballast water discharges are believed to be the leading source of invasive species in U.S. marine waters, thus posing public health and environmental risks as well as significant economic cost to industries such as water and power utilities, commercial and recreational fisheries, agriculture and tourism. The problem is not limited to cruise ships and there is little cruise-industry specific data on the issue.

There are open ocean exchange requirements for ballast water under MARPOL but no regulations apply to ballast water quality. In the U.S., ballast water is explicitly exempt from permit requirements under the *Clean Water Act*. The exemption was challenged by a number of environmental groups in a 1999 petition to the Environmental Protection Agency (EPA). The petition was rejected in September 2003. The environmental groups responded by filing a lawsuit seeking to force the EPA to rescind the exemption, and in March 2005 a federal district court ruled in their favour. The court's decision requires the EPA to remove the exemption by September 30, 2008. In the interim, four environmental groups (Bluewater Network, Environmental Law Foundation, Surfrider Foundation and San Diego Baykeeper) filed suit in state court to force cruise ships to follow a California ballast water law passed in 2000, a law that two-thirds of cruise ships were ignoring. All complied after the lawsuit was heard by a state court (see Bluewater Network 2002).

Air Emissions

Both incinerators and engines are responsible for air emissions from cruise ships. Each type of air emission presents its own problems. The use of incinerators for disposing of solid waste and dewatered sewage sludge has already been addressed in regard to ash discharged into the ocean. Incinerators also produce smoke, which is why many ports ban their use while a ship is docked. California, a leader in environmental protection, prohibits incinerator use when a ship is within three miles of the coast. In contrast to incinerator use on land, which is likely to be strictly monitored and regulated, incinerators at sea operate with few limits. MARPOL Annex VI only bans incineration of certain particularly harmful substances.

Air emissions from engines are an obvious source of pollution. Conventionally a cruise ship's impact on the atmosphere has been likened to that of 12,240 automobiles, but a 2007 study raises even greater alarm. It found that bunker fuel on average has almost 2,000 times the sulphur content of the diesel fuel used by buses, trucks and cars and that one ship can make as much smog-producing pollution as 350,000 cars (Waymer 2007). This figure can vary widely depending on the fuel being burnt. A small number of ships began using gas turbine engines in the late 1990s and early 2000s, well before the spike in fuel costs in 2007. These gas turbines are considerably better than conventional cruise ship engines in terms of sulphur and nitrous oxide, but on the downside they produce considerably higher levels of greenhouse gases (i.e., carbon dioxide—CO^2).

Most cruise ships burn bunker fuel or fuel oil with reduced sulphur content. With International Maritime Organization standards that set maximum sulphur content at 4.5 percent, it is easy for cruise lines to say they meet or exceed international regulations when the average for bunker fuel is 3 percent. In contrast, low sulphur fuels such as on-road diesel has a sulphur content as low as 0.5 percent. It reduces particulate matter 58 percent, sulphur 11 percent and oxides of nitrogen 99.6 percent over bunker fuel.

Cruise lines have been resistant to adopting these fuels. A case in point is the situation of the Port of Seattle. When undertaking construction of a new terminal (T-30) in 2002 the port gave assurances to the Puget Sound Clean Air Agency and the Army Corp of Engineers that ships using the terminal would be required to use fuel with a sulphur content of 0.5 percent or less. On January 8, 2003, it told the Army Corp:

> In order to make sure that all applicable air quality standards are met, diesel-powered cruise vessels using T-30 as a homeport will use on-road diesel fuel, or a similar fuel with less than 0.05 per cent sulphur. Turbine-powered cruise vessels will use fuel with no more than 0.5 per cent sulphur while home porting at T-30. (McClure 2003)

When it was learned in August 2003 that ships docking at Terminal 30 were not using low sulphur fuels the port responded that its expectation was voluntary, not mandatory.

While cruise lines knew the conditions when they committed to using Terminal 30 they subsequently argued they couldn't use low sulphur fuels. Tom Dow, vice president of Princess Tours, said his company planned to remedy the problem the following year by substituting two cruise ships with cleaner burning engines for the single vessel calling in 2003 but he didn't address the current year. He also minimized the impact of Princess Tours' ships, stating that his ship will be in Seattle for only eighteen days, and for only part of those days. "That's a tiny fraction of the parade of ships that enters and exits Puget Sound" (McClure 2003).

These statements get at the core of a problem—a problem of credibility regarding environmental concern. The industry promised it would use low sulphur fuels when it agreed to shift ships from Vancouver to Seattle, but the promise didn't correspond with practice. And it minimizes the value of using low sulphur fuel by concentrating only on the time the ships spends in Seattle (a small proportion of the full week).

The way this became public is interesting. As the California legislature was considering a bill that would require use of low sulphur fuel in California state waters, cruise industry lobbyists at the last minute claimed that it wasn't technically possible for a ship to shift to low sulphur fuel. Being aware of the commitments made to Seattle and of Seattle's requirements, Bluewater Network (which was a proponent of the legislation) contacted the Port of Seattle and asked: "Aren't you using low sulphur fuel there?" The answer: "Well, no they're not. Not any more." The disclosure had the effect of killing California's initiative to have cruise ships do in its waters what was believed to be the practice in Seattle (Klein 2005a: 166–169).

To address the problem of emissions from auxiliary engines run for electricity while a ship is docked, some ports and cruise lines have made arrangements for ships to hook into the shore-side power grid. This was first introduced in 2001 in a partnership between the port of Juneau and Princess Cruises and is slowly expanding to other locations.

Another initiative that appeared at first blush to have potential was introduced by Holland America Line in June 2007. It announced a pilot project that used a saltwater air emission scrubber on its *Zaandam*. When *Zaandam* operated on the west coast of North America (British Columbia and Alaska) it used fuel with a sulphur content of about 1.8 percent; while operating during the winter months in the Caribbean the sulphur content was as much as 3 percent (Montgomery 2007a). The scrubber, at a cost of $1.5 million, was supposed to reduce emissions, chiefly sulphur.

The scrubber was used in June 2007 to counter a campaign initiated by Denise Savoie and Peter Julian, members of Canada's parliament from British Columbia. Savoie, representing Victoria (a quickly expanding cruise port), called on government to begin a process that would lead to a clean cruise ship act. The industry responded that the scrubber and AWTS were examples of why legislation wasn't needed. Both lent support to the industry's claim of its voluntary exercise of responsibility.

Ironic to some, at the end of the summer cruise season in the Pacific Northwest it was learned that the scrubber system, which uses seawater pumped through the stacks to chemically scrub sulphur and other contaminants from ship emissions and then dumps the water back overboard, was actually contributing to increased greenhouse gases. Research out of Sweden and the U.K. indicated:

> When sulphuric acid is added to seawater by scrubbers, carbon dioxide is freed from the ocean surface. Each molecule of sulphuric acid results in release of two molecules of carbon dioxide as the ocean attempts to retain its alkaline balance. (Montgomery 2007b)

Air emissions continue to be a concern, with no quick fixes in sight. Reducing the sulphur content of the fuel appears to be the most promising short-term solution. In June 2007 Norway announced a complete ban on heavy fuel oil onboard ships inside the two large nature reserves covering most of the waters of eastern Svalbard. It also announced a nitrous oxide tax on all cruise ships beginning in 2009 (fifteen kroner per kilo for bunker fuel, as low as four kroner per kilo for fuel with low nitrous oxide). Rather than embracing Norway's concern Holland America Line announced it would cancel all of its Norwegian itineraries in 2009 (*Shipping Gazette* 2007).

The Industry's Environmental Record

At the same time as projecting a positive environmental image the cruise industry paid tens of millions of dollars in fines for environmental offences. These include dumping garbage in plastic bags overboard, discharging into the ocean hazardous wastes and oily bilge water that by-passed the oily water separator, releasing into coastal waters sewage and other wastewater in contradiction of promises and water quality standards and violating air quality regulations (particularly in Alaska). Violations were most frequent in the 1990s. Enforcement efforts (initially in Bermuda and Grand Cayman and later in the U.S.) have impacted industry practices and behaviour.

The U.S. began stricter enforcement for pollution offences in 1993 following a number of unsuccessful attempts to have the problem addressed by the state where offending ships were registered. In October 1992, it notified the International Maritime Organization's Marine Environmental Committee that it had reported MARPOL violations to the appropriate flag states 111 times, but received responses in only about 10 percent of the cases. Subsequently, between 1993 and 1998, the U.S. Government charged 104 ships with offences involving illegal discharges of oil, garbage and/or hazardous wastes (GAO 2000). It also began levying fines: one-half million dollars from Princess Cruises for dumping more than twenty plastic bags full of garbage off the Florida Keys; one million dollars from Palm Beach Cruises after Coast Guard surveillance aircraft videotaped the Viking Princess intentionally dumping of waste oil 3.5 miles from the port of Palm Beach; one-quarter million dollars from Regency Cruises after it admitted two of its ships dumped garbage-filled plastic bags in Florida waters; and one-half million dollars from Ulysses Cruises for two incidents of plastic-wrapped garbage being thrown from the *Seabreeze* off Miami and two cases of dumping oily bilge water. And there were many more. But the most significant, in 1998, 1999 and 2002, were fines levied against Royal Caribbean ($30.5 million), Holland America Line ($2 million), Carnival Corporation ($18 million) and Norwegian Cruise Line ($1.5 million) (see Klein 2002: 83–89 and Klein 2005a: 135–143).

Fines brought unwanted and negative media attention to the cruise industry. At the height, just after U.S. Attorney general Janet Reno chastised Royal Caribbean for using the nation's waters as its dumping ground while promoting itself as an environmentally "green" company, the International Council of Cruise Lines (ICCL) issued a press release affirming the cruise industry's commitment to maintaining a clean environment and to keeping the oceans clean.

> Regrettably, there have been violations of environmental laws involving cruise lines in the past few years. These incidents have served as an important wake up call, causing our industry to redouble its efforts to improve its environmental performance. (ICCL 1999)

Two years later, in July 2001, while Carnival Corporation and Norwegian Cruise Line were under investigation and immediately after Alaska's senate cleared the way for final vote on the Alaska Cruise Initiative (which would set standards for wastewater discharges into the state's waters), ICCL released *Cruise Industry Waste Management Practices and Procedures*. The standards contained in the document effectively were the same as what already existed in U.S. law and or international conventions such as MARPOL. They represented a commitment to abide by existing laws and regulations.

Despite being mandatory, violations appeared to have no impact on a cruise line's ICCL membership or status in the organization. Carnival Corporation, for example, was back in federal court within a year of pleading guilty in 2002 to six counts of falsifying records in relation to oil discharges from five ships operated by Carnival Cruise Lines. It had been summoned in July 2003 after a probation officer reported that the company failed to develop, implement and enforce the terms of an environmental compliance program stemming from the 2002 plea agreement. Holland America employees reportedly submitted twelve audits that contained false, misleading and inaccurate information (Dupont 2003). Carnival Corporation replied to the court that three environmental compliance employees had been fired for the reports but it did not admit violating its probation. In a settlement signed August 25, 2003, Carnival agreed to hire four additional auditors and to provide additional training for staff (Perez 2003: D1).

The corporation was again under investigation in March 2004 for illegal discharges. Holland America Line, a wholly owned subsidiary of Carnival Corporation, notified the United States and Netherlands governmental authorities that one of its chief engineers had admitted to improperly processing oily bilge water on the *Noordam*. According to the company's filing with the U.S. Securities and Exchange Commission, a subsequent internal investigation determined that the improper operation may have begun in January 2004 and continued sporadically through March 4, 2004. Several months later, in July 2004, Holland America Line was again in the news when its former vice president for environmental compliance pleaded guilty to certifying environmental compliance audits that had never been done (Klein 2005a). ICCL's lack of comment and absence of action contrasts starkly with how it proudly promoted its mandatory practices and procedures.

Violations (or as the industry often calls them, accidents) continued. In February 2002, Cunard's *Caronia* was detained and fined $410,000 by Brazilian authorities after nearly 8,000 gallons of heavy fuel oil spilled into Guanabara Bay near Rio de Janeiro. In August 2002, Holland America Line's *Ryndam* discharged as much as 40,000 gallons (250 gallons according to HAL) of sewage sludge into Juneau harbour. The case went to a grand jury in Anchorage and after more than two years Holland America pleaded guilty to a single misdemeanour count of negligently discharging 20,000 gallons of untreated sewage. It paid fines and restitution amounting to $700,000 and agreed to spend $1.3 million to improve its ships' handling of waste.

In January 2003, Carnival Cruise Lines reported an incidental discharge of grey water while anchored one-half mile from land while in Avalon Bay (Catalina Island, California) (Klein 2005a: 142). One month later a Canadian couple aboard the *Norwegian Wind* reported observing whole beer bottles, whole wine bottles, beer and pop cans, corks, plastic plates, plastic utensils, plastic cups and organic material being tossed into the ocean from the back while the ship was between Hawai'i and Fanning Island. The company insisted it did nothing illegal even though discharge of plastics is strictly forbidden anywhere at sea. The couple reported what they saw to U.S. authorities but no action was taken against the company because the ship was in international waters at the time.

In March 2003 Crystal Cruises admitted that its *Crystal Harmony* had discharged 36,000 gallons of treated bilge, treated sewage and grey water into the Monterey Bay Marine Sanctuary the previous October. The discharge violated a written promise the company had made to discharge nothing while in the sanctuary. The discharge was discovered by a state official in a review of the ship's logs. When the company was challenged about the non-disclosure, the company's vice president defended their silence by saying the company hadn't broken any laws; they had only broken their word (Klein 2003a: 14).

Then in May *Norwegian Sun* was cited for the illegal discharge of 16,000 gallons of raw sewage into the Strait of Juan de Fuca; in October Carnival Cruise Lines paid a $200,000 administrative fee to settle with the California State Lands Commission over the cruise line's non-compliance with the state's ballast water law; and in December it became public that the industry had logged fourteen violations of a voluntary agreement it had with the state of Hawai'i that set clear limits on where discharges could take place.

Environmental violations have become less frequent more recently, but they still occur. In October 2005, NCL America's *Pride of Aloha* discharged approximately 300 gallons of effluent into Hilo Harbour; five months later the same ship discharged about seventy tons of treated effluent into Honolulu Harbour. Its sister ship, *Pride of America*, discharged a small amount of what appeared to be diesel fuel into Hilo Harbour in September 2007. And there have been multiple violations of voluntary memoranda of understanding between the cruise industry and the states of Hawai'i and Washington.

Two case illustrations give insight into the way some in the industry think. On November 13, 2006, *The Sunshine Coast Daily* in Australia reported taxi drivers in Vanuatu had gone on strike, refusing to transport passengers aboard P&O Australia's *Pacific Sky*, forcing them to walk five kilometres to town. The taxi drivers had just learned that the Vanuatu government was investigating the illegal dumping of one-half million litres of oil on the island. Apparently, deep holes were dug, lined with thin plastic and then filled with oil and raw sewage. The site was within one kilometre of a village and school and just above a river used for drinking, washing and swimming. The motivation: it would cost US$30,000 to appropriately dispose of the waste at approved facilities in the region whereas dumping illegally cost less than $200. The company faced a potential fine of $35 million but in the end was able to convince the government that an apology and commitment to clean up the mess were sufficient.

A violation by Celebrity Cruises' *Mercury* gives further insight into the industry's thinking. The company was notified by the state of Washington in November 2006 that it would be fined for dumping one-half million gallons of sewage and untreated grey water into Puget Sound ten times over nine days in September and October 2005. The company initially denied the claim but it acquiesced when shipboard documents indicated otherwise. It then appealed to state officials for relief from penalty—each incident carried a $10,000 fine—because three of the violations occurred on the Canadian side of the international boundary and Washington did not have jurisdiction. As well, the cruise corporation argued the discharges, while a violation of its memorandum of understanding with Washington, were not illegal in Canada (McClure 2006).

The state of Washington agreed to reduce the fine from $100,000 to $70,000, but the company paid the full $100,000 after all. It said the money was never the issue; its concern was to ensure there was accurate information. It went on to say that paying the full amount was in order to demonstrate its commitment to protecting and preserving Washington State's marine environment (McClure 2007). It never apologized to Canada for the discharges and expressed no complementary commitment to the marine environment of British Columbia or Canada. It is as though the wastewater discharged in Canada was immaterial because it was legal. This appears inconsistent with industry claims to have a genuine and strong commitment to the environment.

Memoranda of Understanding versus Legislation

Violations in Washington State are against a memorandum of understanding (MOU) between the state and the cruise industry as represented by the Vancouver-based Northwest Cruiseship Association (NWCA). The MOU in large part adopts standards contained in the International Council of Cruise Lines' *Cruise Industry Waste Management Practices and Procedures*. Unlike MOUs in other jurisdictions such as Florida and until 2006 Hawai'i, Washington has prescribed penalties for non-compliance. Enforcement is based on review of ship logs. There is no direct monitoring in real time.

A MOU is a voluntary arrangement. As such it has limited enforceability in law and is largely based on trust. For this reason, MOUs are criticized by those concerned with the cruise industry's environmental practices. Their scepticism is supported by a 2003 report from the Paris-based Organization for Economic Co-operation and Development (OECD). The report directly questions the environmental effectiveness and economic efficiency of voluntary approaches and, focusing specifically on environmental policy, notes there are few cases where voluntary approaches have improved the environment beyond a business-as-usual baseline (OECD 2003).

The issue of trust has been raised by many concerned with cruise industry practices, especially in light of past violations. California Assemblyman Joe Simitian expressed it clearly when he introduced legislation to regulate cruise ship discharges in state waters: "Regrettably, cruise lines have a history of violating their agreements and gaming the system. 'Trust us' is no longer an effective environmental policy" (Weiss 2003: B1). Like folks in other states, he viewed legislation with enforceable standards and penalties as the only way to go.

However legislation isn't always better. Hawai'i is a case in point. In 2005 the cruise industry successfully lobbied for legislation that was much less stringent than the existing MOU between Hawai'i and the NWCA. The legislation was enacted on July 12, 2005. Two months later the NWCA gave notice that it was transitioning out of the MOU because of ambiguity and confusion caused by having two sets of standards. Rather than continue to voluntarily abide by the more stringent terms contained in the MOU the industry chose the less comprehensive legislation (which it had supported). The industry gave notification without fanfare; it was made public two months later after it was learned by KAHEA—the Native Hawaiian Environmental Alliance.

Florida and Washington are the only two U.S. states to use a MOU to set environmental standards for cruise ships. Three states, Maine, California and Alaska, have enacted legislation. The advantage of legislation is that it codifies standards and permits legal recourse for violations.

In April 2004, the state of Maine enacted legislation governing discharges of grey water or mixed black/grey water into coastal waters of the state. The legislation applies to cruise ships with overnight accommodations for 250 or more passengers and allows such vessels into state waters only if they have advanced wastewater treatment systems, comply with discharge and record-keeping requirements currently in place in Alaska and secure a permit from the state Department of Environmental Protection. Maine's legislation also directed the state to apply to the U.S. Environmental Protection Agency for designation of up to fifty "No Discharge Zones" (NDZs) in order that Maine could then prohibit black water discharges into state waters. In June 2006 the EPA approved the state's NDZ request for Casco Bay, which is where Portland is located.

California enacted three bills in 2004. One bars cruise ships from discharging treated wastewater while in the state's waters, another prohibits vessels from releasing grey water and the third prevents cruise ships from operating waste incinerators. A year earlier the state enacted laws banning passenger ships from discharging sewage sludge and oily bilge water as well as prohibiting vessels from discharging hazardous wastes from photo processing and dry cleaning operations into state waters. In 2006 California enacted a law that required the state to adopt ballast water performance standards by January 2008 and sets specific deadlines for the removal of different types of species and bacteria from ballast water by the year 2020.

Alaska Takes the Lead with Legislation

Alaska is both the first and the most recent to enact environmental legislation applying to the cruise industry. Broad-based concerns about pollution from cruise ships arose in the state after Holland America Line in 1998 and Royal Caribbean International in 1999 pleaded guilty to criminal charges of dumping oily wastes and hazardous chemicals in Alaska's Inside Passage. In addition to the federal fines paid by both companies for their violations in Alaskan waters, Royal Caribbean International was levied a $3.5 million fine in January 2000 in state court. These fines, and the behaviour for which they were assessed, spurred an increased interest in monitoring cruise ships; not just for oil pollution but sewage and air pollution. The State Department of Environmental Conservation (DEC), with the U.S. Coast Guard, launched a cruise ship initiative in December 1999.

The initiative began with meetings between the State, Coast Guard, Environmental Protection Agency, cruise industry and environmental groups in order to discuss the activities and operations of cruise ships, with a view toward an assessment of possible environmental issues. When the workgroups realized there was little technical data to support industry claims they developed a scheme for sampling wastewater from cruise ships and for monitoring air emissions. Participation was voluntary. Thirteen of twenty-four ships refused to participate, choosing instead to go beyond twelve miles to dump raw sewage without monitoring and without limitations.

The findings from monitoring during the summer of 2000 were, in the words of Alaska's governor, "disgusting and disgraceful." Concern was raised about both wastewater and air emissions. The results led in December 2000 to introduction by Alaska's Senator Frank Murkowski of federal legislation that prohibited discharge of raw sewage in specific areas of Alaska's Inside Passage and set standards for discharge of treated sewage. Vessels with AWTSs that were tested and certified to meet minimum standards were permitted to discharge treated sewage and grey water as close as one mile from shore and at speeds less than six knots.

Monitoring results also produced a response from the state. In March 2001 Alaska Governor Tony Knowles introduced legislation that would enforce state clean-air and -water standards for cruise ships and that would have monitoring and inspections, which would be funded by a one dollar fee per passenger. The legislation took effect July 1, 2001.

The Alaskan law was not more stringent than current U.S. law regarding the disposal of sewage or pollution from smokestack emissions. But it was unique in that it established enforceable standards and included a verified program of sampling, testing and reporting of wastewater and air discharges. Alaska became the first U.S. state with the authority to inspect ships, prosecute violators and regulate air pollution as well as sewage.

Alaska's Cruise Ship Initiative, as it was called, also established a scientific advisory panel to evaluate the effectiveness of the law's implementation and to advise the state on scientific matters related to cruise ship impacts on the Alaskan environment and public health. In February 2004 the state reported that the standards had prompted large ships to either install advanced wastewater treatment systems that meet the effluent standards or to manage wastes by holding all of their wastewater for discharge outside of Alaskan waters (beyond three miles from shore).

In 2006 Alaska took another major step when, as a result of a citizen's ballot initiative, it required cruise lines to pay a corporate income tax on casino revenues plus $50 for each passenger entering the state. The initiative also increased fines for wastewater violations, mandated new environmental regulations for cruise ships, such as a state permit for all discharges of treated wastewater and introduction of environmental observers (ocean rangers) on all cruise ships in state waters. Revenues from the taxes would be disbursed to local communities affected by tourism and would fund public services and facilities used by cruise ships. Supporters of the initiative contend that the cruise industry does not pay enough in taxes to compensate for its environmental harm to the state and for the services it uses. Opponents argued that the initiative would hurt Alaska's competitiveness for tourism. The cruise

industry worked hard to defeat the legislation, first at the ballot box (a campaign that reportedly spent more than $2 million) and later in the courts,
but was unsuccessful. Elements of the ballot initiative continue to be fought
over in the Alaska legislature.

The Case of Canada

It is interesting that while Alaska raised its standards for cruise ships and
increased its enforcement and Washington signed a MOU that it believed had
comparable effects, the government of Canada remained relatively passive,
essentially looking the other way. In January 2003 the cruise industry publicly
announced at a community forum in Monterrey Bay, California, that it was
working with Canada on a voluntary set of regulations. This was the first
public disclosure that such a plan was in the works. The Canadian Centre for
Policy Alternatives subsequently issued two reports challenging the guidelines
and questioning a wholly voluntary approach (Klein 2003a, 2003b). Issues
were also raised by the Georgia Straight Alliance and Vancouver Island
Public Interest Research Group (see Gorecki and Wallace 2003). Some minor
changes were made.

A year later, in January 2004, Transport Canada issued *Pollution Prevention
Guidelines for the Operation of Cruise Ships under Canadian Jurisdiction*. The guidelines were voluntary, essentially stating Canada's expectations for the industry.
There was no mechanism for monitoring or enforcement, leaving the status
quo unchanged. Transport Canada replaced the guidelines with regulations
in May 2007, which again lacked a mechanism for monitoring cruise ships
and therefore for enforcement of stated standards.

The government appears to have a longstanding belief that cruise ships
don't discharge wastes in Canada. There are violations in Alaska and violations in Washington but somehow the same cruise ships clean up their act
when they are in British Columbia. It is possible but unlikely. The industry's
own data casts some suspicion. Maps produced as part of a 2006 study
commissioned by ICCL and conducted by Conservation International show
discharges close to shore and within close proximity to Marine Protected
Areas in B.C.'s inside passage (OCTA 2006: Appendix 2: 20, 21). As well,
known violations on both coasts of Canada appear to have been effectively
ignored.

Given the state of affairs, Denise Savoie and Peter Julian, NDP members
of Parliament from British Columbia, called on Canada's federal government
to begin work on a clean cruise ship act. They held a press conference in June
2007 to announce their initiative, which included Private Member's legislation calling for hearings in Parliament. No government action followed.

The cruise industry opposed the initiative, stating that it didn't need any
more regulation, especially in view of its exemplary environmental record.

As in the past, it said "it has considerably less impact on the environment than cities like Victoria that still dump raw sewage into our coastal waters" (Shaw 2007). To some the industry's opposition to the initiative is surprising. If their behaviour is so environmentally sensitive and responsible then the obvious question is why they wouldn't embrace legislation that sets regulations consistent with practices they claim are already in place. Without a strong environmental movement behind Savoie's and Julian's efforts, it didn't go far.

South of the Border

The concept of a clean cruise ship act first surfaced in the United States in the early 2000s. Then in April 2004 Senator Richard Durbin (with nine co-sponsors) and Representative Sam Farr (with forty-two co-sponsors) introduced in the U.S. Congress a bill that would regulate wastewater discharges from cruise ships in U.S. coastal waters. The legislation was free-standing and would not require U.S. ratification of Annex IV of MARPOL (*Regulations for the Prevention of Pollution by Sewage from Ships*), an Annex that came into force September 27, 2003, but from which the U.S. continued to withhold its consent. Without U.S. support it had taken nearly thirty years for Annex IV to be ratified by more than seventy-five countries representing more than 50 percent of the world's ocean going ship tonnage.

The provisions of the *Clean Cruise Ship Act* were much more stringent than MARPOL. Cruise vessels entering a U.S. port were prohibited from discharging sewage, grey water or bilge water into waters of the United States, including the Great Lakes, except in compliance with prescribed effluent limits and management standards. It directed EPA and the Coast Guard to promulgate effluent limits for sewage and grey water discharges from cruise vessels that were no less stringent than the more restrictive standards under the existing federal law regarding Alaska's Inside Passage. The legislation also sought to broaden federal enforcement authority, including inspection, sampling and testing.

In effect, the *Clean Cruise Ship Act* would require all cruise ships discharging in U.S. waters (within two hundred miles) to have an advanced wastewater treatment system and would subject these systems to regular monitoring and testing; no discharge would be permitted within twelve miles of the coastline. The legislation failed to move out of Committee in 2004; it was reintroduced in 2005 and again failed to be considered before the end of that session of Congress. It was redrafted and reintroduced in April 2008. The new legislation would prohibit discharge of sewage, grey water and bilge water within twelve miles of shore. For discharges beyond twelve miles the Environmental Protection Agency will be charged with standards based on the best available technologies.

Cruise industry groups opposed the legislation, arguing that it targeted an industry that represents only a small percentage of the world's ships and that the industry's environmental standards already meet or exceed current international and U.S. regulations. Conservation International (CI) was enlisted in a joint project that effectively "green washed" the cruise industry to bolster its case (see Klein 2005a: 150–156). With funding from the International Council of Cruise Lines, CI's Centre for Environmental Leadership in Business issued a report in March 2004 complimenting the industry on its environmental record and leadership. In December of that year the industry funded CI's Ocean Conservation and Tourism Alliance (OCTA).

The OCTA focused on four priority areas: best practices for wastewater management, establish destination partnerships, promote environmental education and promote vendor environmental education. Except for best practices for wastewater management, which essentially encouraged the industry to continue its installation of advanced wastewater treatment systems (despite opposing similar calls from environmental organizations such as Bluewater Network and Oceana), OCTA's priorities dissuaded attention from cruise industry practices. Instead they focused on what could be done by those on land, such as ports, to improve the cruise industry's environmental impact; or placed the industry in context as a smaller threat to the health of the oceans than things such as runoff from farming in the U.S. Midwest. OCTA activities proved to be excellent as a public relations campaign.

While opposed by the industry, the *Clean Cruise Ship Act* was actively supported by a broad-based coalition of environmental groups that were at the core of the move for its promulgation and introduction (see Klein 2007a). Some of these groups were national in scope, such as the act's key proponents: The Ocean Conservancy, Oceana and Bluewater Network; others had mainly a local focus. As the cruise industry has continued to project a more positive image, environmentalists' interest in cruise ship issues and the *Clean Cruise Ship Act* have waned. Since 2006 many national environmental organizations in the U.S. have shifted to what they perceive to be higher priorities or to areas that foundations and other organizations are willing to fund. Local organizations are consequently left even more on their own. It is still useful to take a glimpse at those involved in the campaign for the *Clean Cruise Ship Act*.

Environmental Organizations and the Clean Cruise Ship Act

One of the first organizations to openly criticize the cruise industry's environmental practices was The Ocean Conservancy (TOC). Formerly known as the Centre for Marine Conservation, TOC became directly involved with cruise industry issues when it released in May 2002 *Cruise Control: A Report on How Cruise Ships Affect the Marine Environment.* Royal Caribbean, which had provided a grant of $450,000 ($150,000 per year for three years) through its Ocean Fund for TOC's non-cruise ship projects, expressed its "disappointment and dismay" over the report and withdrew funding from The Ocean Conservancy's projects. In contrast to the publicity given when the grant was awarded no publicity or press release was issued when funding was withdrawn. In correspondence to the president of TOC Royal Caribbean criticized the report and said, "You have dredged up and unloaded upon the public a bucketful of mostly tired, old accusations and downright inaccuracies about present day environmental practices and impacts." Royal Caribbean had tried unsuccessfully to quash TOC's publication of the report.

The Ocean Conservancy engages in both national and local activities. Its field offices in Monterey Bay (California) and Key West (Florida) were key players in local initiatives to contain and prevent cruise ship pollution in adjacent national marine sanctuaries. In Monterey Bay specifically, a partnership that included TOC, Friends of the Sea Otter and Save Our Shores was a critical force protecting the sanctuary and in taking decisive action against violators.

Vancouver-based Oceans Blue Foundation (OBF) was involved with cruise industry issues well before TOC but by 2003 had become marginalized. The OBF was established in 1996 through a cooperative effort involving the Vancouver Port Authority, Tourism Vancouver, Tourism British Columbia, the Canadian Tourism Commission and private foundations and business leaders in British Columbia. A key project was the OBF's Cruise Ship Stewardship Initiative. The initiative focused on a plan whereby the cruise industry would voluntarily adopt standards of environmentally responsible tourism. The OBF planned to implement an eco-certification program that would identify and reward cruise lines that took meaningful and positive steps. This was at the forefront of the international wave to establish green certification of travel and tourism products.

The OBF held a series of meetings with environmentalists and the industry and in 2002 convened a roundtable involving representatives of the cruise industry and environmental organizations. The OBF hoped it could influence the industry's environmental practices. However, increasing dialogue led the organization to believe the cruise industry was insincere in its talk of changing practices and instead was using the cooperative process to undermine the OBF's efforts. As the organization learned more about the industry's practices and experienced the industry's political games (including the industry's use of Canada-based David Suzuki Foundation (see Klein 2003b: 8)) it became more confrontational. In October 2002 the OBF published *Blowing the Whistle and the Case for Cruise Ship Certification*, a report that directly confronts contradictions between industry claims and practices. The OBF lost most of its funding.

Tourism Vancouver criticized the report and said "There are better ways of being able to encourage that kind of discussion and debate," that the matter would be raised with the Canadian Tourism Commission (CTC) and that Tourism Vancouver would consider ending support for the OBF. An official with the CTC was also critical, suggesting that "the CTC supports a balanced approach between environmental protection and economic development" (Tjaden 2002). The OBF closed its doors a year later. A follow-up to the October 2002 report, completed in September 2003, was never published.

San Francisco-based Bluewater Network was another key player in pushing for the *Clean Cruise Ship Act*. It has been on the forefront of environmental activism related to the cruise industry since the late 1990s. It merged with London-based Friends of the Earth in 2005. Bluewater Network has used a mix of strategies in its efforts. It used the courts to pressure the U.S. Environmental Protection Agency to promulgate regulations to control vessel emissions, to force cruise lines to stop their habitual violation of laws prohibiting the discharge of ballast water in California waters and in 2003/2004 (and again in 2007) to challenge EPA standards for air emissions from ships. It also engages in political lobbying. Bluewater Network was successful in 2003 in having enacted two of three bills it sponsored in the California legislature; it sponsored three bills that were enacted in 2004. This legislation, discussed earlier, regulated grey water, black water, incinerator usage, sewage sludge, hazardous waste and oily bilge water. And teaming with San Franciscans for a Clean Waterfront, Bluewater Network was involved in ensuring sufficient environmental protections around construction of a new cruise terminal in San Francisco. Friends of the Earth continues to seek regulations for cruise ship discharges and is focused on both the legislative front and the judicial front as a means for pressuring the EPA to finally issue regulations for cruise ship waste streams.

Bluewater Network/Friends of the Earth also supports efforts of organizations in other jurisdictions. It participated in a lawsuit in Washington State following discharge of raw sewage in Puget Sound by Norwegian Cruise Line, brought to light cruise line violations of emission standards set by the Port of Seattle and has engaged in public education and social action campaigns in San Francisco, Seattle and nationally. In Seattle it partners with Ocean Advocates, an environmental organization that actively monitors and comments on development in the port, especially those involving the cruise industry.

The most recent actor on the scene is Oceana. Established in 2001 with funding largely from the Pew Charitable Trusts, Oceana merged with the American Oceans Campaign in 2002. It identified cruise ship pollution as one of its key areas of interest and undertook a cruise ship campaign in early 2003. Similar to the OBF, Oceana began by collaborating with the cruise industry. It engaged in discussions with Royal Caribbean Cruises Limited (operator of Royal Caribbean International and Celebrity Cruises) and asked for a commitment to upgrade wastewater treatment systems. At the same time Oceana engaged in public education and mild forms of social and political action.

Discussions between Oceana and Royal Caribbean broke down in July 2003. In Oceana's words they had been negotiating with Royal Caribbean; Royal Caribbean said it had engaged in meetings as part of its routine outreach to interest groups, environmental organizations, academic institutions and others (Londner 2003). Oceana launched a media campaign beginning July 21, 2003, and held rallies and media events in several cities across North America. The CEO of Royal Caribbean issued a form letter on September 24, 2003, responding to letters he received as part of Oceana's campaign. He clearly stated that the company discharged its black water and its grey water "only when we are 12 or more miles from the shore and moving at at least 6 knots." The letter proudly promoted Royal Caribbean's policies and procedures for exceeding Coast Guard requirements and as more strict than U.S. law requires. These claims appear to contradict a State of Hawai'i report in December 2003. It cites the company for twelve violations of a memorandum of understanding that prohibits discharges within four miles of the coast (Yamanouchi 2003).

Oceana escalated its campaign in October 2003, calling for a national boycott of Royal Caribbean, and in February 2004 placed advertisements for its cruise ship campaign on Google.com. After two days the ads, which did not mention Royal Caribbean by name, were banned. Google claimed that the ads violated its editorial policy, which prohibits ads criticizing other groups or companies. The ads reappeared two weeks later on Yahoo. In May 2004 Royal Caribbean announced a commitment to install AWTSs on all of its ships by 2008—exactly what Oceana was calling for. But RCCL said that Oceana's campaign had nothing to do with its decision. At the start of 2008 twelve of Royal Caribbean International's nineteen vessels and two of Celebrity Cruises' eight vessels did not have an AWTS. Oceana had already moved on to other issues after winning and scarcely took notice.

One other national organization involved with advocating for the *Clean Cruise Ship Act* was the Campaign to Safeguard America's Waters (C-SAW). Like Bluewater Network, the C-SAW began as a project of Earth Island Institute. It is dedicated to closing loopholes in federal and state water pollution regulations that allow millions of gallons of polluted wastes to be dumped into public waters and is actively engaged in the debate about the use of mixing zones to circumvent water quality standards. The cruise industry advocates thinking in terms of mixing zones, in effect saying "dilution is the solution" to discharge of its wastes.

The C-SAW's efforts around water quality standards and the EPA are national in scope (including efforts to include cruise ships under the *Clean Water Act*). However the campaign is also intimately involved in Alaska's efforts to contain and control pollution produced by cruise ships. The organization's founding is related to discharge of hazardous chemicals (dry cleaning fluids, photofinishing chemicals, and more) in Alaska's Inside Passage, including waters around Haines, on which the Campaign's founder had depended for salmon. The C-SAW was a key player in the Alaska Cruise Ship Initiative in 1999/2000 and in the 2006 Alaska ballot initiative, which created a $50 per passenger fee on cruise ships using Alaska's waters.

Several local organizations were also intimately involved in discussions leading to the *Clean Cruise Ship Act*. These included Friends of Casco Bay, which was instrumental in pushing for legislation in Maine; Ocean Advocates, which is a key player in Washington state; and KAHEA, The Native Hawaiian Environmental Alliance, which has been behind a number of efforts and public education campaigns in Hawai'i (see Klein 2007a).

Since a peak in 2003 national organizations' interest in cruise industry environmental practices has subsided. Except for Bluewater Network/Friends of the Earth, the major national organizations have moved on to other issues and maintain a relatively small interest if any in cruise tourism. Most successful efforts in recent years have been initiated by local organizations motivated by local issues and concerns.

It Isn't Just Environmentalists

Environmental concerns go beyond those normally focused upon by environmental organizations. Cruise ships also present a problem of people pollution—overcrowding—in the places they visit. Ports in Europe can see as many as ten ships in a single day, leading one journalist to observe:

> It's an unfortunate fact but the popular spots on Europe's cruise trail have become nightmare destinations—both for the locals, unless they live on tourists, and the hapless cruise passengers who suddenly find themselves in a maelstrom of humanity. (Archer 2007)

The number of ships and passengers is even higher in some Caribbean ports. A single port can receive 25,000 passengers or more in a single day, numbers that take their toll on local communities—not just wear and tear on the physical environment but on the people who live there year round. Consider Cozumel, Mexico, where in 2004 an average 9,000 cruise ship passengers visited per day. Because the distribution is not consistent from one day to the next there are quiet days and huge spikes. For example, on December 26, 2002, the port received its all-time record—approximately

38,000 cruise ship visitors.

Problems caused by huge numbers of cruise passengers led to community-based citizen action in Key West, Florida. Cruise passenger numbers had risen sharply from 375,000 in 1995 to close to a million in 2004. Many on the two-by-four-mile island saw cruise tourism as a major reason for the "getting ugly" label assigned by *National Geographic Traveler's* 2004 "Destination Scorecard." Key West scored forty-three out of one hundred (it received forty-six points in 2007).

Concerns extended beyond the congestion at tourist attractions, the kitschy shops that had sprung up around the port, the disruption caused by Conch Trains running cruise passengers around the town and the assertion by *National Geographic Traveler* that the city's character was lost. Restaurant and hotel owners saw that cruise tourism was displacing people who in past would stay at a hotel for a week, spend money in restaurants and bars and shop in the stores. The president of the Lodging Association of the Florida Keys and Key West says cruise passengers change the nature of a destination.

> Our whole advertising and marketing program is around Key West being an easy-going, laid-back, relaxed destination with interesting shops and stores and great cultural and historical resources…. Put yourself in the position of a visitor who comes for the first time, checks into one our fine hotels, and then decides to take a stroll down this town's main drag—Duval Street—and encounters crowds more reminiscent of Times Square. (Babson 2003)

Citizens in Key West directly confronted the problem in January 2003. A grassroots organization, Liveable Oldtown and its political action arm Last Stand, held a panel discussion entitled "Keys in Balance," which looked at the good, the bad and the ugly of cruise ships in Key West. While acknowledged that cruise ships generate approximately $2.5 million in disembarkation and docking fees for the city's yearly budget, there were questions about the impact of cruise ships on the fragile marine environment surrounding the lower keys, the risk of dependence on cruise ship dollars and the social impact of thousands of cruise passengers pouring into town each day. The overarching question was stress on Key West's 27,000 residents from the daily influx of cruise ship passengers. A public education and political action campaign followed from the forum.

Anger peaked in March 2004 when local residents learned that the city had been violating a 1993 resolution that placed a limit of seven cruise ship visits per week at Pier B—a privately owned dock adjacent to the Hilton Hotel. Liveable Oldtown called for a protest on March 11, 2004, when there would be five ships visiting the city. They encouraged residents to drive up and down Duval Street between 11 a.m. and noon. Though cruise passengers barely noticed the added congestion the point was well made with city residents and city councillors by the hundred or so protestors (see O'Hara 2004).

The protest had the desired effect. Solidarity increased in calls from the community to cutback cruise tourism. The city was forced to address the concerns, which a year later were leant support by a city-funded quality of life study (see Murray 2005). City councillors who favoured scaling back cruise tourism were elected following the study's release, and the city began reducing cruise passenger numbers.

Half a world away in Gold Coast, Australia, another community-based action took on problems associated with cruise tourism. The Queensland government in 2004 announced plans to build a cruise terminal on the spit overlooking the entrance to the bay where Surfer's Paradise sits. A broad-based coalition of business, recreational users of the area and environmental interests joined together and formed Save Our Spit. Though comprised of groups with sometimes diverse and competing interests the organization's sole purpose was to prevent construction of a cruise terminal and to preserve the spit for recreational boaters, surfers and citizens who would spend a leisurely day out in Douglas Jennings Park. Its efforts also reflected concern about over-blown expectations for income from cruise tourism and displacement of an already thriving tourism industry. A two-year fight included public rallies, community education campaigns and lobbying of state and federal governments.

Success appeared elusive but an election call in 2006 led to the main election campaign period coinciding with an already planned major event. An international expert was brought in for press conferences and media work, and Save Our Spit planned a rally expected to attract more than 5,000 people. Two days after the media blitz began and a day before the rally the Queensland Government announced it was cancelling plans for the cruise terminal. Save Our Spit had succeeded. Its success, like the success of citizens in Key West, is attributed in large part to the fact that the organization and effort had a single focus and goal. As a result it could not be sidetracked or bought off by competing interests or trades that would give concessions on a different issue. Though coalition partners were approached with deals that gave them individual concessions on others issues, Save Our Spit as the collective organization couldn't be bought and remained steadfast (see Johnston and Gration 2008).

A grassroots coalition in Moloka'i, Hawai'i (Hui Hoopakele Aina) similarly had a single focus and, like Save Our Spit and Liveable Oldtown, realized its goal. With concern about negative environmental, economic and social impacts from cruise tourism, the group challenged plans for cruise ship port calls in 2002 by taking the State of Hawai'i to court over its failure to undertake a full environmental impact assessment. Local residents holding placards and chanting that the passengers were not welcome met the first ships planning to stop. The first two calls were cancelled in the face of this public display. Future calls were also cancelled. Some in the know suggest there was a negotiated settlement between the State and industry in order to make the lawsuit and demonstrations go away (Klein 2005a). In any case, Moloka'i remains free of cruise ships.

And on an ongoing basis, James Bay Neighbourhood Environmental Association in Victoria, British Columbia, keeps a watch on environmental impacts from cruise ships docking at the city's Ogden Point. The James Bay community is concerned about air quality on cruise ship days, both from ship emissions and from increased vehicle traffic for passenger and crew tours and taxis. The organization engages in public education, conducts community forums and regularly engages in discussion with the port. With a relatively singular focus on their community the neighbourhood organization has reasonable impact and visible successes.

Bar Harbor, Maine, has also taken a proactive approach. After hearing complaints from residents and business owners that passengers from cruise ships overcrowded downtown the town council voted in January 2008 to restrict the number of passengers that can disembark at one time: 3,500 in July and August; 5,500 from May through October. The decision effectively limits one ship per day during the peak summer months, a sensible approach that attempts to keep cruise passengers from overwhelming other forms of tourism.

The Environmental Debate

The chapter began with the cruise industry's assertion of environmental sensitivity and responsibility. The claim is laudable but put into context, it is one that must be viewed with scepticism. The problem isn't only the volume of wastes produced by a cruise ship but the industry's tendency to put economic interests above environmental concerns. Decisions about wastewater treatment systems are influenced by space considerations, including the loss of onboard space that could otherwise be used for revenue, and are not guided by a commitment to have a system that produces effluent comparable to major U.S. cities. The industry's claims of drinking water quality sound good, but they would be more convincing if they were true.

A key element of the cruise industry's defence around environmental issues is that cruise ships are a small part of the problem; they are a relatively small proportion of all ships on the world's oceans. This argument is reasonable in consideration of shipboard wastes that cruise ships have in common with all ships: oily bilge water, ballast water and emissions from burning fuel.

But other waste streams, such as solid waste (including incinerator emissions), toxic waste from photo processing, printing and other onboard consumer related services, and the volume of both grey and black water create issues unique to a cruise ship because of the size of its human cargo.

The cruise industry has an ongoing problem of credibility. Past behaviour doesn't correspond with pronouncements about environmental responsibility and commitments to protection. And the industry's word doesn't follow in action. Changing positions on fuel usage is an excellent example. When it suited its purpose the industry agreed that ships using a new terminal in Seattle would use low sulphur fuels but it didn't follow through on its promise. The reversal became known some time later when California sought, through legislation, the same practice it understood to be in place in Seattle. Or take Holland America Line, which, when it announced installation of saltwater smokestack scrubbers to reduce the environmental impact from fuel, unabashedly told the media that it used fuel with less sulphur content in the Pacific Northwest (1.8 percent) than on the exact same ship when it was deployed in the Caribbean (3 percent). The duality (using poorer grade fuel in the Caribbean versus Alaska) undermines a claim of sincere environmental concern. Perhaps more illustrative is that cruise ships in Hawai'i typically burn fuel with a sulphur content ranging from 1.4 to 2.5 percent, while land-based power plants in contrast burn mostly 0.5 percent sulphur fuel (Eagle 2008).

A common way for the industry to counteract criticism is to say, "We meet or exceed all international and local regulations." It is a claim that is mostly true, but it needs to be seen in light of the industry lobbying against more progressive rules and regulations. It doesn't embrace efforts to extend greater protection to the environment, and it minimizes the issue by saying that cruise ships are only a small part of a much larger problem. The industry dissuades focus from cruise ships as unique in terms of the volume of people onboard and the volume of waste produced. In contrast to cities, which have high standards for discharge of wastewater and disposal of solid waste based in enforceable rules and regulations and which often includes systematic monitoring, the cruise industry operates largely in a system of voluntary arrangements in which they police themselves. The rules and regulations that apply when they are in international waters are those of the flag state, maybe half a world away. Like prosecution of sexual assaults, prosecution for environmental offences are difficult and made complex by the foreign-flagged status of the ship.

The largest volume of waste discharged into the oceans consists of black and grey water. The cruise industry's view on these effluents is simplistic: dilution is the solution. The basic concept is the oceans are so vast and huge that a little bit of sewage or grey water will be quickly assimilated and won't make much difference. The argument makes intuitive sense until consideration is given to the fact that many ships follow the same routes, so it isn't just one ship discharging but, in the case of Alaska, twenty-seven ships discharging along the same routes every day. The matter is even worse in the Caribbean and elsewhere. Advocates of "dilution is the solution" ignore cumulative effects, which are also relevant for air emissions, especially while ships sit stationery in harbours and as they transit to and from a cruise terminal.

In addition to the environmental impacts from normal operations of cruise ships there are risks when a ship has an accident or when it sinks. Take for example the year 2007. In January Hurtigruten's *Nordkapp* discharged as much as 750 litres of fuel oil when it scraped bottom near Deception Island in Antarctica causing an eighty-two foot gash in the ship's outer hull. Three months later in the Mediterranean Louis Cruises' *Sea Diamond* sunk off Santorini and discharged more than 300 tons of fuel oil—it contained some 450 tons of fuel and lubricants on board (see *Shanghai Daily* 2007). About ten weeks later, in July, the Spanish passenger ferry *Don Pedro* sunk after striking a tiny barren island one mile from Ibiza. The ship had 150 tons of diesel fuel in its tanks, which were reported to be leaking. Then in September the cruise ship *Dream* was detained in Rhodes after it severely listed and discharged sewage. An inspection found that holding tanks had overflowed and caused the spill; the ship had more than 3,000 tons of waste that had to be pumped out. And in November the expedition ship *Explorer* hit ice and sank 120 kilometres off the Antarctica peninsula, leaving an oil stain five by eleven kilometres in length and debris; the ship had onboard 185,000 litres of fuel oil, 24,000 litres of lubricant and 1,000 litres of gasoline. The hundred passengers and fifty-four crew boarded lifeboats and were rescued within hours. There were no injuries. In December Norwegian Cruise line's *Norwegian Dream* collided with a cargo ship as it left Montevideo, causing automobiles and containers with chemicals to be dumped into the harbour.

There are more than the obvious pollutants when a ship sinks. A major concern expressed by the Greek government over the *Sea Diamond* is the number of hydraulic and air conditioning systems that contain toxic liquids and the hundreds of television and computer screens in the vessel that could leak arsenic and other harmful substances. Similar concerns were raised after *Explorer* sank off Antarctica.

As much as the cruise industry would like its ships to be seen as innocuous and posing no threat to the environment, a careful accounting suggests cruise ships should be a serious concern for all of us. The growth of cruise ships and cruise tourism needs to be managed, and regulations and laws need to be tightened and enforced.

A good example is Antarctica, where cruise tourism is growing exponentially. In the 2002–2003 season (which runs from November to March) 13,500 people travelled to Antarctica. In 2006–2007 the number had increased to 35,000—a 160 percent increase in just four years. Many cruise tourists visit the area on larger ships offering cruise-only tours to the peninsula which allow passengers a view of icebergs from the comfort of heated cabins and lounges but not trips ashore. Princess Cruises' describes its Antarctica and South America trip as scenic cruising involving glaciers, penguins and a dazzling landscape. It makes no mention that Antarctica remains a thoroughly hostile environment, prone to savage storms, sub-zero temperatures even in summer and howling winds of up to 320 kilometres per hour. Though these larger ships offer many luxury extras, most are built for cruising in warmer waters and lack ice-hardened hulls. Aside from the issue of safety, consider the daily volumes of grey water (1.4 million litres), treated sewage (120,000 litres) and solid waste. Just as it takes lots of money to build a ship with a reinforced hull, an expense cruise lines are reluctant to take on, it costs money to effectively reduce the footprint of a cruise ship in any environment, but particularly in the sensitive and pristine environment of Antarctica.

Before You Embark

The first question before embarking on a cruise ship is whether you still want to go. The environmental issues and the impacts of cruise tourism may cause you to choose a different type of holiday. One issue is air emissions. Travel by plane contributes less CO_2 than a cruise ship. According to a report prepared by Intertanko, global emissions from shipping are twice the level of aviation (McGrath 2007). The Port of San Diego further estimates in a September 2007 report that cruise ships create more air pollution than anything else in its waters.

> They emitted more nitrogen oxides than any other type of ship—more than 500 hundred tons per year. Combined with freight and cargo ships, they produce more greenhouse gases than any other port-related sector. (Fox 2007)

If a cruise is still your vacation choice, then it makes sense to support efforts to force government bodies such as the U.S. Environmental Protection Agency to regulate emissions from cruise ships and to support local government initiatives such as one in Seattle that is considering a plan for cruise ships to offload sewage sludge for onshore treatment at the county waste plant (see Bolt 2007). This isn't a matter of shutting the cruise industry down but of citizens and governments undertaking initiatives that force cruise ship operations to significantly reduce their ecological footprint.

Passengers are potentially valuable as witnesses of environmental violations. It isn't rocket science to see an oily sheen on the ocean surface, discolouration of water from discharge of ash or liquid waste or to watch for solid waste being tossed overboard. Taking a picture of these violations can be rewarding given that U.S. law rewards passenger informants with one-half of fines collected for environmental violations in U.S. waters. A couple earned $250,000 for photographs showing garbage bags being tossed overboard from *Regal Princess* in 1993. And a ship's assistant engineer was given $500,000 for reporting to authorities the illegal discharge of oily bilge water from *Rotterdam* in Alaska's Inside Passage in 1994. Keep your camera handy. The problem however is when garbage or other discharges are thrown in the seas outside U.S. jurisdiction. There is no MARPOL police. Enforcement is the responsibility of the country where the ship is registered; few of these countries are likely to take any action.

Passengers can also be instrumental in changing cruise industry practices by letting companies know they will not tolerate harmful environmental practices and by supporting politicians who put forward initiatives for enforceable regulations with active monitoring. They can also actively choose ships that are relatively cleaner environmentally (by having an AWTS) and shun ships with outdated technology. This strategy depends on information being available so consumers can make fully informed choices. Information (somewhat like crimes) the cruise industry doesn't readily share.

Like any business, the cruise industry has making money as its primary goal. It does what it can to maximize profits and to minimize the costs associated with behaving environmentally responsible. Behaviour is most likely to change when economic disincentives derive from irresponsibility. Fines are one type of disincentive. Another is when passengers go elsewhere with their vacation dollars because of environmental policies and practices.

Chapter 4

Passengers Bring It with Them

Several days after embarking a cruise a letter is slipped under your door. It says a larger than usual number of passengers is reporting ill—the subtext is that there is an outbreak of illness, likely norovirus—and it encourages frequent washing of hands and practice of good personal hygiene. It isn't as though you wouldn't have already known something was happening given the absence of self-service condiments in buffet lines, the smell of chlorine permeating the air and a film of bleach covering glass and metal surfaces.

Passengers in these situations are often faced with conflicting messages. The cruise line is more than likely saying the illness was brought onboard by a passenger. That has been the industry's mantra since late 2002, during a cluster of outbreaks of norovirus on cruise ships operating from ports in the United States. But passengers often hear from crewmembers that the illness began on a previous cruise—that it was present before the cruise began.

Who to believe? This was the question in August/September 2003 after 300 passengers and 45 crewmembers reported ill on a transatlantic crossing by *Regal Princess*. The cruise line used the industry's mantra, saying it believed one or two passengers brought the illness aboard in Copenhagen (see Morgan 2003). But a passenger disembarking the ship in Copenhagen said in a private e-mail sent to Cruise Junkie dot Com:

> During our trip, several days of overflowing toilets in the public restrooms, as well as in the passengers' cabins occurred. Carpets were changed; plastic over carpet in several areas seemed the norm. Several crew members fell ill including our assistant waiter who was quarantined for days.

Other passengers later confirmed what she wrote; that passengers and crew had been ill on the previous cruise.

This chapter looks at the problem of illness outbreaks on cruise ships with a view to understanding what is really going on. Is it, as the industry says, a matter of cruise passengers coming onboard and spreading around disease, or is there some other explanation? The chapter also discusses other onboard health issues, including food and water safety, medical services and the cruise line's responsibility for providing those services.

Illness Onboard Cruise Ships

The complexion of illnesses found on cruise ships has shifted over the past two decades. In the 1980s and 1990s outbreaks were commonly caused by food borne bacteria such as shigella, salmonella and E coli, but these gave way to norovirus as it increased in incidence in 2001. Also in 2001 the Food Standards Agency in the United Kingdom announced that it would give health officials the statutory right to enter and inspect cruise ships (similar to the Vessel Sanitation Program in the United States). It was reacting to a report from the Consumers' Association that indicated an increase of food poisoning cases among cruise ship passengers. The Consumers' Association had received complaints about fourteen ships in 2000 and 2001, with illnesses ranging from salmonella poisoning to the potentially fatal Legionnaires' disease (Gadher 2001).

With better food processing and refrigeration, and more careful testing and treatment of drinking water loaded from shore, incidents caused by bacteria have reduced significantly. In fact, from 2002 through 2007 there are only four known outbreaks caused by salmonella, affecting just two ships (back-to-back cruises of Celebrity Cruises' *Mercury* in July/August 2002 and Radisson Seven Sea's *Seven Seas Mariner* in 2002 and again in 2005) and three caused by E coli (Cunard Line's *Caronia* in 2002, Holland America Line's *Amsterdam* in 2004 and Cunard Line's *Queen Mary 2* in 2006). There were four reports of Legionnaires' disease during the same six-year period (*Ocean Monarch* and *Pacific Venus* in 2003, *Legend of the Seas* in 2005 and *Black Watch* in 2007).

As bacteria-caused illness has decreased, the incidence of illness caused by norovirus has increased significantly. Between 1999 and 2001 the U.S. Centres for Disease Control (CDC) recorded four or five illness outbreaks per year on cruise ships that were attributed to norovirus (3 percent of passengers or 2 percent of crewmembers must report illness to be considered an outbreak). In contrast, the CDC's reported numbers jumped to twenty-nine illness outbreaks in 2002 (most of which were caused by norovirus); in total there were forty-four cases of gastrointestinal illness reported on cruise ships in 2002. The jump in incidence is reflected in an increase in the CDC's rate of outbreaks from 0.65 per 1000 cruises in 2001 to 6.45 per 1000 cruises in 2002—a ten-fold increase (see Cramer et al. 2006). The number of outbreaks has fluctuated since 2002 with a high of fifty-four in 2006 and a low of thirty-five in 2005 (see <www.cruisejunkie.com/outbreaks2008.html>).

Because illness outbreaks on cruise ships are highly visible, especially when more than 20 percent of passengers become ill, norovirus has come to be nicknamed the cruise ship virus. The obvious question of course is whether norovirus is more common on cruise ships than elsewhere. The cruise industry claims the label is unfair because the virus is often found in institutional settings such as schools, camps, prisons, nursing homes and hospitals. Their point is technically correct but it fails to acknowledge that a cruise ship is the perfect incubator for norovirus and a host of other viruses and bacteria.

Norovirus Explained

Norovirus refers to a family of unclassified, small round-structured viruses previously referred to as Norwalk-like virus. It is named after Norwalk, Ohio, where the first outbreak was documented in a school cafeteria. There are more than one hundred known viruses within the norovirus family (Ando, Noel and Fankhauser 2000). These break into at least five norovirus genogroups, which in turn are divided into at least thirty-one genetic clusters.

Norovirus causes nausea, vomiting, diarrhea and abdominal pain and sometimes a headache and low grade fever. The most frequent complication is dehydration, especially among the very young and elderly. The disease usually develops twenty-four to forty-eight hours after contaminated food or water is eaten (a median of thirty-three to thirty-six hours, but as short as twelve hours) and lasts for twenty-four to sixty hours. Recovery is usually complete and there is no evidence of any serious long-term problems. A person will normally be asymptomatic after four or five days but continues to shed the virus for as long as two weeks. For this reason conscientious and correct hand-washing is as essential on cruise ships as anywhere else.

Norovirus is transmitted by a fecal-oral route. It is contracted either by consumption of fecal-contaminated food or water or by direct person-to-person spread. Person-to-person spread includes through objects touched by an infected person who hasn't washed their hands. It also includes transmission due to aerosolization of vomit, where minute particles contaminate a surface or are transmitted by air and enter the oral mucosa and are swallowed. There is no evidence that infection occurs through the respiratory system.

Noroviruses are highly contagious and as few as ten viral particles may be sufficient to infect an individual. There is no known immunity to becoming ill after coming in contact with the virus although some suggest there may be short term (a few months) immunity that is strain-specific. Given the genetic variability of noroviruses individuals can be repeatedly infected. But this may not be totally random. Recent findings suggest people with blood type O are more susceptible than others (CDC 2007). As well, research reported in 2003 found that 29 percent of a study population lacked the gene required for norovirus binding—they did not become infected after receiving a dose of the virus (Lindesmith et al. 2003). It remains unclear whether a person who is asymptomatic transmits the virus through fecal shedding.

Transmission through water or through food prepared or served by an infected food handler was the norm in the 1980s and 1990s. Forty-two percent of outbreaks in one CDC study were attributed to water or food; only 12 percent were linked to person-to-person contact (MMWR 2001). Food and water contamination has clearly been reduced as a result of the Vessel Sanitation Program's twice-yearly ship inspections. But the scores reflect cleanliness and are not a safe indication of risk for illness from norovirus (Cramer, Gu and Durbin 2003).

If cruise industry claims are correct, transmission today is more common through direct person-to-person physical contact or from contact with a surface that has been touched by someone with the virus on their hand. This makes norovirus a nasty challenge for a cruise ship. Once the virus goes public the immediate goal is containment. Given wide-scale infection, the source of the virus may never be determined.

In recent years, the largest percentage known to be infected at one time on a single ship was on Holland America Line's *Ryndam* in 2005: over 46 percent of passengers and 6 percent of crewmembers reported ill. P&O's *Aurora* had the largest number of people reporting ill: over 600 passengers and crew in October/November 2003. The illness was so widespread that Spain shut its border with the British colony of Gibraltar for the first time in two decades on November 3, 2003, when the ship arrived in Gibraltar's harbour. Those who were judged to be healthy were allowed to disembark in Gibraltar but the frontier to Spain was closed and their travel severely restricted. The same passengers were forced to stay onboard while the ship took on supplies at Piraeus (Athens) three days earlier because local authorities would not allow them to disembark. P&O Cruises said the infection was believed to have been brought onboard by a passenger. A year earlier Aurora's sister ship *Oceana* was denied permission to dock at Philipsburg, St. Maarten, because 269 passengers and 24 crewmembers had contracted a stomach illness. The incident came a day after four people working in St. Lucia's tourism industry reported stomach illness after meeting visitors when the ship docked there (Hokstam 2002).

Are Passengers the Source?
That passengers bring norovirus with them was first asserted in November 2002 after three successive illness outbreaks sickened more than four hundred passengers and fifty crewmembers on Holland America Line's *Amsterdam*. The company's vice president of public relations, Rose Abello, stated at a press conference, "The ship is not sick. There are sick people getting on the ship" (LaMendola and Steighorst 2002).

With large-scale illness outbreaks affecting other cruise ships as well, the industry's trade group, International Council of Cruise Lines (ICCL), adopted Abello's statement and began its "passengers bring it with them" mantra. The ICCL laid out the strategy used in a session focused on illness outbreaks and the media at the World Cruise Tourism Summit in Miami in March 2003. The session opened with an almost inspirational video about the situation in which the industry found itself and how it successfully responded on the public relations front.

At the start the industry was depicted as receiving an inordinate amount of attention for a series of norovirus outbreaks on cruise ships. Illness on cruise ships had been the topic of stories on mainstream television: *Inside Edition*, CNN, NBC and many others. The industry had even become the brunt of jokes on late night television—Jay Leno and David Letterman among others. Evening news with increasing frequency showed people who had become sick onboard ships.

But there was also misinformation. Peter Greenberg on the 8 a.m. segment of NBC's *Today Show* on November 22, 2002, really messed up. He inflated the number of passengers reporting ill on *Amsterdam*, incorrectly assumed that two affected ships operated from the same port and thereby contradicted the CDC's conclusions, which ruled out food or water as a source, and suggested that terrorism could not be ruled out. Greenberg's misinformation was a source of humour and a turning point in the video. This is when the industry began its offensive.

The industry's media strategy had three elements: provide talking points to cruise executives and others in a position to present the industry's position, arrange as many media interviews as possible and flood the media with positive information about the cruise industry. It proactively distributed pictures and video footage showing ships being disinfected and engaged in positive messaging. Carnival Cruise Line's president, Bob Dickinson, framed the problem as part of a national epidemic and said there was no cause and effect with regard to norovirus on cruise ships. Colin Veitch, NCL's CEO, pointed to the incidence of norovirus in the general population in an effort to minimize the problem as unique to cruise ships. The industry also enlisted the help of third parties in its campaign, most significantly the Centers for Disease Control. It helped promote the idea that people get sick on airplanes too, but they don't experience symptoms until they get home so they don't associate it with air travel.

ICCL's video concluded with "Smooth Seas Ahead." The industry had successfully fought off the negative media attention and reframed the issue. Its message was two pronged: cruises are a great vacation at a good price and why worry about norovirus—it is as common as the common cold. You can't argue with that. The media became desensitized to the issue, and the vast majority of the 200 outbreaks effecting more than 25,000 passengers in 2003 through 2007 went unnoticed.

Incidence of Illness

The industry's assertion that passengers bring norovirus with them implies the cruise line is as much a victim as the passenger. The idea that passengers bring it onboard and spread it around places the problem beyond the cruise line's control. Their only response is to attempt containment of illness outbreaks. This resists assignment of blame, presumably including liability, for the outbreaks. As the cruise industry might say, "We're doing everything humanly possible, so don't penalize us."

The industry's position implicitly assumes outbreaks are random. But a review of cases suggests this is not the case. For one thing the frequency of illness outbreaks is related to cruise length: shorter cruises have lower rates than longer cruises. A study reported in 2006 found 27.4 outbreaks per 100,000 passenger days on cruises of three to six days, 26.5 per 100,000 passenger days on cruises of seven days, 38.8 per 100,000 passenger days on cruises of eight to fifteen days, and 48.7 per 100,000 passenger days on cruises of sixteen to twenty-one days (Cramer et al. 2006). It is tempting to conclude from these numbers that one is safer on a short cruise but that might not be the case. To register as an outbreak more than 3 percent of passengers or 2 percent of crewmembers must report illness. The 3 percent figure is more easily reached over a longer period of time. Thus, one might conclude that while the rate of outbreak is higher for cruises that are longer, it is more likely that risk is greater on a short cruise, where the 3 percent threshold is reached within a very short time.

It may be more enlightening to look at whether there is a relationship between illness outbreaks and cruise line or cruise ship; for example, are some cruise lines or ships more prone to illness outbreaks than others? Table 4.1 shows the number of outbreaks by cruise line from 2002 through 2007. It reveals that Princess Cruises and Holland America Line are disproportionately represented as a percentage of all reported outbreaks. Both cruise lines are considerably smaller in size than Carnival Cruise Lines and Royal Caribbean International but their share of outbreaks is greater.

The degree to which they are out of line with other cruise lines can be seen in Table 4.2, which shows each cruise line's share of illness outbreaks beside its percentage share of the North American market. The ratios indicate Princess Cruises' rate of illness is relatively equal to its share of the North American market. In contrast, Carnival Cruise Lines and Royal Caribbean International are considerably below what would be expected if illness outbreaks were random (between one-third to one-half less than their proportion of the cruise market share). The rate of outbreak on Norwegian Cruise Line, Celebrity Cruises, Cunard Line and Regent Seven Seas is a shade higher than market share. This is significant given how low the rate is for some other cruise lines. But Holland America Line is the most visible

Table 4.1 Illness Outbreaks by Cruise Line, 2002–2007

Cruise Line	2002	2003	2004	2005	2006	2007	Total	Percent of All Outbreaks
Holland America Line	10	5	6	5	9	8	43	16.7
Princess Cruises	2	5	10	6	7	4	34	13.2
Royal Caribbean Int'l	4	1	3	8	12	2	30	11.6
Norwegian Cruise Line	5	5	7	2	3	4	26	10.1
Celebrity Cruises	3	0	2	4	8	2	19	7.4
Carnival Cruise Lines	5	6	1	3	0	2	17	6.6
Clipper Cruise Line	4	7	3				14	5.4
Cunard Line	1	1	3		1	2	8	3.1
P&O Cruises	1	3	1	1			6	2.4
P&O Australia Cruises	1	1	3		1		6	2.4
Regent Seven Seas	1			1	1	2	5	1.9
Disney Cruise Line	4						4	1.6
Cruise West	1			1		1	3	1.2
Fred Olsen Cruises					2	1	3	1.2
Hurtigruten						3	3	1.2
Seadream Yacht Club				2	1		3	1.2
Seabourn Cruises	2	1					3	1.2
Travelscope					3		3	1.2
NCL America					1	2	2	0.8
Silverseas Cruises			2				2	0.8
Sun Cruises		2					2	0.8
Windjammer			2				2	0.8
Windstar Cruises	1			1			2	0.8
Crystal Cruises				1			1	0.4
Other	3	8	3		1	2	17	6.6
TOTAL	48	45	46	35	50	35	258	

Source: Cruise Junkie dot Com

anomaly. Its share of illness outbreaks is more than twice what it should be if illness was proportionate to market share—it is more than seven times higher than Carnival Cruise Lines.

Looking at ship specific outbreaks further supports the impression that illness outbreaks are not entirely random. Table 4.3 shows ships having three or more illness outbreaks from 2002 through 2007. It also shows cases where there were outbreaks on two or more successive cruises. The table shows ships with the most frequent illness outbreaks; it reveals wide variation between ships within a single cruise line. Not only can it be said that Holland America Line has the highest rate of illness but that three or four of its ships are proportionately more problematic than others in its fleet. This raises more questions than it provides answers.

The Role of Crew

Cruise ship outbreaks reflect how easily norovirus can be transmitted from person to person or via food in a closed environment such as a cruise ship. The continuation or resurgence of outbreaks on consecutive cruises on the same ship, or even on different ships of the same company, suggests that environmental contamination may be an issue. Infected crewmembers might serve as reservoirs of infection for passengers (MMWR 2002). This view is supported by research that found that approximately 50 percent of all norovirus

Table 4.2: Percentage Outbreaks by Cruise Lines with North American Capacity, 2002–2007

Cruise Line	Percent of North American Capacity	Total Outbreaks	Percent of All Outbreaks	Ratio of Capacity to All Outbreaks
Seadream Yacht Club	0.1	3	1.2	12.00⁺
Seabourn Cruises	0.3	3	1.2	4.000⁺
Holland America Line	7.5	43	16.7	2.227
Windstar Cruises	0.3	2	0.8	1.778^
Regent Seven Seas	1.1	5	1.9	1.727*
Cunard Line	2.0	8	3.1	1.550
Silverseas Cruises	0.6	2	0.8	1.333^
Norwegian Cruise Line	7.7	26	10.1	1.311
Celebrity Cruises	6.6	19	7.4	1.121
Princess Cruises	12.8	34	13.2	1.031
Disney Cruise Line	1.6	4	1.6	1.000
Royal Caribbean Int'l	20.2	30	11.6	0.450
Crystal Cruises	0.9	1	0.4	0.444
Carnival Cruise Lines	21.3	17	6.6	0.301
NCL America	2.7	2	0.8	0.296
Clipper Cruise Line	N/A	14	5.4	–
Cruise West	N/A	3	1.2	–

Table 4.2: Percentage Outbreaks by Cruise Lines with North American Capacity, 2002–2007, continued...

Cruise Line	Percent of North American Capacity	Total Outbreaks	Percent of All Outbreaks	Ratio of Capacity to All Outbreaks
Fred Olsen Cruises (U.K.)	N/A	3	1.2	–
Hurtigruten (Norway)	N/A	3	1.2	–
P&O Cruises	N/A	6	2.4	–
P&O Australia Cruises	N/A	6	2.4	–
Sun Cruises (U.K.)	N/A	2	0.8	–
Travelscope (U.K.)	N/A	3	1.2	–
Windjammer	N/A	2	0.8	-
Other	N/A	17	6.6	–
TOTAL		258		

* The ratio for Regent Seven Seas (previously named Radisson Seven Seas) should be viewed in light of the fact that half of the illness outbreaks were attributed to salmonella; the other half were caused by norovirus.
+ The ratio for Seabourn and Seadream Yacht Club must be treated with caution given the small size of their ships. Seabourn's ships accommodate 200 passengers, which means the 3 percent threshold requires only six passengers to report ill; Seadream Yacht Club's ships are half the size, which means an outbreak requires only three ill passengers.
^ The ratio for Silverseas and Windstar must also be treated with caution given the relatively small size of their ships (i.e., 200–300 passengers).
Source: CLIA 2005.

outbreaks are linked to ill food service workers (Widdowson et al. 2005). At the very least we should not see passengers as the sole source of illness.

The industry argues that crewmembers are not a key because of the relatively small number of reported illness among crew as compared to passengers. As far back as the 1980s and 1990s reported illness among crewmembers are at levels lower than passengers. Perhaps they are less susceptible to gastrointestinal attacks or are stoic when they suffer. More likely however is that strong disincentives exist that mediate against crewmembers reporting when they are ill (see CDC 2002). Crewmembers who depend on tips are not paid when they don't work, so they are likely to work even when they aren't healthy. As well, there is some indication that crewmembers risk losing their job if they are absent for more than two or three days and that they feel pressure to return to work even when they are not well.

This poses a serious problem for controlling spread of the virus. Ill crew-

Table 4.3: Cruise Ships with Three or More Reported Illness Outbreaks, 2002–2007

Ship (Cruise Line)	Total Outbreaks	Number of Back-to-Back Outbreaks
Amsterdam (Holland America)	10	4
Ryndam (Holland America)	10	4
Veendam (Holland America)	7	1
Norwegian Crown (Norwegian)	7	2
Sun Princess (Princess)	7	1
Mercury (Celebrity)	6	2
Pacific Sky (P&O Australia)	5	1
Volendam (Holland America)	5	0
Island Princess (Princess)	5	1
Zenith (Celebrity)	4	0
Queen Elizabeth II (Cunard)	4	0
Norwegian Dream (Norwegian)	4	0
Norwegian Sky (Norwegian) / *Pride of Aloha* (NCL America)*	4	1
Oceana (P&O)	4	0
Regal Princess (Princess)	4	0
Seven Seas Mariner (Regent)	4	0
Celebration (Carnival)	3	1
Holiday (Carnival)	3	1
Constellation (Celebrity)	3	1
Disney Magic (Disney)	3	1
Zaandam (Holland America)	3	0
Zuiderdam (Holland America)	3	0
Norwegian Sun (Norwegian)	3	0
Royal Princess (Princess)	3	0
Empress of the Seas (Royal Caribbean)	3	0
Radiance of the Seas (Royal Caribbean)	3	0
Serenade of the Seas (Royal Caribbean)	3	1

* *Norwegian Sky* was transferred to NCL America and renamed *Pride of Aloha*. Three outbreaks were under the former name; one under the latter.
Source: Cruise Junkie dot Com.

members may continue to work. And crewmembers who are quarantined in their cabin—a cabin that is normally shared with others—for forty-eight to seventy-two hours are likely to return to work when they are symptom free but will continue to shed the virus for as long as two weeks. The virus can easily be reintroduced and carry over from one cruise to another, especially by kitchen workers, food and beverage servers and others engaged in regular and direct contact with passengers. Crew as much as passengers are potential sources of person-to-person contact. But the problem cannot be addressed until the problem is seen more broadly—that outbreaks are caused by passengers and by crew.

Ship maintenance and cleanliness is another factor, but it is hard to quantify. Review of postings at online discussion boards such as Cruise Critic and Cruisemates give many examples of toilets backing up and of other sewage-related problems. While the accounts are anecdotal they cannot be ignored. Take an e-mail received by Cruise Junkie dot Com from an officer on a large U.S.-based cruise ship:

> I worked on one ship where the guys fixing the plumbing had no clue. When a line would get clogged, they would drill a hole to find the clog, but the hole was then just fixed with duct tape. When they eventually did get the clog out, the compartment where the clean out had occurred would be left as is. You'd open the door and find feces and urine just sitting there. This was found throughout the ship. This was noted in an internal audit; only after the chief engineer made a big deal out of it to the auditors (the chief engineer had enough of the company and had a new job to go to).

Granted that this may be an anomaly, but for those planning to take a cruise it suggests the need for caution. For those in the industry, it suggests the need for a comprehensive review and analysis of the problem of norovirus with a view toward honest and objective assessment. The industry clearly invented the mantra "passengers bring in with them" to resolve a crisis thrust upon them by a large wave of illness outbreaks within a short period. It is about time the industry replace its public relations stance, designed to absolve it of responsibility, with a clear statement to passengers and crew of risks and methods for prevention.

Part of this shift would include ceasing the practice of penalizing passengers when they are ill. Many passengers tell of saving for years for a cruise only to find they are quarantined in their room for the majority of the cruise and with little compensation for their lost vacation. Passengers who avoid illness give accounts of discomfort and inconvenience caused by thick chlorine in the air and having mirrors, metal surfaces and walls covered with a film of disinfectant. That is not the vacation they expected from the slick advertising.

The practice of quarantine is beginning to impact passengers in the same way as crewmembers. It creates a clear disincentive to report one's illness, which further complicates containing spread. Passengers are coming to realize they have a choice: report the slightest sense of illness and be quarantined in their room for a couple of days or more and miss the ports they were looking forward to seeing, or keep their illness quiet and go about enjoying their vacation. If the industry is truly interested in getting these folks out of the general circulation on and off ship, then it needs to remove the economic and other disincentives to reporting illness. It also needs to think more sensitively about how people who are quarantined are treated. Many passengers report room service that is not responsive and housekeeping staff that leave to the passenger the cleaning of their own room.

In a perverse way, the cruise line benefits by maintaining disincentives to passengers reporting their illness. Outbreak statistics kept by Centres for Disease Control are based on the percentage of passengers reporting ill (with specific symptoms and criteria) during a cruise—if a cruise ship reduces the number of persons reporting ill (whether by better disease control measures or by greater disincentives to reporting) it also reduces the officially recorded number of outbreaks. Non-reporting by passengers and crew can actually work to the cruise ship's advantage when the number reporting ill falls short of the outbreak threshold.

Food and Water Safety

The discussion of illness makes one wonder whether the food and water on a cruise ship are safe. Food safety is somewhat overseen by twice-yearly ship inspections conducted by the Vessel Sanitation Program of the Centres for Disease Control for ships using U.S. ports. Similar inspection programs are in place in Canada and the U.K. These inspections are credited with preventing food borne illness by focusing upon and auditing shipboard practices. Many problems are found requiring immediate remedial action. That is a positive; however, one wonders why inspection by an outside government body is needed to determine that drinking water is not safe for human consumption, that kitchen surfaces are not properly cleaned, that refrigerators don't seal properly and are not at correct temperatures, that dishwashers aren't properly calibrated and that food is not stored at or served at temperatures that assure safety.

It is tempting to give a list of problems by ship but the number would be too large, and choosing some for illustration would obviously be arbitrary and potentially misleading. These reports are available online and prospective passengers may look up the reports for ships being considered for their holiday. Inspection reports for ships visiting U.S. ports are available at the Centres for

Disease Control and Prevention website under Vessel Sanitation Program <wwwn.cdc.gov/vsp/InspectionQueryTool/Forms/InspectionSearch. aspx>.

In September 2005 U.K.-based *Which?* magazine published "Behind the Scenes in the Cruise Ship Galleys." Based on inspection reports secured through the U.K. *Freedom of Information Act*, the article mentions veal being thawed for use that was ten months out of date, cheese and a frozen goose of uncertain vintage, cockroaches and swarms of flies in food larders and problems with refrigerators. The article culled considerable media attention in the U.K., and its findings are consistent with many reports found from the U.K. and the U.S.'s Vessel Sanitation Programs.

While some inspection reports provide fascinating reading, they should be viewed with some scepticism. Inspections are supposed to be a surprise to those onboard (i.e., unscheduled), but many ships appear to know in advance when they will occur. An officer on one ship writes:

> I have witnessed U.S. health inspections where the cooks/galley/ wait staff were told by senior management to hide things in their cabins when the inspectors came onboard. There were meat cutters, delivery carts and trays stored in garbage rooms only to be taken out and reused after the inspectors left (in one case the garbage room had such an infestation problem that it had to be sprayed weekly with insecticides/pesticides). There were foodstuffs such as cheese and rice stored in crew member cabins that had been regularly sprayed with insecticides in order to contain a bed bug infestation; these too were returned to the galley after inspectors left. When informed about such things, the captain just laughed. The reason: the inspection scores figure into their bonus, so if they can get a higher score, they get more money. (Private correspondence 2007)

This brings us back to the question of food safety. There is nothing to indicate that food on a cruise ship is any more unsafe than food from a restaurant onshore. Thus, consumers need to treat the cruise ship as they would a restaurant. If things don't appear right or if food doesn't taste right, then trust your intuition. Be cautious and sensible and report issues and concerns to the agency charged with the ship's health inspection.

One should use the same caution with drinking water. Cruise ships offer the option of bottled water, a choice that may be wise to make. Concern is based on a court case about which there is incomplete information: it has been sealed by the British courts, and those involved are not permitted to comment for fear of fine or incarceration. The lack of transparency suggests there is a real basis for fear. The Log a Complaint website at <www. logacomplaint.com> had information about toxicity in potable water aboard certain cruise ships in October 2005, but that material has disappeared, as has all information about the case that followed. (The case, *Hempel A/S v B Bradford* [2006] EWHC 2528, is cited at the website of the attorney for the industry, but otherwise no information may be found anywhere).

From what was on the website and from appeals filed with the High Court of Justice in the U.K. and European Court of Human Rights, we can extrapolate that a paint coating used in potable water tanks on a series of cruise ships built in Pappenburg, Germany (at least four ships owned by two major companies serving North America and Europe), was found to be defective. It could purportedly break down and potentially release toxins into the water systems of these vessels. The problem was apparently discovered and repairs undertaken.

Rather than take the ships out of service for proper repair, the work was done while ships were in service with passengers and crew onboard. The work required sanding the interior surface of water tanks and then applying a new, safe coating. If done properly, repairs would also address contamination that had already occurred and was now part of the water delivery system. While the problem coating was being "solved," the repair itself may have produced another set of problems. There is no certainty that fine dust produced from the sanding did not make its way into other areas of the ship, including air ventilation and food preparation areas. On one ship the fine dust clogged vent pipes that allowed air to escape as water tanks were filled, creating a serious and dangerous situation when one of the tanks was put back into use.

The lack of information is frustrating. There is a clear basis for knowing that there was (and may still be) a problem. It appears that industry and government authorities know of the problem and the threat to public health, but that industrial profit and secrecy have a higher value than the public need to know. The lack of transparency about the case, and the way in which the information has been sealed from public knowledge, gives good reason for a passenger on any cruise ship to be cautious. The purportedly defective paint coating was manufactured by a large scale provider (Hempel A/S) to shipyards building cruise ships, and it is hard to know, without adequate testing for chemical contamination, on which ships there is reason for concern. This isn't a matter of opinion or conjecture—there are apparently affidavits admitting to the problem of toxicity but these too are sealed. Under the circumstances one should be cautious about tap water on cruise ships.

Onboard Medical Care

Most people planning a cruise don't give a second thought about medical care onboard. Their assumption that a ship has a physician-staffed infirmary is reinforced by cruise brochures. One states, "Should you require medical attention while onboard, our infirmary staff are available to assist you twenty-four hours a day." It then goes on to explain that the infirmaries meet or exceed Medical Facilities Guidelines established by the International Council of Cruise Lines and that medical services are rendered at a customary fee. What the brochure doesn't say is perhaps more important than what it says.

Most passengers are surprised that a cruise ship is not required under international maritime law to have a physician. The only legal requirement, under the Standards of Training, Certification and Watchkeeping for Seafarers (SCTW) Convention, is that there be identified crewmembers who have various levels of first aid and medical training. Regardless, all modern cruise ships maintain an infirmary and almost all have a physician and nurse on staff. These medical professionals work under contract as concessionaires and receive a fee plus commissions on medical services, prescriptions and medical supplies.

The precise qualifications of onboard medical care providers can vary widely. A 1996 survey administered by two Florida physicians to eleven cruise lines found

> that twenty-seven percent of doctors and nurses did not have advanced training in treating victims of heart attacks, the leading killer on ships, and fifty-four percent of doctors and seventy-two percent of nurses lacked advanced training for dealing with trauma. Fewer than half of shipboard doctors—forty-five percent—had board certification, an important credential that is granted after three to seven years of residency and a written examination in a specialty or its equivalent.... As for equipment, the survey found that sixty-three percent of ships did not have equipment for blood tests for diagnosing heart attacks, and forty-five percent did not have mechanical ventilators or external pacemakers. (Frantz 1999b)

The study concluded that the quality of maritime medical care was less than adequate, from the medical facilities to nurse and physician credentials.

The study led the American Medical Association (AMA) to call for greater awareness of the limited medical services available aboard ships. The AMA also called on the U.S. Congress to develop medical standards for cruise ships. But the cruise industry's lobbying organization, the International Council of Cruise Lines (ICCL), has so far been successful in keeping the issue off the Congressional agenda. The ICCL neutralized the issue when, in response to the AMA's call, it adopted industry guidelines for medical facilities and personnel on cruise ships.

The guidelines, written by the American College of Emergency Physicians, are entirely voluntary and (like environmental guidelines) are not enforced. While they play well for public relations and for defusing criticism, they do not establish predictable standards of care for the industry. As they say, "They simply reflect a consensus among member lines of the facilities and staffing needs considered appropriate aboard cruise vessels" (ICCL 2002).

The guidelines have serious gaps. For example, they do not require certification in emergency or critical care, which is significant given that 90 percent of deaths on cruise ships are caused by a heart attack. But the greatest weakness is the wide variation in actual equipment onboard a ship. While the guidelines suggest one infirmary bed per 1000 passengers and crew, one intensive care unit bed per ship and a variety of equipment (e.g., two cardiac monitors; two defibrillators; an electrocardiograph; advanced life support medications sufficient to run two complex codes; capability for measurement of hemoglobin/hemocrit, urinalysis, pregnancy tests, glucose tests; x-rays on ships delivered after January 1, 1997, with more than 1000 passengers; and a range of emergency medications and supplies), there is no guarantee that these are in place. The actual equipment onboard varies depending upon the itinerary, size of the ship and anticipated demographic makeup of passengers. It also varies by cruise line. In 2000 I was given a tour of the *Radisson Diamond* and was impressed that the ship had an x-ray machine—at least that is what the caution sign said on the outside of a door. My positive reaction was quickly replaced by disappointment when the physician giving the tour said the machine had been broken for quite some time and there was no plan for it to be repaired or replaced.

Infirmaries on ships essentially are equipped to deal with minor injuries, including workplace injuries of crew, and to stabilize a patient experiencing a heart attack and many other acute conditions. Realistically speaking it is more like a neighbourhood clinic than a hospital emergency room. It can most effectively deal with routine problems such as scrapes and cuts, sunburn and indigestion. It also is equipped to serve as the "family doctor" for all the ship's crew, treating anything from the common cold and flu to high blood sugar and hypertension. This reflects the types of problems ship infirmaries tend to deal with. The most common diagnosis in passengers is respiratory illness (26–29 percent). Injuries, most frequently sprains, and superficial wounds and contusions also account for a significant proportion of ship-board medical visits (10–18 percent), as do gastrointestinal illness (accounting for 9–16 percent). Interestingly, the rate of medical consultation on cruises is higher than on shore. Crewmembers, although significantly younger than passengers, make proportionately more medical visits (CATMAT 2005: 2–3).

The Medical Staff

There is wide variation in the training and background of medical personnel. Some cruise lines draw their physicians only from the U.K., the U.S. and/or Canada and pay $10,000 or more a month; all are board certified in one of these countries. In contrast, personnel on other cruise lines are drawn from a range of countries, have salaries reported to be as low as $1,057 a month and may not be board certified. A 1999 *New York Times* article reports that only 56 percent of the doctors on Carnival Cruise Lines' ships had board certification or equivalent certifications; 85 percent of the physicians on Royal Caribbean Cruise Lines were board certified (Frantz 1999b).

Board certification itself may not be altogether reassuring. For example, the physician on one cruise ship had thirty years of experience as an anaesthesiologist; his expertise to deal with some of the possible emergency situations on a cruise ship was untested. The physician on another ship had a specialty in oncological colorectal surgery. Though well respected within his specialization he was not regularly required to exercise skills in emergency medicine.

The intent here is not to question the competence of all onboard physicians. Rather, the information presented illustrates that the medical qualifications and facilities can vary widely from ship to ship and from cruise line to cruise line. As a potential patient one needs to take proper care and cannot assume the same level of care on a cruise ship as one is accustomed to receiving at home. There are many case examples of misdiagnosis and, just like at home, a patient may need to secure a second opinion, whether at a port of call or via a telephone consultation with one's family physician. The following, written to Cruise Junkie dot Com by an officer on a major cruise line, states the situation well:

> In regards to the doctors I have seen a drastic change in treatment. We used to have teams of doctors and nurses from Norway, Sweden, Denmark, Finland. They were very good. The company has since started using an agent that deals only with South Africans and Central and South American doctors. Questionable practices can now be seen. Imagine this: you live in a country where as a doctor you earn $800 a month. You are now on a cruise ship earning well over $12,000.00 a month—and you earn more money (commission based) when you keep adding up the charges on guests. The possibility for unethical behaviour with this scenario is rampant. I have seen the exact opposite with the Scandinavian teams—their earning potential is about the same at home as it is on the ships. They seem to provide better treatment, at minimal costs. Also, you also have to look at the view of "upper caste" vs. "lower caste" from both teams. The Scandinavian doctors are fantastic with everyone, regardless of what rank they are—could this just be a result of what naturally happens in their own countries? Whereas the Central/ South American teams seem to provide less than desirable treatment

to crew members that are not officers. I've seen situations where the doctors keep crew members confined in the hospital until they have diarrhea and can prove it before they put them on the GI list. Would you ever imagine going to a doctor and having to produce a bowel movement just to prove you are sick? This also has a double edge to it because if crew members have to fear this type of treatment, then what incentive do they have to come forward when they are sick? Why not keep your mouth shut, deal with it, keep working?

Liability for Medical Care

No doubt there are cases of malpractice on cruise ships. Most Americans and Canadians assume they have the same rights and the same protections as they would on land when something happens. But that is not the case. Even though a physician wears the uniform of a senior-ranked officer, is introduced to passengers onboard as the ship's physician (implying s/he, like the captain, is an employee of the cruise line), like other senior officers has his/her picture displayed and likely hosts a dinner table for invited guests, cruise lines without exception say the physician is a private concessionaire and as such the cruise line accepts no liability for mistakes made. It is a hard concept to get one's head around given that the service is offered by the cruise ship and the cruise ship collects the fees. But this position was supported by the Florida Supreme Court in February 2007 and by the U.S. Supreme Court in October 2007.

The case began ten years before in March 1997. Fourteen-year-old Elizabeth Carlisle was on a Caribbean cruise on *Carnival Destiny* with her family. On the second night out of Miami she developed severe abdominal pain. She consulted the ship's physician, Dr. Mauro Neri, who had finished medical school in his native Italy in 1981 and had held nine medical jobs in Italy, Africa and England in the fifteen years before joining Carnival Cruise Lines. His salary was $1,057 a month. Dr. Neri advised that Elizabeth was suffering from the flu and sent her on her way. But her pain became worse. On the third visit to the infirmary, after Elizabeth's parents specifically asked whether the problem could be appendicitis, Dr. Neri conducted his first physical exam. He responded that he was sure the problem was not the girl's appendix.

When the pain continued to grow worse Elizabeth's parents called their family physician in Michigan, who advised they return home. The family took the advice, and shortly after arriving home Elizabeth underwent emergency surgery to remove her ruptured appendix. The infection had rendered the fourteen year old sterile and caused lifelong medical problems. Elizabeth sued Carnival Cruise Lines in Florida state court, a case she lost on Carnival's motion for summary judgement. The cruise line claimed it was not responsible for the medical negligence of the doctor on board and pointed to the fine print in the passenger cruise contract to support its position.

The family appealed the Circuit Court's decision to Florida's Third District Court of Appeal, where the parents argued the cruise line was vicariously liable for the doctor's negligence. Judge Joseph Nesbitt agreed and reversed the lower court's decision. The judge held that the cruise line had control over the doctor's medical services for agency law purposes; the doctor was to provide medical services to passengers and crew in accordance with the cruise line's guidelines. And as it was foreseeable that some passengers at sea would develop medical problems (and that the only realistic alternative for such a passenger was treatment by the ship's doctor) the cruise line had an element of control over the doctor–patient relationship. As such, the cruise line's duty to exercise reasonable care under the circumstances extended to the actions of a ship's doctor placed onboard by the cruise line. The doctor was an agent of the cruise line and his negligence was imputed to the cruise line. This invalidated the cruise ticket's purported limitation of the cruise line's liability for the negligence of its agents.

Judge Nesbitt's decision was groundbreaking. It was likely the very first case where a cruise line was held responsible for the care provided by a ship's physician. Not surprisingly, Carnival appealed the case to the Florida Supreme Court. While the court almost agreed with the lower court's assertion that times had changed and that a doctor's negligence at sea also shows negligence by the cruise line, it ultimately found in favour of Carnival. Justice Peggy Quince wrote in her opinion:

> We find merit in the plaintiff's argument and the reasoning of the district court. However, because this is a maritime case, this Court and the Florida district courts of appeal must adhere to the federal principles of harmony and uniformity when applying federal maritime law. (Supreme Court of Florida 2007: 18–19)

The case was appealed to the U.S. Supreme Court and the court refused to hear it. The Florida Supreme Court's decision was the final word. If the Carlisle family wanted to pursue the case they would have to sue the physician directly. But this would be difficult in their case, and in most involving medical malpractice on cruise ships, given that they'd first have to locate the physician in his present home. Cruise lines historically have not provided assistance with locating former staff members. In addition, malpractice cases involving treatment in international waters must be filed in the courts of the physician's country of origin, which is both difficult and expensive (see Chen 2007: D1).

Other passengers have had experiences with onboard medical care that are similar to Elizabeth Carlisle's. For example, a year earlier on another Carnival Cruise Lines ship, *Jubilee,* Russell Lum, a fifty-two-year-old aircraft mechanic from Berkeley, California, died as a complication from a norovirus outbreak on the ship. He had complained that he wasn't feeling well the second night of the cruise and following a bout of nausea spent the following day in his cabin. At 1:30 a.m. on the third day, Russell's wife found him collapsed in the bathroom. She called the ship's infirmary, resisted the nurse's attempt to discourage her from bringing him in and insisted he be put on an intravenous solution to avoid dehydration.

After a time, the nurse took Lum's blood pressure and said he was improving and could return to his cabin. Russell's wife returned to their room to retrieve fresh clothing and within five minutes was back in the infirmary. She was met by the nurse and physician and asked to wait in the waiting room. Several minutes later they came in and told her Russell had taken a turn for the worse and died. His death was a result of extensive blood loss from a tear in his esophagus caused by vomiting. His family sued Carnival Cruise Lines for his wrongful death. The cruise line's lawyer contended the company was not responsible because the death was an act of God and that Russell had failed to seek timely or appropriate medical care. He said Russell Lum's own negligence contributed to his death and injuries (Frantz 1999b).

There is also the 1997 case of a woman on her honeymoon on Carnival Cruise Lines' *Sensation.* The woman and her husband returned to the ship from a walk ashore and went to the infirmary because the woman, a diabetic, felt flushed. There the nurse and doctor checked her blood sugar and because it was very high the woman was administered fast-acting insulin to bring the blood sugar down. According to the husband:

> Instead of getting better, she got worse and worse.... She was totally unconscious and went into a diabetic coma and was wringing wet. I called for the nurse and she said she'd come around. I waited and she started jerking real bad. (Frantz 1999b)

He rushed back to their cabin to get his wife's glucose meter and returned to the infirmary to measure his wife's blood sugar himself. He found that her blood sugar was not too high, but rather too low. The nurse administered glucose, and the woman regained consciousness after about fifteen minutes. The couple claims that the incident caused brain damage that has left the woman disoriented and unable to return to her job.

More recently, in 2006, a seventy-three-year-old woman allegedly died as a result of mistreatment and misdiagnosis onboard *Carnival Legend.* According to a lawsuit filed September 4, 2007, the woman was suffering from a build-up of fluid in her lungs. She went to the infirmary, and after examination they pumped her full of fluid, exactly the wrong thing to do.

In effect, the suit alleges, the medical staff allowed the woman to drown in her own fluids, and while she was in distress the captain would not allow a medical evacuation to a land-based medical facility.

It isn't just Carnival Cruise Lines that has a history of medical care problems—the *Wall Street Journal* reports that more than four malpractice cases are filed against Florida-based cruise companies each year (Chen 2007: D1). The problem spans the industry and is well exposed in Douglas Frantz's 1999 article on medical care aboard cruise ships. For those who choose to cruise, the stories are a reminder to seek a second opinion (when needed) and to not blindly trust a physician chosen by a cruise line. Take a case in 2000 of a passenger who had been using patches behind the ear to control seasickness. Because he didn't think they were working, he used a new patch each day; by day four he wasn't feeling well. He went to the infirmary, complained of abdominal discomfort, was advised by the nurse to take a laxative and sent on his way. When told of the situation, a fellow passenger who was a physician pointed out the possibility that he had an overdose from the scopolamine patch. The symptoms were compounded by the fact that he was also taking Ditropan. The man went to the infirmary, asked about the other physician's theory and was catheterized. He was fine thereafter (Klein and Halley 2001: 78–81).

Before You Embark

People taking a cruise are somehow blinded to issues about which they would probably give careful thought if travelling on land. Someone who would view it as common sense to be cautious about medical care provided in a foreign country may not give a second thought to medical care provided by a physician from somewhere else, on a cruise ship registered in Panama or the Bahamas. If anything, their concern should be heightened on a cruise ship. On land there are alternative care providers and there is legal recourse when something goes wrong. But at sea there are few if any alternatives and there is no legal protection when something goes wrong. In effect, the cruise line provides medical care for which it assumes no liability. The best advice to a passenger: don't get sick. And if you do, be proactive in your care and don't hesitate to seek a second opinion from your family physician back home or from a physician in the next port of call. The alternative can be catastrophic.

The same is true of other services provided on a cruise ship. Take a 2007 case where a passenger on a two-week Mediterranean cruise decided to treat herself to a teeth-whitening treatment at the ship's beauty salon. She assumed it was safe because it was sold on the cruise ship. But it didn't turn out as expected. The treatment used a chemical typically used for disinfecting swimming pools, stripped away the top layer of enamel from her front teeth and left her with yellowing teeth that were easily stained and dry. The damage is permanent and she is now faced with the huge expense and inconvenience of complex cosmetic procedures to ameliorate the problem (Rose 2007). The beauty salon, like the onboard physician, is a concessionaire, and the cruise line accepts no liability. The ship earns a portion of what the passenger spends and bills the passenger on behalf of the salon but that is the end of its connection.

Should the woman have known this in advance? If she had read the cruise contract that was delivered with her documents and which she accepted by stepping onto the ship she'd have been forewarned. There in clear language is a variation of the standard caveat—text stating that the ship's masseuse, barber, hairdresser, manicurist, fitness or golf instructor, videographer, art auctioneer, gift shop personnel, wedding planners or providers of other personal services are employees of independent contractors and the cruise line is not responsible for their actions. The same statement of nonliability applies to medical services, shore excursions, ground transportation provided from an airport to the ship, and more. As Carnival Cruise Lines' contract states, these services are provided as a convenience for the guest, and guests are free to use them or not. The contract goes on to say that the company assumes no responsibility and does not guarantee the performance of these independent contractors. This is something to think about carefully before taking a cruise and something to keep in mind if you choose to avail yourself of any onboard service or amenity.

The cruise-line mantra that "passengers bring it with them" in referring to anything from norovirus to bed bugs is another means for escaping liability. If something infectious is brought onboard, over which they claim they have no control, then their liability is limited. But if they admit that a virus or bed bugs were present before a passenger arrived, they'd have some responsibility. The industry's position is made clear in a response by Carnival Cruise Lines' public relations department to a lawsuit brought after a norovirus outbreak was listed as a contributory cause of a passenger's death. The company said the seventy-six-year-old passenger had serious pre-existing conditions, including cardiovascular disease, which was the primary cause of death. It added: "Cruise ships do not create viruses; however, Carnival does work closely with the CDC to monitor and prevent the spread of any illnesses brought on board our vessels" (Brannigan 2007).

This means that passengers have little recourse when something goes wrong. They must take their own precautions and are responsible for avoiding risk. In the case of bed bugs this may include a practice common among those travelling in developing countries—before getting comfortable in a room, pull the bed away from the wall and look for signs of bed bugs along the baseboard and the bed's headboard. And if there are signs of gastrointestinal illness among the passengers or crew, avoid contact with people, avoid high risk foods and if you become ill accept that it's your fault. It must be, because according to the cruise line it isn't theirs.

Those still willing to take a cruise in the face of these conditions should review the sanitary inspection reports available online for the ship(s) being considered. While these reports are not an indication of the level of risk for illness—there is no direct correlation between vessel sanitation scores and norovirus outbreaks (Cramer et al. 2006)—they do give insight into maintenance practices and will help inform expectations for cleanliness in food preparation and food service areas. Even when a corrective action report is included with the initial inspection report, we have to wonder why it took a government agency to come onboard before fixing violations as visible as cockroaches, dirty food preparation surfaces, refrigerators and food warmers that are not properly calibrated and much more.

Chapter 5

We Contribute Millions of Dollars
to the Local Economy

The belief that cruise ships are an economic boom to a port community's economy seems almost universal. There are few ports with the capacity to accommodate cruise ships that have not thought about cruise tourism as a cash cow. They believe the proverbial "if we build it they will come." They invest in enhanced piers, build new cruise terminals and wait for the dollars to roll in. Their motivation is the assumption that cruise passengers spend lots of money in each port they visit. In December 2007 Princess Cruises issued a press release stating the 1950-passenger *Sun Princess* will generate an average $500,000 at each New Zealand port it visits. Communities make decisions based on industry claims such as these.

Embracing cruise tourism appears at first blush to be a good business decision for many ports and islands. But governments and communities tend to overlook or minimize the downside. The cruise industry in contrast has an enviable business environment, where ports compete for cruise ships, and cruise lines negotiate deals most favourable to their bottom line. If the deal with a port isn't optimal, a ship's mobility means it can go someplace that will give a better deal. Ports as a result often earn less than expected. There are a number of possible reasons. One is that, increasingly, ports are in direct competition with the cruise ship for passenger spending.

From Necessity to the Economic Bottom Line

Carnival Cruise Lines revolutionized cruising in the 1970s when it introduced onboard revenue generation as a significant element of the cruise product. Carnival opened larger casinos and discos and devised new ways to make money onboard its ships. This was the beginning of the "fun ships" concept, devised less as a grand plan and more as an immediate strategy for meeting the weekly payroll. By the 1990s, most cruise lines had a manager of onboard revenue whose job was to oversee and increase generation of income onboard. Modern cruise ships were on their way to becoming "little more than floating bedfactories with shops and restaurants attached. Time spent at sea is simply a matter of getting from A to B with an emphasis on cajoling those trapped inside into spending their money on shopping, drinks, and other extras" (Ashworth 2001).

Cruise pricing in the 2000s remained somewhat stable but corporate profits continued to increase significantly. Onboard revenue had become a key element in the new economic reality of cruise tourism. Income previously made from ticket sales is now generated after passengers are onboard. Cruise columnist Mary Lu Abbot warned in November 2004 that extras can cost more than the cruise.

A 2002 report from the U.S. Federal Trade Commission succinctly captures the most recent shifts:

> Cruising has evolved from a minor offshoot of the oceanic passenger industry of the past into a broad-based vacation business.... Today's cruise ships, bearing a far stronger resemblance to floating luxury hotels, or even amusement parks than to traditional ocean liners, offer their thousands of passengers amenities such as full scale, "Main Street"-style shopping districts, multiple restaurants, spas, basketball courts, and even ice skating rinks and rock-climbing walls. (Federal Trade Commission 2002)

A typical cruise ship today is in a manner of speaking a 1500-room resort with lifeboats—about equal in guest capacity to six of the largest resorts on St. Lucia combined: three Sandals properties, two Almond resorts and the Westin Le Paradis. And some ships are even larger. Royal Caribbean's Freedom-class ships, first introduced in 2006, carry more guests than can be accommodated at all seven Sandals resorts combined on the island of Jamaica. Royal Caribbean's Genesis-class ship, debuting in 2009, is 50 percent larger again. Each ship will carry more than 6000 passengers. Cruise ships today dwarf land-based resorts in the number of people accommodated and do this in a fraction of the space.

Onboard revenue has also become huge. In 2006 the Big Three cruise operators had combined net revenue of $3.5 billion from onboard revenue. That translates into a profit of $43 per passenger per day (more profit than generated from ticket sales) and constitutes 24 percent of the total net revenue for all cruise companies combined; the percentage is significantly higher for the large U.S.-based mass market cruise lines (Cramer 2006). This perspective is reflected in what one speaker said at the industry's annual trade show in Miami, Seatrade Cruise Shipping Convention: "Never give away something you can charge for, as long as you can provide a really good experience. Consumers are willing to pay for a quality experience" (Seatrade Insider 2007).

Top Sources of Onboard Revenue

One of top three generators of income is a ship's bars. In the early 1970s cruise ships had a reputation for providing drinks at inexpensive prices. Between purchasing liquor at duty free prices and a marginal attempt to generate income from the bars a mixed drink could be had for between thirty-five and fifty cents. A decade later prices had tripled. Today the price is comparable to that in a bar or hotel in any major city on land.

Also in contrast to the 1970s there are a range of bars, including pool bars, wine bars, piano bars and any number of theme bars (e.g., martinis, single malt scotch, champagne, etc.). Bars are effective money-makers given that about 80 percent of revenue is profit (Huie 1995: 50). Beverage sales are further maximized by prohibiting passengers from bringing soft drinks or alcohol onboard. Cruise lines in the late 1990s began the practice of not allowing passengers to bring onboard their own wine, liquor, beer and soft drinks (including bottled water). Any beverages found at embarkation (including when luggage is x-rayed) or during a port call is vulnerable to confiscation and is returned at the end of the cruise.

Casinos, in some cases the second largest generator of onboard revenue, are a relatively recent source of significant income. In the 1970s a cruise ship casino typically had several rows of slot machines, a roulette wheel and a black jack table or two. By the 1990s, casinos were commonplace and ships were competing for the biggest or the best casino afloat. Some ships' casinos had two or three floors. Others offered settings comparable to any top-of-the-line Las Vegas-style casino. And like Las Vegas and Atlantic City the cruise ship casino uses strategies to draw people in, including tournaments and providing complimentary cruises to players who agree to a minimum level of gambling. Over the years casinos have grown in size as the ships have and, because they are an effective source of income, take up proportionately more space. Many of the casinos, like other revenue centres on cruise ships, are operated by a concessionaire rather than the cruise line itself. The concessionaire pays for the space and shares a proportion of the revenue.

Often the third largest centre for revenue is art auctions. First introduced by Norwegian Cruise Line in the mid-1990s art auctions have become commonplace today. Passengers are attracted to auctions by the offer of free champagne and because of the entertainment value. They are shown serigraphs, lithographs and signed prints from well-known artists such as Picasso, Dali, Erte, Miro and Chagall. The auctioneer provides background about the art and emphasizes the excellent price available, suggesting that pieces may be had for as much as 80 percent off shore-side prices. *USA Today* cited a number of people who dispute this claim (see Yancey 2001: D–1). In one case, the same piece of art bought on the ship was found at the neighbourhood K-Mart for a fraction of the price. No matter whether this is correct, art auctions are big business. Park West Gallery, only one of the onboard art auctioneers, reported selling 200,000 pieces of art in the year 2000. The auctioneers do not work for the cruise line and depend entirely on sales for their income. To this end, some auctioneers are known to use phantom bidders in order to raise bids and also to give the impression that items are selling. The cruise line is not responsible or liable for the auctioneer's actions.

Art auctions have come under considerable scrutiny by the media. Take a passenger who in 2005 was contacted by Princess Cruises (which operates its own art auctions at sea) about artwork bought on *Golden Princess* in 2003. The company requested the return of two pieces of art—a Picasso and a Miro, both of which had been sold with a certificate of authenticity—as apparently they were fakes. The cruise line sent a refund cheque, which the passenger refused to deposit. She said she didn't want a refund; she simply wanted the original artworks for which she paid over $22,700.

> What I don't understand is both Picasso and Miro, as well as four pieces of Salvatore Dali and a dozen or so pieces of rare artwork we purchased all came with their fancy, gold stamped, signed, dated and guaranteed certificates of authenticity.... We purchased this and other artwork during our cruise vacations over the years either from Princess Cruises or their parent company Carnival Corporation. I don't even know anymore if any of the artwork they sold us is original or they are worth anything. As far as I'm concerned they might be worthless fake pieces of coloured paper. I won't be surprised if these cruise ship auctions with cheap glasses of champagne turn out to be a big multimillion dollar scam. (Sys-Con Media 2005)

Others have had similar problems. Two women took a Princess Cruise from Fort Lauderdale in the spring of 2002 and were attracted by the advertising for onboard art auctions. They ended up spending $86,000 on artwork, which caught the cruise line's attention. The women were subsequently invited to take a cruise free of charge and in the summer of 2003 embarked from Barcelona. They spent another $250,000 on this cruise and were again invited for a free cruise, which they took the following summer from Copenhagen. On that cruise they outbid other passengers for a "one of a kind original" entitled *Tranquil Remorse* by Martiros Manoukian, for which they paid $71,640. A year later, in the summer of 2005, they again returned for a free cruise—a twelve-day cruise of the Mediterranean. They attended the art auctions and were stunned when they saw another copy of their "one of a kind original" being auctioned. This time it sold for $20,000 less. When they challenged the company about the copy, they were told the painting they bought was different than the one being sold this year. They hired an art expert and learned that "their painting was one of a series of 'oil reproductions where the artist cleverly tries to represent each version of the *Tranquil Remorse* as an original'" (Cramer 2006). The expert told the women they had been "raped" and said they needed to call the police. They contacted Princess Cruises, which offered to buy back the artwork for the price paid. The women decided instead to take the cruise line to court.

The problems are not unique to Princess Cruises. In 2001 a group of passengers filed a class action suit against Carnival Cruise Lines and Park West Gallery (the company that operates art auctions on Carnival's ships) alleging, among other things, driving up prices by using phantom bidders. There are reports about Park West that are similar to those from Princess. For example, Gary Holloway spent $17,836 on three limited-edition prints by Rembrandt van Rijn plus one by Salvador Dali. He was thrilled with what he thought was a sophisticated investment backed by appraisals and letters of authenticity. The Dali piece alone showed a total retail replacement price of about $24,000. But when it was advertised on e-Bay six months later the highest bid was less than $1,000. The passenger complained to Park West but did not receive a satisfactory response. As a newspaper reporter put it, it's all in the fine print:

> If Holloway had read the invoice on his purchase, he would have found a disclaimer: "No verbal agreements or representations [by Park West agents] shall be of any force or effect unless set forth in writing." If he had read the certificate of authenticity, he would have learned that it did not apply to guarantees about the work's title, lot size, rarity, provenance or importance. And if he had inspected the appraisal, he would have seen that Park West "assumes no liability for claims that our appraisal is inaccurate." (Wagner 2007)

Another side of the issue is reflected in Park West Gallery's statement to TV's *Inside Edition* in February 2008 that it has a policy of not selling art as an investment (*Inside Edition* 2008).

The Expanding Sources of Onboard Revenue

There are other traditional sources of income, including bingo, spas, shops, photography, photo printing and communication services. Except for bingo, each is typically provided by a private contractor that pays the cruise line a fee plus commission for the concession. Each of these services has grown in recent years. For example spas and beauty shops, operated by Steiner's Leisure Limited on the majority of cruise ships, have become larger and provide an increasingly wider range of services. Prices for services are comparable to those found at major resorts on land.

Communication services have also grown considerably in recent years. Passengers no longer need to wait until reaching a port to use a cyber café or to use their mobile phone. In addition to usual forms of telecommunications (telephone and fax), cruise ships introduced cyber cafés in the early 2000s, and mobile telephone service in 2004, and by 2006 many ships had internet access through ship-wide WiFi networks. These fee-based services are provided by different concessionaires.

An area where there has been particularly significant change is in the size and variety of onboard shops. In the 1970s and 1980s there would have been a small shop carrying a few sundries and some duty free items. Today ships like Royal Caribbean's Voyager-class have a four-storey shopping mall deep in the bowels running longer than a football field. The ships have Ben and Jerry's Ice Cream, a Johnny Rockets restaurant, a cappuccino bar and shops selling a wide range of products: spirits, wine and cigarettes; beachwear and other clothing; jewellery and collectibles; and almost anything else a cruise passenger is likely to consider buying, including items they are likely to shop for on shore. This pattern is found in varying degree across the industry. Onboard shops further engender business by guaranteeing they will not be undersold by stores in port.

On top of traditional sources of income there is a range of onboard revenue centres, including rock climbing walls, bungee jumping platforms, golf simulators and ice skating rinks. These are part of a growing group of activities and recreation options offered for an additional fee. The list includes virtual reality games, pay-per-view movies, in-room video games, yoga classes, fitness classes (including pilates), wine tasting events, culinary workshops, self-improvement classes and art and craft classes. And it goes further. Most ships have ATMs, in-room mini bars and in-room gambling. Norwegian Cruise Line offers same-day delivery of select newspapers on some of its ships—for $3.95 a day—and in 2003 it introduced the concept of premium entertainment, for which passengers pay extra (Smart 2004). And Costa Cruises (like many other cruise lines) charges a fee for shuttle service from the dock to a drop-off point in the city, a service that is required: "Passengers cannot walk on their own at these ports, so if you don't pay the fee you can't leave the port area, which equates to not leaving the ship" (Hilton 2007).

Similar to charging for shuttles, most cruise lines have begun charging a daily service fee of $10 or more to passenger onboard accounts. This is in lieu of the traditional expectation for tips. Some cruise lines, such as NCL America, make the fee mandatory. Others say the fee is optional and it can be raised or lowered. But passengers who try to alter the fee do not always find an easy time of it. A journalist reports on his attempt to lower the "optional" fee by 50 percent while on a cruise on *Costa Classica*. He planned to distribute the money instead to specific workers who had provided him service:

> The clerk at reception told me to come back later, saying that the supervisor who could make the adjustment was away and, on the second try, that he couldn't find the correct form. He found the form and got clearance from his boss on my third attempt, but only after I threatened to reduce the service fee by 100 percent if he didn't allow me to make the change right there and then. (Hilton 2007)

Similar experiences have been told by passengers on other cruise lines.

Whether mandatory or not, money paid to a cruise ship as a service fee (or as they want it called, a gratuity) is a source of income used to pay staff and presumably to support other activities. Many workers report they earn less money under this system than when they were paid tips directly by passengers. The service fee, like fuel surcharges introduced by most cruise lines in late 2007, allows the cruise line to generate income for its operations without altering the advertised price for a cruise holiday. Unlike a hotel or resort, which typically advertises upfront all costs associated with a vacation stay, a cruise line advertises one price and then between fuel surcharges, government taxes and fees, and service fees adds as much as another $140 per person per week; a bargain cruise for $500 or $600 quickly becomes less of a bargain.

Another area in which income has significantly grown is from food. In contrast to the late 1990s, when cruises were sold as all-inclusive (in that context, Princess Cruises was criticized for charging extra for Haagen Dazs ice cream and Royal Caribbean for charging at its Johnny Rockets restaurant), most cruise ships today charge extra fees for certain food options. Passengers can spend money at cafés for pastries and premium coffees and at extra-tariff restaurants, which provide an alternative to the normal dining venue and where charges can range from $3.50 to $30 or more plus beverages and tip. These optional dining experiences are available across the industry, from the a la carte supper club on the Carnival Cruise Lines' ships to ten or more dining options on Norwegian Cruise Lines' ships with "freestyle cruising." Many cruise ships also offer restaurants with celebrity chef affiliations such as *Queen Mary 2*'s Todd English restaurant.

Onboard Revenue Generated from Onshore

Another major source of onboard revenue is derived from onshore activities, particularly shore excursions and port shopping programs. Shore excursions—land-based tours sold by the cruise ship—accounted for 30 percent ($100 million) of Royal Caribbean International's 2002/2003 profit of $351 million. A typical Royal Caribbean ship generated close to half a million dollars in tour income with a single call at St. Petersburg, Russia (Peisley 2003: 5). Income from shore excursions, like other sources, has continued to increase.

Shore excursions are convenient for passengers (between 50 percent and 80 percent buy an excursion in each port) and provide solid revenue to the cruise line in the form of sales commissions. In some locales as little as 10 percent of the amount collected for a shore excursion is paid to the person that actually provides the tour; in others it is more commonly a 50/50 split. At the extreme, a shore excursion costing a passenger US$99 may yield the in-port provider just $10 (CMC 2007). The cruise line and its shore excursion concessionaire share the remainder. This leaves the shore excursion provider in the uncomfortable position of being paid $10 for a product that passengers expect to be worth $99. If passengers are disappointed, they blame the port, not the cruise ship.

Port-based excursion providers are further marginalized by the terms of their contract with cruise lines. Carnival Cruise Lines' standard contract, for example, gives the cruise line the authority to refund the cost of an excursion to a passenger who complains, and the ship charges the refund back to the excursion provider, even if the complaint is unfounded. Further, the provider is only paid for tickets collected from passengers. This means that the cruise line keeps all monies, even when a passenger loses his/her ticket and is allowed on the shore excursion anyway or when a passenger is a no-show.

North American-based cruise lines generally use one of three companies to run their shore excursion programs: International Voyager Media, On-Board Media and the PPI Group. The concessionaires arrange the excursions, hire port lecturers and handle shore excursion sales. The model is slightly different in Alaska, where the major cruise lines operate their own tour companies. Carnival Corporation through Westours and Princess Tours operates more than 500 motor coaches and twenty domed railway cars in Alaska. They also own hotels and sightseeing boats (see Klein 2005a: 28, 42).

The same companies that provide shore excursion programs offer port lecture and port shopping programs. Along with lectures on shore excursion options passengers learn about shopping, are provided a map with preferred stores and are advised that they will get the best prices at the recommended stores. Passengers on shore excursions are also taken to preferred stores, which pay hefty fees and may also kick back money to tour guides.

Onboard promotion of shore-side shops evolved into a mini industry by the mid-1990s and continues to thrive today. "What used to happen is that the tour directors on a major line would earn a quarter of a million dollars a year in royalties from port merchants" (Reynolds 1995: L-2). Now, the money is collected as an annual promotion fee and/or a commission fee for all sales and it is shared between the concessionaire and the cruise line. The largest concessionaire, Onboard Media, is owned by Louis Vuitton Moet Hennessey (LVMH). Like the PPI Group and International Voyager Media, Onboard Media also offers art auctions.

Private islands are another way to generate onboard income from onshore. Norwegian Cruise Line was the first to introduce the concept. The innovation provided an alternative to landing passengers in already congested ports. It could also be used on Sundays when passengers would often complain about shore-side shops being closed.

The private island has several economic benefits for the cruise line. For one thing, passengers on a private island are a captive market. The cruise line runs all beverage sales and concessions such as tours, water activities and souvenir and convenience shops; all money spent on the island contributes to its revenue and profit. Holland America Line has fine-tuned the private island concept by offering fifteen beach cabanas that accommodate four people comfortably at a cost of $249 per day. The rental package includes priority tender use, cabana with refrigerator, ceiling fan, air conditioner and deck chairs, a misting shower on the private terrace, fresh fruit, vegetables with dip, chips and salsa, and an assortment of soft drinks and bottled water. An optional Butler Service Upgrade Package for a $270 adds unlimited beverages and house drinks, a picnic lunch and butler assistance from cabin to cabana and while ashore.

More affluent passengers can choose the Private Oasis at Half Moon Cay. The oasis, able to accommodate up to twenty-five people, has its own hot tub and water slide, an indoor teak dining table seating six people, outdoor teak lounges and bar stools accommodating twelve, barbecue area, full wet bar and refrigerator, massage table, iPod music system, multi-coloured Bahamian tapestries, men's and women's changing rooms, indoor and outdoor showers with heated fresh water, 100 foot walkway with misting stations and privacy gate. The cost for up to twelve guests, non-alcoholic and alcoholic beverages, fresh fruit and snacks, BBQ lunch buffet, butler, personal chef, and lifeguard is $1,195 (additional guests up to a maximum of twenty-five are $99 per person). Upgraded packages are also available for the less than eight hours onshore. The Ultimate Oasis Package ($5,995 for up to twelve guests and then $395 per person up to twenty-five) includes a wider food variety including Russian caviar served with iced vodka in an ice bowl, iced crab legs and unlimited Dom Perignon champagne in the open bar. Passengers also receive an escorted transfer from the ship to the cabana and return in the afternoon, tables with white linens, fine china and silverware, full butler service and wait staff, private chef, made-to-order celebration cake, an 8 x 10 group photo for everyone in the package, complimentary water sports equipment, a floating bar on a surf board near the cabana and a Greenhouse Spa masseuse is available for short massages.

Private islands further contribute to the economic bottom line of the cruise line because of their location. Most are located in the Bahamas or Haiti. With a stop at the island, ships are able to save fuel by cruising at a slower speed between two primary ports. Rather than sailing non-stop from St. Thomas to Miami, for example, a ship may reduce speed between the two ports with its scheduled stop at the private island. The ship saves money and at the same time increases passenger satisfaction.

Is Anything Left for Spending Onshore?

There is little question that the cruise industry has effectively constructed a system for separating passengers from their money. Cruise lines have done well for their owners and stockholders. But what are the implications for ports used by the ships? They too depend on passenger spending for their income, but as the ship takes a larger piece of the pie they are left to be content with the remaining crumbs—money passengers were able to resist spending onboard.

Not only do ports compete with the cruise ship for passenger spending, they also compete with one another. Consequently most ports find they earn much less than expected. This disappointment is reflected in local media coverage. The President of the Federation of the Small and Medium Businessmen in Cartagena, Spain, following a cruise ship visit said he took a sample of five shops in the town centre and found total sales to all tourists combined amounted to no more than 39 euros (h.b. 2007). In Tasmania, a ship that was touted as bringing passengers who would spend more than $150 per person, in reality had businesses reporting lacklustre trade. Predictions of steady streams of business through the door of local shops and restaurants have not materialized (Duncan 2007). Projections that 50,000 cruise passengers and crewmembers would spend more than $7 million in Tasmania in 2007/08 were beginning to be viewed with scepticism.

Ports agonize over schemes to improve spending by cruise passengers but they rarely look at ways their plans are undermined by the context. The most obvious question is whether passengers have any money left for spending onshore given the range of spending options onboard. This is particularly salient given that cruises in the 2000s attract a wider segment of the population, including people who choose a cruise over a land-based vacation because it appears to be a better bargain (based on the advertised selling price). Many of these folks save for years for their "cruise of a lifetime" and have limited funds after paying for the cruise itself. Their spending onboard will most certainly influence their ability to spend onshore.

An even larger problem for many ports is their uncritical acceptance of the cruise line's claims that passengers on average spend US$100 in each and every port of call. Port officials and national governments extrapolate the cruise industry's economic impact on this basis. Few undertake independent empirical research to determine actual passenger spending. When they realize there is less passenger spending than they believe is the norm, port officials think they are getting the short end of the stick. For example, in the Bahamas, where average spending is estimated to be $60 per passenger per port of call, there is great effort to find ways to bring spending up to par with what they perceive is the norm elsewhere (McCartney 2007). The furthest thing from the government's mind is that $60 may be the norm for passenger spending, even at neighbouring ports. Empirical study of passenger spending is limited and sorely needed.

The bit of research that has been done suggests passenger spending in the Caribbean is going down rather than increasing. A 1994 study commissioned by the Florida–Caribbean Cruise Association (FCCA) found passengers on average spent $372 on the island of St. Thomas (see Huie 1995: 50)—adjusting for inflation, the equivalent in 2007 is $475. The average for the Caribbean region was $154 per passenger per port (adjusting for inflation, $195 in 2007). A study done for the FCCA six years later found that spending on St. Thomas had fallen to $173 per passenger ($202 in 2007 dollars); the overall average in the region decreased to $89.72 per passenger per port (PWC 2001)—$105 in 2007 dollars. Excluding Cozumel and St. Thomas, spending per port ranged from $53.84 to $86.81, with an average per port of $72.81 (well below $100 in 2007 equivalence).

Despite significant decreases in spending over the 1990s and levels of spending well below the $100 expectation, ports still act as though cruise passengers spend $100 or more in each port of call. Perceptions are hard to change, especially when the cruise industry continues to tell ports to expect the higher figure. This is not unique to the Caribbean. Ports worldwide have adopted the $100 per passenger figure and they appear surprised when their research proves otherwise. A study in Croatia in 2007 found passenger spending averaged 41.44 euros (less than US$60). The study also found that spending varied widely between different ports, between different ships, and with the time of day and length of stay (Marusic et al. 2007: 266–267). While Dubrovnik and Korcula had average passenger spending of 36.65 euros and 34.11 euros respectively, passengers in Split spent an average of 70.51 euros and in Zadar an average of 82.16 euros.

The Croatian study is one of the few in recent years based on data gathered directly from passengers by an organization not sponsored by the cruise industry. Its findings are similar to those from research done in Central America by the Centre on Ecotourism and Sustainable Development. Cruise passenger spending in Costa Rica (including that spent for tours) averaged $74.84 for each passenger who went ashore; when adjusted for the number staying onboard onshore spending averaged $44.90 for all passengers aboard cruise vessels (CESD 2007: 67). Passenger spending in Belize was much the same: $44 per passenger. Stayover sector visitors by comparison spend on average $96 per person per day. Though stayover visitors are only 25 percent of tourist arrivals they account for 90 percent of the employment in the tourism sector (CESD 2006: 14).

In addition to the decreasing amount of money spent by cruise passengers and the wide variation in spending from one port to the next, one would expect differences with variation in the number of hours in port and time of day. Not all ports make this adjustment in expectations. Victoria, British Columbia, for example is like other ports and estimates the economic impact of cruise tourism based on the $100 per passenger figure. The port has even undertaken its own study of passengers but it hasn't analyzed for differences in the day of the week, time of day, length of time in port or time of year. These are particularly important considerations given three distinct patterns in cruise ship schedules across a typical cruise season. Each pattern conceivably produces different levels of passenger spending. (See Appendix for more details.)

Using 2007 for illustration, the first pattern is in the early season (before May 18), during which 79 percent of ships are in port during the daytime (between 8:00 a.m. and 5:00 p.m.). These visits are in advance of the main season for cruises to Alaska and mostly involve ships repositioning from their winter activities in the Caribbean or Pacific to their summer itineraries to Alaska. With a full day in port, passengers are likely to explore the city and surrounding area and to stop into shops and eateries. There are fourteen port calls during this period of time.

The second pattern, with 123 port calls, is found during the core season for Alaska cruises, between May 18 and September 15. During this period 89 percent of cruise ships stop in the evening between 6:00 p.m. and midnight and they spend one-third less time in port (6.1 hours versus 9.1 hours). As well, port calls in the second pattern are often the night before the cruise ends the next morning in Seattle. It is passengers' last night on the ship, which means they are likely to already be packed for disembarkation the next morning and are unlikely to have much money left after seven days on the cruise. Given that the ship arrives in port at dinnertime, many passengers will choose to have their last meal onboard and then go ashore; they are unlikely to go ashore for dinner. Interestingly, unlike cruises in the early and late seasons, which are likely to call at other Canadian ports in addition to Victoria, the core Alaska cruises have Victoria as their only port in Canada. A ship leaving Victoria at midnight is easily in port at Seattle six hours later.

The third pattern occurs when the Alaska season is winding down and ships are beginning to migrate to their winter home. There is also a small number of ships offering short cruises focused on British Columbia ports. During this third period 74 percent of ships spend daytime hours in the port and their length of time in port is similar to the early season. Passengers are again more likely to have time to explore the port and to enjoy what it has to offer in daylight hours. It is reasonable to expect that passengers will have greater economic impact during these visits than they have during midseason. But with multiple port calls in Canada, spending during this period is likely to be distributed across the ports given that each is offering the same basic souvenirs and products.

Despite the wide difference in the number of hours and time of day spent in port, the Victoria Port Authority assumes each cruise passenger leaves behind the same amount of money, regardless of the time of year. The port, like others in British Columbia, also ignores the importance of

U.S. cabotage laws (i.e., the *Passenger Vessel Services Act of 1886*, which requires a foreign-flagged cruise ship beginning and ending in a U.S. port to include a foreign port in its itinerary) in the reason for why cruise ships stop at the port. For example, Victoria is the only Canadian port of call in all but one of 123 cruises during the midseason, when ships are mainly focused on getting from Seattle to Alaska. Victoria like many other ports appears to have lost perspective about its economic value.

Maintaining Perspective

With promises of significant economic benefit, most ports are quick to develop or expand capacity for cruise ships. They listen to the cruise industry and often consider themselves fortunate to have a cruise ship bless them with a port call. The mayor of Campbell River, British Columbia, reflected this view when he stated: "Everyone is very excited.... To be selected as a port of call is a real honour and it creates a rather glamorous side to our community." The $14 million cruise terminal, built with public funds, opened in 2007 but has failed to lure many cruise ships. It had a couple of calls from small ships in 2007 and 2008, but even these have changed plans for 2009 (Wilson 2008). There are several reasons for the port's difficulty, not least of which is that ocean currents and the nature of the approach to the port are difficult for navigation, especially for large ships. These were known to be issues before construction was undertaken.

Ports tend to suffer from two problems. First, like Campbell River, they believe the adage, "if you build it they will come." They don't think about whether they are marketable, and they tend to ignore the fact that increasing the supply of ports potentially decreases the value of other ports in the area. Second, ports fail to realize they have more power than the cruise industry; cruise ships need ports more than the ports need them. Passengers take a cruise with expectations to see new places. If these places are not offered then a cruise loses its attraction. Most passengers prefer a day in port over a day at sea and would not take a cruise if there were no ports of call. This potentially gives ports an advantage in their relationship with the cruise industry. If ports work together they can all derive greater benefit.

The problem is that the cruise lines effectively place ports in competition with one another for cruise ship visits, and while the industry players maintain a degree of solidarity with each other, ports are willing to undercut one another in order to secure their piece of a finite pie. St. Vincent's Tourism Minister Glen Beache warned in October 2007 that unless the Caribbean region develops a united approach it will continue not to benefit significantly from the cruise sector. He pointed to a recent case where a cruise line had negotiated a certain arrangement with his government, but one of their neighbours offered the ship free water, garbage disposal and a reduced head tax so they went there instead. Further, he commented that it was like pulling teeth to get a cruise line to contribute to the upkeep of sites cruise visitors frequent, especially ones that are relatively unused by locals and stayover visitors. He concluded: "We have to stop stabbing each other in the back and find common ground in our negotiations with the cruise sector as this is the only way we will obtain maximum benefit, by working together" (CMC 2007). This aversion to cooperation and collective action was also seen in relation to the Caribbean Tourism Organization's idea of a twenty dollar levy for all passengers cruising to the Caribbean. The plan died before it was fully aired because several governments broke solidarity in favour of benefits offered to them individually by the cruise industry (see Klein 2005a: 117–120).

The Caribbean is not alone in this type of scenario. It is played and replayed almost everywhere cruise ships visit. Take British Columbia for example. Until 1999 Vancouver was the starting point for virtually all cruises to Alaska's Inside Passage; other ports in the province had negligible business. Vancouver's growth was largely a product of two factors. First, as mentioned above, U.S. cabotage laws prohibited foreign-flagged vessels from carrying passengers between U.S. ports so Vancouver conveniently served as the foreign port in itineraries that were otherwise wholly based in Alaska. Second, ships could not cruise at a speed that would allow a seven-day cruise to begin from Seattle. It is in this context that the Port of Vancouver in 2000 announced it would spend $79 million to construct a third cruise berth at Canada Place, on top of the $49 million it had already spent on re-development of the Ballantyne Cruise Terminal.

But new ships appearing in the late 1990s cruised at higher speeds and could use Seattle as an alternative to Vancouver. The result is that Seattle's cruise business grew from 6,600 passengers in 1999 to over 800,000 passengers (about 200 port calls) in 2008. Over the same period of time Vancouver saw its passenger numbers decrease from a high of 1.125 million in 2002 to about 900,000 in 2008; the number of ships decreased 25 percent from 342 to approximately 255 (see Klein 2005b: 7; Constantineau 2007). The port's huge investment to accommodate more cruise ships appears to have been poorly timed.

Vancouver's loss was a gain for other B.C. ports given that foreign-flagged cruise ships still needed a non-U.S. port between Seattle and Alaska in order to comply with U.S. cabotage laws. Victoria is booming. Its passenger numbers grew to 324,000 in 2007, reflecting a 730 percent increase from 1999; the number of ships increased 382 percent over the same period. Other British Columbia ports also captured a share of cruise tourism. But their success too is at the expense of others. NCL announced in August 2003 that *Norwegian Sky* would call at Prince Rupert's newly constructed $9 million terminal eighteen times as part of its 2004 Seattle-based seven-day roundtrip itineraries;

in 2003 the ship had a seven-hour port call at Victoria. Celebrity Cruises' *Mercury* also committed to use Prince Rupert in 2004, scheduling thirteen Wednesday evening stops from 8:00 p.m. to midnight; it had shifted from Vancouver to Seattle as its home port so needed an intermediate Canadian port. Then at the start of the cruise season Celebrity announced the Prince Rupert stop would be reduced to a one-hour technical stop with no passenger disembarkation. The stop would satisfy U.S. requirements but would have no economic impact on the city. Cruise ship calls in subsequent years normally were five or six hours in length. In 2007, Prince Rupert welcomed sixty cruise ships with a total of approximately 100,000 passengers.

Watching Prince Rupert's and Victoria's success brought other British Columbia ports onside. As mentioned, Campbell River built a multimillion-dollar terminal with high expectations of a cruise boom. And Nanaimo expanded its capacity for cruise ships and began courting them. The city's mayor in 2005 stated that the port was not competing with other B.C. ports; he knew that Nanaimo was better than the others and that cruise ships would choose Nanaimo based on this apparently incontrovertible fact.

In 2008, there are five B.C. ports (Vancouver, Victoria, Nanaimo, Campbell River, Prince Rupert) competing for the same cruise ship business. The industry has the same scenario there as in the Caribbean, Eastern Canada and elsewhere, where ports are interchangeable and are chosen based on which gives the cruise line the best deal. Rather than recognizing their inherent value to the cruise industry—to not include a Canadian port in an Alaska cruise means a $300 fine for each passenger onboard—these ports clamour so much for cruise ship business that they effectively bargain from a position of weakness rather than strength. They not only undercut one another but their lack of perspective causes them to short-change themselves. While ports may make some money from cruise tourism their larger contribution is a subsidy to cruise corporations (in the form of discounted services and under-priced port fees) that earn billions of dollars in net profit and which pay no corporate income tax in Canada or the U.S.

All of this begs the question of who needs who. Although cruise ships need ports more than ports need cruise ships, the industry has successfully turned the tables and put ports in competition with one another for ships that are touted as cash cows. Ports don't question the assertion and as stated earlier lose perspective as to in whose interest they are acting. Rather than behaving as a business and working to maximize income and profits, which is the stance taken by cruise lines, ports seek ways to facilitate the cruise industry in the mistaken belief that a cruise ship in port means lots of money in local coffers.

Put simply, ports forget about the economic law of supply and demand—rather than allying with others to control the supply of ports (thereby increasing the value of each), they glut the market and leave cruise lines in a position to pick and choose the port offering the best deal. The abundance of ports also provides the industry a ready source of alternatives, such as when Cozumel was heavily damaged in October 2005 by Hurricane Wilma and Costa Maya by Hurricane Dean in August 2007. In both cases ships easily shifted to other ports eager for the business. These alternatives are also effectively used to persuade other ports to keep fees steady or to provide additional services.

It isn't just countries competing with each other but they build multiple ports that compete with one another for the same business. We see this on Canada's west coast. Jamaica is doing the same with the construction of cruise terminals in Negril and Falmouth (Plunkett 2007). Each of these will directly compete with existing ports in Montego Bay, Ocho Rios and Port Antonio for the same business.

Competition is likely to be even greater given that cruise tourism in the Caribbean is at a plateau in growth, as reflected in a marginal increase in the number of bed days, from 31.2 million in 2004 to just under 32 million in 2007. During this period relatively smaller cruise ships (2000 passengers and less) shifted from the Caribbean and were replaced by relatively larger ships, such as Royal Caribbean's *Freedom of the Seas* and *Liberty of the Seas*, each of which accommodates more than 4,000 passengers, and Carnival Cruise Lines, which has introduced since 2002 six ships accommodating almost 3,500 passengers each. The marginal growth is not so much from more ships but from deployment of larger ships.

The Demand for Newer and Bigger Cruise Terminals

With larger ships comes demand for new and enlarged port facilities. Major design and structural changes were needed when Carnival Cruise Lines and Princess Cruises introduced megaships in excess of 100,000 ton, again for Royal Caribbean's Voyager-class ships, which were 140,000 tons, and in 2008 for Royal Caribbean's Genesis-class vessels, which will be 220,000 tons. Fort Lauderdale will spend $37.4 million to renovate one of its current terminals so it can accommodate the 6,400 passenger, 2,000 crewmember vessel. Other ports are also making sizable expenditure so Jamaica's port at Falmouth is anticipated to cost US$250 million in order to accommodate the Genesis-class vessel, and Philipsburg has assumed a US$130 million in debt as part of its commitment to an expansion and development project that will make "St. Maarten the proud owner of the largest port in the Northeastern Caribbean" (Singh 2007).

As ports enthusiastically prepare for expansion and for a new wave of ships, they tend to ignore the risks. Ports such as Seattle and Mobile (Alabama), which excitedly embraced cruise tourism continue to operate at a deficit. Others make investments and then see business shift to neighbours or to other parts of the world.

This was most obviously the case in 2007, when Norwegian Cruise Line America (NCL America) announced it would reposition one of its three U.S.-flagged ships from Hawai'i because of excess capacity. Cruise ship calls to the islands will fall from 469 in 2007 to 310 in 2008; a loss of one-third. The state will lose almost $34 million in visitor expenditure and approximately 300 jobs (Associated Press 2007). Then in early 2008 the cruise line announced it was withdrawing a second ship in May, doubling the economic loss to the state and its ports. This fall-off is in the context of consistent calls on the state and local communities to improve port facilities and local infrastructure for the benefit of cruise passengers. Investments were made, but the payoff is not going to be what was expected.

Interestingly, NCL America received sizable subsidies and other benefits for initiating its Hawai'i-based service. Not only was the company given a controversial monopoly on Hawai'i-based cruises but it paid fire-sale prices for the failed Project America ships commissioned by American Classic Voyages in 1999 and begun in 2000. Construction ceased when the company went bankrupt in the fall of 2001. A year later, in the fall of 2002, the U.S. Maritime Administration (which guaranteed loans for the project, up to $1.1 billion) sold to NCL America for $29 million the partially completed hull of one ship, parts for the second ship and the ships' designs. Then in January 2003, Hawaii Senator Dan Inouye tacked a provision onto the 2003 Omnibus Appropriations Bill allowing NCL America to operate three U.S.-flagged ships in Hawai'i. The ships were the two Project America ships, which would be completed at Meyer Werft shipyard in Germany, and a current foreign-flagged ship. It is estimated that the Maritime Administration lost $330 million on the deal; money that was to be recouped through taxes paid by the three ships operating in Hawai'i (see Klein 2005a: 55–56).

Grand Cayman Islands is also concerned about the falling number of cruise passengers. For the second half of 2007 numerous newspaper stories focused on the double digit fall in the number of cruise passengers compared to the year before. The numbers dropped as much 30 percent in some months, and lost economic impact was estimated in tens of millions of Cayman Island dollars. Hotel occupancy had also decreased and in September 2007 was the lowest since 2003, at 41.3 percent. By year's end, occupancy was at about 66 percent.

The difficulty for Grand Cayman is that, since 2005, it has developed a dependence on cruise passengers—more than 1.8 million a year. The current drop is back to levels that had been relatively steady from 2003 through 2006, following a 76 percent increase between 1999 and 2003. Figures for 2007 and 2008 are close to those for 2005. In comparison to cruise visitors, the island has about 300,000 stopover visitors arriving annually by air, a figure that has dropped more than 14 percent between 2001 and 2005. Stopover visitors spend twelve times as much as cruise passengers per head (Hughes and Davidson 2005).

Cayman's reaction to changes in cruise numbers reflects a failure to recognize the mobility of cruise ships and the degree which weather and other factors affect cruise tourism. After all, Grand Cayman's increases in 2006 were likely a product, in part, of Cozumel's closure after Hurricane Wilma. But the industry's commitment is to its profits, and Cayman, like Hawai'i, is finding that cruise ships use them when it suits. Ships previously deployed to Grand Cayman are increasingly shifting to ports where the cruise line owns the terminal or where they have more favourable arrangements.

The industry's commitment is not to local economic needs and interests. Tom Oosterhoudt, a Key West city commissioner, captured the essence of the issue:

> Cruise ships have changed the dynamic; it's budget, budget, budget and volume, volume, volume.... There was a time when we all thought of cruise ship customers as high rollers. Today that is not necessarily so.... We need to evaluate where we are going with the extreme increase we are seeing each year with the number of cruise ships.... We need to stand back and evaluate where we are at and make sure we are controlling the cruise ships and they aren't controlling us. (Babson 2003)

The same basic insight is expressed by residents in Hoonah, Alaska, a port of call with a growing cruise ship business, who express the need to manage the industry's growth and size in order to preserve the local community, its lifestyle and its Tlingit (aboriginal) culture (see Cerveny 2007).

A Variety of Financial Arrangements

There are a variety of financial arrangements between cruise lines and ports. Traditionally, ports have been locally owned and operated and have charged cruise ships a head tax or fee for each passenger landed. The fees presumably were sufficient to cover the cost of operating the ports.

As the industry grew and ports began to compete for cruise ship calls, ports began to offer incentives to attract a cruise ship or cruise line. These included reduced or waived port fees. The Puerto Rico Tourism Company in San Juan, for example, had an agreement through 2004 to rebate three dollars per passenger for every 120,000 passenger arrivals in a year per cruise line. Bahamas, which charges a fifteen dollar per passenger head tax, offered incentives that cut the cost in half; the fee would be waived altogether if a company brings one half million people in a year. And Jamaica, which also charged fifteen dollars per passenger, had contracts with individual companies that cut the rate in half (see Klein 2005a: 109–110). Ports are so anxious to bring cruise ships in that they appear to forget about the cost of operating a port. In many cases they end up subsidizing cruise ship operations. Governments that typically charge cruise passengers a head tax of five or six dollars charge stayover visitors twenty to thirty dollars in airport departure taxes. Cruise passengers have a relatively good deal by comparison, especially given they don't pay room taxes, nor do they have other expenditures common for people staying on an island for a few days or a week or two (restaurants, shops, etc).

More recently cruise corporations have developed other arrangements in order to ensure a supply of ports and to have ports with the facilities they need. One arrangement involves a cruise corporation loaning a port money to undertake improvements requested by the cruise line. In return for its investment the cruise corporation is given preferential berthing rights at the pier. An example of this type of arrangement is the agreement between Carnival Corporation and the Port at Phillipsburg, St. Maarten. Carnival loaned the port US$34.5 million for construction of a second pier, which will be able to accommodate ships like the *Queen Mary 2* (owned by Carnival Corporation's Cunard Line) as well as Royal Caribbean's Genesis-class ships. The loan is repayable in twenty years at 5.9 percent interest. To generate income for the port and help facilitate repayment of the loan, Carnival Corporation guarantees approximately 700,000 passengers a year to St. Maarten, where it will have one fixed berth on the new pier and three on the existing pier. Royal Caribbean is loaning the port an additional US$10 million and also has guaranteed a certain number of passengers annually. In return it will have one fixed berth on the new pier and one on the existing one.

On surface it appears that Carnival and Royal Caribbean are being generous, but the loans are good business moves for the cruise lines. They gain positive regard for supporting the port's expansion, which is being undertaken at the request of the cruise lines, and they also make out well financially. Carnival Corporation will earn more than US$24 million in interest payments over the course of the loan; it secured a favourable return given the fixed income securities market in late 2007. The port on the other hand will collect $6 per passenger brought by Carnival Corporation ships and, after applying passenger fees against debt repayment and interest ($2.94 million per year), will be left with approximately US$1.2 million per year for operating and maintaining the port facilities used, an amount that is probably insufficient for covering the actual costs of operation. Local residents and taxpayers will undoubtedly be called upon to subsidize port operations, or the debt will be extended beyond the twenty-year period, or both. As well, it is likely there will be further calls for renewal and improved facilities before the loan is repaid. What looks like a good deal on the surface actually leaves the port to operate with a sizable debt while it provides the cruise lines with facilities and infrastructure that allow them to maximize their profit and minimizes their risk.

Contrast Carnival's apparent generosity to St. Maarten to the arrangement negotiated by Port Everglades (Ft. Lauderdale) for the expansion required for it to accommodate Royal Caribbean's Genesis-class ships. Port Everglades agreed to renovate one of its terminals at a cost of $37.4 million, but neither the port nor taxpayers will foot the bill. Royal Caribbean will instead pay for the work through a $5.70 surcharge on passengers when they leave and arrive. That's in addition to a $9.95 port user fee all passengers pay. The result is that while St. Maarten has to pay for its new piers with existing port fees and is left at the margin with regard to generating enough income to cover all expenses, Port Everglades maintains its user fees and collects an additional fee to specifically cover construction costs. One might argue that Port Everglades is savvier in negotiations, which might be true. But the contrast also draws with clarity the difference in treatment of U.S. ports versus ports in developing countries and small island states. The arrangement with St. Maarten keeps the port and the island in its relatively subordinate position to the cruise industry; to a certain degree it remains under Carnival's thumb.

Terminal Ownership Has Its Privileges

The newest pattern in the industry is for a cruise line or cruise corporation to own the terminal or to operate it under a long-term lease. Carnival Corporation, for example, financed and owns the newly constructed $40 million cruise terminal and welcome centre on Grand Turk. The company benefits directly from port fees collected from its ships and from concession charges for shops in the welcome centre and for transportation services offered in or outside the terminal and centre. The port hosted nearly 300,000 passengers in its first year, 2006, and 367,000 passengers from 173 ships in 2007. These ships would have visited other ports had the corporate-owned terminal at Grand Turk not been available. Carnival Corporation also owns the cruise terminal in Cozumel. It has made a number of efforts to develop other ports, but not always with success. There were two failed initiatives in 2001.

One initiative involved an agreement between the U.S. Virgin Islands and Carnival Corporation and Royal Caribbean reached in August 2001. The arrangement—one previously proposed and rejected by several Caribbean governments—allowed the two cruise corporations to jointly develop port facilities at St. Thomas's Crown Bay. They agreed to invest $31 million to enlarge the two-berth pier so it could accommodate the lines' mega ships. They also planned to improve 7.5 acres of adjacent land into an area offering taxis and tour dispatch, and to include 90,000 square feet of retail, restaurant and amphitheatre space. Five thousand square feet would be reserved for local vendors and include an attraction themed on the islands' sugar cane heritage, a rum distillery and a terminal to accommodate home porting of smaller ships. In return for their investment Carnival and Royal Caribbean would enjoy priority berthing for a thirty-year period, retain 75 percent of the head tax charged passengers and receive a percentage of revenue from the retail operations. Passenger port charges would pay for the investment needed for the project and profit would generate from retail operations at the terminal. The project was approved by the legislature, despite opposition. It appeared on track until March 13, 2002, when the governor announced the agreement was cancelled. He stated that although the agreement had many merits, he believed it was important that the Virgin Islands maintain full control of its harbour and harbour development. The Crown Bay project continued without the cruise lines, after the Port Authority reimbursed them $900,000 in preliminary costs.

Also in 2001, Carnival thought after a nine-year search that it had found the perfect purpose-built homeport from which to operate three- and four-day cruises in the western Caribbean. It settled on an area between Playa del Carmen and Cancun, adjacent to Parque Xcaret's (its partner in the project) nature park, located several miles from the core of hotels in Cancun. The $80 million port would accommodate four homeported cruise ships per week plus twenty-four other ships visiting as a port of call—approximately 800,000 visitors a year. Despite opposition from environmentalists concerned about the cumulative risks posed to the 220 mile coral reef and from hoteliers concerned about further loss of business to the cruise lines the project was approved by all levels of the Mexican government, except the mayor of Playa del Carmen. He agreed to permit construction of the homeport subject to a number of conditions, including a port fee of $30 per head. The project's developers argued the tax was illegal but the mayor responded that the necessary tax legislation would be in place by the time the first passenger was ready to board a Carnival cruise ship at the Xcaret homeport. The planned development was put on hold and has not been resumed.

A project in Belize City also appears to be on hold. In September 2003 Carnival Corporation announced plans for a joint business venture with Belize Ports Ltd. The cruise corporation planned to invest $50 million in a new cruise terminal; it also had an option for a fifty-room hotel and casino adjacent to the terminal. The new terminal would not displace or replace the existing cruise terminal in Belize City, which is owned by Royal Caribbean. The Carnival-owned terminal would accommodate two ships and include a welcome centre with 200 spaces for gift shops, restaurants and other stores and a transport hub for hundreds of buses and taxis. Carnival's investment would be funded through passenger fees for using the port; under the contract all fees to the government were to be waived.

The project was challenged on several fronts, including in the nation's courts. The strongest objection was that the deal would cost the government money given that Royal Caribbean's contract with the government would see it receive $4 for every cruise passenger landed at the Carnival terminal, money that ultimately would have to come from government coffers. Though given the go-ahead by the Supreme Court, delays and negative publicity stalled the project. It appears to have been replaced with a project in Roatan (just up the coast) announced in early 2007, which includes construction of a cruise terminal on the island—to be called Mahogany Bay. Completion of the $50 million terminal is expected by summer 2009.

The cruise facility will be situated on twenty acres on the Roatan waterfront and will consist of a two-berth cruise terminal capable of accommodating super post-Panamax vessels and up to 7,000 passengers daily. Adjacent to the facility will be a 35,000 square foot welcome centre including retail shops, restaurants and bars, along with a sixty foot high lighthouse, a lagoon with cascading waterfalls and a nature trail. A transportation hub with the ability to accommodate taxis, rental cars and tour buses is also planned. Carnival's partner in the project is Jerry Hynds, a local business leader and a member of the Honduran Congress. He is also the owner of Coral Cay, a resort property located adjacent to the planned port facility. Within five years of operation, Mahogany Bay (Roatan) is expected to host 225 cruise ship calls and 500,000 passengers annually.

Ownership and investment in terminals is not limited to the Caribbean. Carnival owns the terminal in Long Beach, California; Costa paid one-third of the construction cost for a terminal in Savona (Italy) in return for a twenty-two-year operating lease; a Carnival/Costa–Royal Caribbean partnership holds the concession for the cruise terminal at Civitavecchia (Rome); and Royal Caribbean opportunistically invested $27 million in the terminal at Kusadasi (Turkey) in return for a thirty-year concession. And the list goes on. Royal Caribbean says its investment in ports

> is based on a variety of circumstances: high volume utilization; inadequate facilities; ports' inability to perform; opportunities for privatization; strategic or competitive advantage and operating cost control. (Seatrade Insider 2004)

The incentives are usually economic and focus on the cruise line's bottom line, not benefits to the port.

The case of Kusadasi provides another example of arrangements that on the surface looked favourable to the port. Royal Caribbean took the port over in 2003 after "winning" a privatization auction. Shortly after assuming control of the port, it extended the port facilities further over the sea and built a centre with fifty-five stores to rent. Laws were changed to accommodate the development, despite angry public protests and a petition.

The new facility yields a tidy profit for Royal Caribbean. Stores on the first floor reportedly rent for as much as $70,000 a year; those on the second floor cost between $20,000 and $30,000. In addition, stores are expected to pay commissions against sales made to cruise passengers. Profit that traditionally would have remained in the country with local merchants and businesses now makes it way into the cruise line's profit margins. The operation is so lucrative that Carnival Corporation has plans to build its own cruise facility, with tens of stores, several miles away at the yacht harbour. In 2008 Royal Caribbean's terminal welcomes more than 670 cruises bringing about 700,000 tourists.

Shops and merchants outside the port have been negatively impacted by Royal Caribbean's development. A vibrant area of shops and cafes through which cruise passengers would wander near the port has lost its business to the shops at the cruise terminal. Most passengers who leave the port area do so with shore excursions. They are likely to visit stores as part of their excursion—most including the ancient site at Ephesus—but unbeknownst to most passengers these stores charge up to 10 percent more to cover commissions to the cruise line (one contract has commissions of 6 percent for carpet sales, 8 percent for sale of other products plus a flat fee that guarantees a minimum number of buses and passengers will visit) and 18 percent to the local agency/tour guide. Some tour operators guarantee commissions in the millions of dollars in order to secure the shore excursion contract. These types of arrangements are not unique to Kusadasi. There, as elsewhere, shops not included in shore excursions or "approved" by the cruise line can charge one-half to one-third less for the same products. But the system makes it difficult for them to be found by the majority of passengers.

Kusadasi is a good example of the privileges and economic value of ownership of a cruise terminal. It also reflects the costs to ports of agreeing to arrangements that increase the economic benefits to cruise lines but that are detrimental to the port. Most ports earn considerably less than they should, much less than they can and, if they are lucky, enough to break even.

Ports need to extract better deals from cruise lines and their passengers. They also need to more accurately and realistically analyze the economic benefits and costs of cruise tourism. While the sheer number of passengers may appear attractive, this needs to be measured against the implications for all segments of the tourism industry, including hotels and resorts, which contribute considerably greater economic benefit per guest. For many ports, a careful analysis might suggest shunning cruise ships in favour of growing a more stable home-grown and locally controlled tourism industry.

Before You Embark

Three suggestions can be drawn from the issues discussed. First, in view of the arrangements cruise lines have with shops, shore excursion providers and local merchants they promote, it is often worth a passenger's time and effort to explore alternatives. This may be easier in some locations than others, though in all cases it is facilitated with a bit of advance research. The internet is an optimal source with its many websites devoted to information about ports, key shopping areas and merchants (to visit and to avoid) and tourist sights to be seen. Independent tours for sightseeing can be arranged in advance in some ports at favourable rates or set up upon arrival. The only risk of going independent is that if you aren't back to the ship on time it may leave without you so you need to plan accordingly. Cruise lines assure that this will not happen to those on shore excursions it sells. The benefits of going independent include freedom from the crowd, stopping where you want and generally having a greater degree of control over the time spent in port.

This chapter also cautions about the danger of runaway onboard spending. Passengers need to be realistic about what a cruise is likely to cost—not just the advertised list price—and compare the cost of their chosen cruise with available alternatives. After all of the add-ons many do not find a cruise as economical as they thought it would be. Spending is of course under the control of the individual so if you do go on a cruise it is within your ability to stay within your budget. The danger of course is temptation. Perhaps advance knowledge and warning can provide some inoculation.

Finally, with the interchangeability and close proximity of many cruise ports passengers need to be prepared for itinerary changes. These may result from operational problems with a ship (e.g., engine problems that cause it to cruise at slower speeds), from weather, from a cruise line's decision to substitute one port for another or from a cruise line's efforts to influence a port. Regardless, a published itinerary is not guaranteed. A passenger needs to be prepared for a cruise to go to different places than planned. According to the cruise contract, the cruise line has this right and has no liability for the consequences to passengers. Most of the changes are relatively minor—substituting one port for another—though others can be dramatic. The itinerary for a 2003 Norwegian Cruise Line cruise from Dover was changed at the last minute to include Amsterdam, Norway and Germany instead of ports calls to St. Petersburg, Helsinki and Talinn (Estonia). A number of cruise itineraries from Boston and New York have similarly been changed from the Caribbean to Canada because of hurricanes—passengers embark with clothes for the warm south and are unprepared for the climate to which they are taken. These changes not only impact passengers but also the ports whose calls are cancelled.

Chapter 6

Our International Crew Is Here to Serve You

Cruise lines project the diversity of their crew as though it were by design to give passengers an "international" experience. To the contrary, most cruise ships employ crew and staff based on who applies. While there are consistently high numbers of Filipinos across the industry, the remaining crew (except officers) is drawn from dozens of countries. In some cases this wide mix reflects a cruise line's preferences (e.g., East India, Indonesia, Eastern Europe), but it is mostly dependent on which labour market provides people willing to work for the remuneration offered. Many workers come from developing countries. The main attraction is money; the possibility of earning $400 to $500 a month (even if it is less than the International Labour Organization's minimum wage for seafarers) is an offer that many can't refuse. They and their families can live like royalty on that kind of money. But they quickly learn that working on a cruise ship stands in stark contrast to the glamour and indulgence on the passenger side of the ship.

The corporations that own the ships, though headquartered in the U.S. and/or U.K, are registered off shore. Carnival Corporation (with ten brands, including Princess Cruises, Holland America Line, Carnival Cruise Line, Costa Cruises and Cunard Line) is registered in Panama; Royal Caribbean Cruises Limited (with its five brands) is registered in Liberia; and Star Cruises (owner of Norwegian Cruise Line) is registered in Bermuda. These three corporations account for 95 percent of the North American market. Foreign registry provides many benefits, including avoidance of corporate taxes. The savings are significant. In 1999, estimates of lost tax revenues to the U.S. from Carnival Corporation were in the half billion dollar range; Florida was losing more than $40 million per year (Frantz 1999c: 14).

Flags of Convenience and Labour

These foreign registered corporations also register their ships off shore, often with a "flag of convenience." Foreign registries provide protection from burdensome income taxes, U.S. labour laws and many other regulations. The ship is effectively governed by the laws of the country where it is registered, and the flag state has responsibility for enforcement of international regulations and conventions. Flags of convenience severely limit employees' recourse to U.S. or other courts in disputes over wages or a workplace injury.

Ship registry is big business and is competitive. Royal Caribbean shifted all of its ships to the Bahamian registry in 2004, claiming this was a means to streamline the management process for all shipboard operations. But the real motive was economic. Not only did the cruise line save on the cost of registration, but the change also affected about 400 shipboard employees covered by collective bargaining agreements, required by the Norwegian International Ship Registry. The cruise line said it planned to keep compensation levels for those employees at or above their current levels during a two-year transition period set to end in January 2007.

Workers on foreign-flagged vessels often work without union protection, and with their pay determined by the employer. They may even have to accept cuts in pay to keep their jobs. In the view of Paul Chapman, a Baptist minister who founded the Center for Seafarer's Rights in New York in 1981, the typical cruise ship is a sweatshop at sea. "A ship owner can go any place in the world, pick up anybody he wants, on almost any terms. If the owner wants to maximize profit at the expense of people, it's a piece of cake." (Reynolds and Weikel 2000: T-5). Though the requirement to pay minimum wage was extended to ships registered in the United States in 1961, Congress left intact the exemption for foreign ships. This exemption was further defined in a 1963 Supreme Court decision that held that U.S. labour laws, including the right to organize, do not apply to foreign vessels engaged in American commerce even if the owners of these ships are from the United States. This is the context in which the modern cruise ship industry developed and took hold.

U.S. Congressional Interest

Working conditions on cruise ships emerged as a momentary concern in the late 1980s and early 1990s. William Clay, Chair of the House Labour–Management Subcommittee of the Education and Labour Committee of the House of Representatives, introduced legislation to extend the *National Labour Relations Act* (NLRA) and the *Fair Labour Standards Act* (FLSA) to foreign-flagged cruise ships operating primarily in the United States (see House of Representatives 1994: 1). At hearings in October 1989, the Committee was told of exploitation of sailors, who had no redress for grievances about their working conditions. Reverend James Lingren, the director of the New England Seaman's Mission, specifically described conditions in the cruise ship industry:

> We have discovered that on several of the largest cruise ship lines calling in U.S. ports a typical seafarer works 100 hours each week with no days off during his one year of employment. Many of them work without benefit of anything resembling a true contract of employment. They often earn less than 75 cents an hour.... I personally saw the contract of... [a] seafarer who signed for $192

a month to work for seven days a week for one year. He was to be paid overtime for any hours over eight hours a day, and while he was required to work 12 hours a day, the company refused to pay the overtime. This meant he was effectively making 53 cents an hour. When he complained he was relieved of his duties and sent home. (House of Representatives 1994: 3)

The Subcommittee approved the bill in the summer of 1990, but it never went any further. It was reintroduced in the next Congress on February 27, 1991, and again died in Committee.

On March 30, 1993, Clay introduced H.R. 1517, another version of the same legislation. Hearings were again held; they yielded no new information. However, for the first time the cruise industry, through its main lobbyist, the International Council of Cruise Lines (ICCL), threatened that if the House of Representatives passed the legislation the cruise industry would be forced to relocate to non-U.S. ports. In testimony before the Subcommittee on Labour Standards on May 13, 1993, the president of the ICCL, John Estes, stated:

> Some have told you that we will not relocate. I am here to tell you that this industry will relocate if the Bill is passed. It won't happen all at once, but it will happen. (Estes 1993)

He pointed out the ease with which cruise ships can be moved from one homeport to another and that

> in order to keep international costs competitive we do in fact on occasion move from country to country. International shipping will always seek a hospitable economic and political climate from which to operate.... It would be an unfortunate failure of United States policy not to recognize that homeports are unimportant to passengers. (Estes 1993)

The legislation this time made its way to the floor of the House of Representatives, but it failed to be heard by the full House and died with the end of the Congress.

Pro-industry legislation introduced in 1995 by Representative Don Young had much greater success. He attached a tort reform measure to the Coast Guard Reauthorization Bill passed on May 9, 1995. The amendment, referred to by Young as a "noncontroversial manager's amendment," was for the most part written by the ICCL (Glass, 1996: 1). It raised a number of concerns.

For one thing, the amendment limited the rights of foreign seafarers to sue in U.S. courts for grievances against foreign cruise lines. This went against the stream of court cases taken up by the U.S. Government several years earlier. In 1991, the U.S. Equal Employment Opportunity Commission (EEOC) won two cases against foreign-flagged cruise vessels. In one, the court enjoined a foreign cruise line from discriminating on the basis of sex against any actual or potential job applicant. In the other, NCL was charged with sex discrimination by an assistant cruise director who alleged she lost her job after becoming pregnant, and with discrimination by race and national origin by a bar manager who says he was forced to resign. NCL disregarded two subpoenas, claiming the EEOC lacked jurisdiction. NCL won in the U.S. District Court in Miami, but the decision was reversed by the U.S. Court of Appeals in Atlanta, which affirmed the EEOC's jurisdiction. This was a dangerous precedent for the cruise industry, and Young's amendment gave them an out.

There were two other provisions in the amendment. One was designed to protect ship owners from unlimited liability in suits brought by passengers or crewmembers who were harmed by medical malpractice at a shoreside facility. The other, directed at mounting claims from injuries and sexual assaults, limited liability to passengers and crew for "infliction of emotional distress, mental suffering or psychological injury" unless negligence or an intentional act could be proven. This was discussed in chapter two.

The final version of the legislation followed intense lobbying by opponents to the amendments and by the cruise industry. As finally passed, the legislation allows a cruise line sued by one of its workers in regard to treatment at a U.S. health facility or doctor's office to invoke an award cap allowed medical practitioners under the laws of the state in which the care is provided. The provision limiting seafarer's use of U.S. courts was replaced with a provision that seafarer employment contracts can block the worker from seeking legal remedies in U.S. courts (Glass 1996: 1). This provision has crept into seafarer employment contracts and has thus far been ruled enforceable by U.S. courts.

U.S. Courts and Labour

There is a long history of court cases where cruise ship workers have successfully sought relief in cases of, among other things, breach of contract, injury and death. Claims have often been under the *Passenger Vessel Services Act* (also known as the *Jones Act*) or the federal *Seaman's Wage Act*. But access to the U.S. courts appears to be waning for seafarers on foreign-flagged cruise ships that operate out of U.S. ports.

A federal court decision issued in October 2003 and upheld on appeal in January 2005 ruled that the families of Filipino cruise ship workers injured and killed during a 2003 boiler explosion aboard Norwegian Cruise Line's *Norway* had to resolve claims in the Philippines per their employment contract. The decision meant that claims for the eight crewmembers killed in the accident were limited to $50,000. This is considerably less than a U.S. court would likely award, especially given that the U.S. National Transportation Safety Board subsequently ruled that the accident, which also severely injured about twenty crewmembers, was the result of "deficient boiler operation, maintenance, and inspection practices of Norwegian Cruise Line, which allowed material deterioration and fatigue cracking to weaken the boiler" (NTSB 2007: 42).

The court's ruling had more far reaching consequences. It upheld employment contracts that require disputes to be resolved through arbitration and only in particular places—for Filipino workers the place is Manila. It also lent support to Carnival Cruise Lines' desire to have a clause inserted in its new crewmember contracts requiring all claims against the employer to be arbitrated internationally in London, Manila, Panama City or Monaco, whichever is closer to the crewmember's home.

Carnival Corporation included an arbitration clause in its settlement of a 2006 class action suit brought by workers claiming unpaid overtime. The clause requires crewmembers to arbitrate any future wage claims and waives their right to seek wages under the federal *Seaman's Wage Act*, and their right to arrest the vessel as security for wages. There had been other settlements in cases involving unpaid overtime to cruise ships workers—Norwegian Cruise Line was the first, followed by Royal Caribbean, Carnival and Princess. However, only the settlement with Carnival included the arbitration clause.

Regardless, arbitration clauses are becoming more commonplace, and they are effective in almost any situation. Take a case brought by a Filipino worker with Holland America Line, filed in U.S. federal court in Seattle, Washington, on April 27, 2007 (Case #C07-0645) and that sought class action status. The suit claimed the company illegally forced crewmembers to pay back the cost of airfare to and from the ships and fired them if they failed to do so. The worker was a bartender who had signed a standard twelve-month contract with the cruise line. He received a monthly guaranteed salary of $442 (inclusive of overtime, vacation pay and allowances) and was required to repay $212 per month for "deployment costs"—leaving a net income of $230 per month. Deployment costs include round trip air fare, uniforms, medical exams, visas, recruiting costs and union dues.

The U.S. court refused to hear the case given terms of the employment contract between the crewmember and the cruise line; it referred the case to the Philippines for arbitration. The arbitration board ruled in favour of the individual claimant, but there was no basis on which it could certify a class action claim. The cruise line benefits because the penalties assessed by an arbitration board are small by comparison to those historically garnered through the U.S. courts and it avoids a payout to other workers in the same situation.

Life Below Passenger Decks

Long hours of work is a common part of employment on a cruise ship. The typical dining room waiter works a minimum seventy-seven hours per week (eleven hours per day), plus potentially another ten or more hours overtime. They likely get the required ten hours' rest in a twenty-four-hour period, but except for six hours overnight, the remaining time (which includes the time needed for bathing and other personal care requirements) is broken up with work assignments. This pace of twelve-hour days, seven days a week, continues for months—up to twelve months on some cruise ships.

A similar pace of work is maintained in most positions in the hotel department onboard the ship; some in the deck and engine department more typically work ten hours per day. Officers and bridge staff tend to work at least twelve hours per day. Workers in the galley have reported working more than sixteen hours per day, but this is not common. These long hours and other issues with working conditions were the focus of a "Sweatships" campaign launched in September 2002 by the International Transport Workers Federation and U.K.-based War on Want. The campaign had some impact on public awareness.

There is some variation in the nature of employment contracts. Not surprisingly, officers and senior management are paid more and have shorter contracts (three or four months) than those they supervise. However workers in many positions have pay scales and contract lengths based solely on the country from which they come. Most cruise lines pay higher salaries and give shorter contracts (five or six months versus ten or twelve months) for the same positions when filled by European workers versus Asian, Mexican or South American workers. Consequently, two people working side by side in the exact same position are paid different salaries and work under different conditions solely because of where they were born. These basic inequities can exacerbate already existing racial and ethnic tensions.

Though it varies widely, the pay on cruise ships is generally low for what the job involves. A waiter or room steward on a Holland America Line ship, where gratuities are centrally collected through a service fee, earned in 2006 an annual guarantee of $17,316 ($1,443 per month, approximately $4 per hour). At the same time, an assistant baker earned an annual guarantee of $11,424 ($952 per month, approximately $2.85 per hour) and a food service worker earned an annual guarantee of $6,885 ($442 per month, $1.34 per hour). In addition, workers have deployment costs of approximately $2,000 deducted from their income. This level of remuneration is relatively consistent across the industry. Those in unskilled labour positions earn $500 or less per month; semi-skilled and skilled workers can earn $1000 or more.

A study done by the International Transport Workers Federation in 2000 found more than half of cruise ship workers reported a monthly income of less than $1000; 16 percent earned less than $500. Of those surveyed, 19 percent earned between $1000 and $14,999, 17 percent between $1,500 and $1999, and 12 percent earned over $2000 (Klein 2002: 135). Wages today have probably not increased significantly. To the contrary, most service workers, who previously depended on tips, report earning less under the new system, where gratuities are centrally collected as a service fee.

Income earned is only one issue. Most workers secure their job through a recruiting agent. Though International Labour Organization (ILO) regulations prohibit agents from collecting fees from the worker—they are supposed to be paid by the employer—workers are often required to pay to secure a position. These fees can amount to as much as $4,000. According to the International Transport Workers Federation, Filipinos normally pay $1,500 to join a ship (ITF 2000: 17). A 1997 story in the *Wall Street Journal* cites a Croatian worker who paid $600 to an agent to confirm his employment. In addition, he started work with a $1,400 debt to Carnival Cruise Lines, which had advanced the cost of his transportation to the ship (Prager 1997: B1). In February 2000, an article in the *Miami New Times* described a cook on Carnival Cruise Lines' *Paradise* who had given a Bombay agency $2,000, which included airfare. That sum, much of which he borrowed from relatives, is almost one-third of the $7,000 he will make during his ten-month contract (Nielsen 2000). And in 2001 it was reported that an agent in Rumania was charging $500 to interview for a position with Norwegian Cruise Line; if the person is hired an additional $1,000 was required to secure the position (Klein 2002: 128).

The recruitment fees and deployment charges remain the financial reality for many of those securing employment on a cruise ship. They present a particular problem for workers who go into debt to pay them; the worker is effectively forced to work in order to pay the debt. Their choices are limited even when situations become difficult.

If the hours and issues of remuneration were not challenging enough, workers onboard find themselves in a system that is strictly hierarchical and in which there are clear lines of authority and responsibility. Supervisors expect obedience to their authority, something easily enforced given how easily they can terminate a worker's employment and send them home. Officers are revered and obeyed, especially by members of the crew. Holland America Line, for one, reinforces the line between officers and service staff with its traditional use of Dutch officers and Indonesian workers, thereby replicating onboard the colonial relationship. Other cruise lines are more subtle but they create a similarly hierarchical system.

The hierarchy is even reflected in food budgets. A premium cruise line that sells itself on its high quality dining in 2008 allocated $12.40 per day per passenger for food and $8 per day per officer. The food budget for each crewmember was $4.20 per day, less if there were cost overruns for passenger food. In contrast to the dozens of choices given to passengers and officers, crewmembers were served four different items for lunch and dinner plus steamed rice. The crew mess rarely had fresh fruits or vegetables, though very occasionally there was an apple. Some suspect crew galleys of preparing poor quality food purposely so that the crew won't eat as much; lower consumption saves money and means less work. Crew dissatisfaction with food is not unique to a single line. Another large premium cruise line completed a fleet-wide survey of its onboard crew. Compared to an average approval rating of 70.1 percent for accommodations, crewmembers' approval rating for food quality was 54.8 percent. The assessment of food was the lowest rated item in the company-sponsored sixty-five-item survey.

The hierarchy is further reinforced by cultural stereotypes. Some cultures favour light over dark skin, and this plays out in the onboard social hierarchy, often in odd and uncomfortable ways. The *Miami New Times* interviewed a worker on a Carnival Cruise Lines ship:

> "We are black. Sometimes there is some kind of discrimination on-board." For example he claims some light-skinned security guards act like prison wardens. "As soon as we put on reggae music [in the crew bar], the guards come and turn it off," he says. "They come and treat us like we're in jail or something. We're not making any trouble." Guards also hassle him when he is off-duty and passing through the hotel portion of the ship. "If I stand too long in the public area, the security guard comes along and asks, What you doin'?" A lot of bullshit goin' on…. You have some crew members who don't like black people. You expect it from the passengers, but not from the crew. (Nielsen 2000)

Skin colour can be a factor in opportunities for advancement and in the job roles that are available. One cruise line prohibited dark-skinned people who worked as busboys from becoming a waiter. Another cruise line replaced Filipino wine stewards with workers of European descent, believing the different optics would influence the dining experience and presumably increase wine sales.

Cultural attitudes about sex and gender also influence employment. Citing the diverse cultural perceptions among crewmembers on a cruise ship, Greenwood (1999: 3) says a "possible risk factor is their cultural view of male/female interaction and what constitutes sexual harassment and unwanted attention." Greenwood was referring to sexual harassment and assault of female crewmembers, a problem that is an ongoing concern for most women working on cruise ships.

A glimpse is given by comments made by a fifty-four-year-old woman who worked at the ship's gift shop on the *Crystal Harmony*. She had instituted a lawsuit against Crystal Cruises claiming the she had been fired for refusing the captain's advances. She says that from the start, she saw that parties and love affairs were common among crewmembers.

> But more disturbing, she said, was how the ship's top brass hit on stewardesses and other lower-ranking crewmembers.... One ship stewardess confided... that she was "stressed" over sleeping with 31 crewmembers. And she heard that an officer tried to hang himself after finding his girlfriend in bed with the ship's doctor.... She also said she once encountered the captain and a stewardess in a sex act below deck. (*SF Gate News* 1998)

The woman characterized the cruise ship as a more blatant sexually promiscuous environment than she had ever seen and said, "The officers and captain think they can take liberty with anyone.... Nobody wants to complain, because they would lose their job" (*SF Gate News* 1998). Such behaviour, often role modelled by senior officers, is defined as acceptable by the onboard culture. Things are improving on some ships, but changing such a culture takes time. There are two necessary elements: officers must serve as positive role models and there must be universal intolerance for any form of sexual harassment or sexual assault.

Prospects for Collective Action

Most cruise ship workers are technically represented by a seafarers' union or association, but on a practical level this means nothing to individual workers. Most, especially those in the hotel department, are not aware of any union affiliation. And the unions are not the type to engage in collective bargaining while using the threat of job action as a means for enforcing their demands. Cruise ship workers don't collectively negotiate or approve a collective agreement.

The International Transport Workers Federation (ITF) model contract for cruise ship workers is used by some lines, at least in part. ITF has also come to the aid of workers left stranded on cruise ships that have been abandoned or where a company has gone bankrupt, and in the early 2000s it ran a cruise ship campaign from an office in Port Canaveral and internationally advocated for the rights of women working on cruise ships. Conditions on cruise ships have not improved much in recent years and certainly not to the extent that they would in a traditional labour-management environment with collective bargaining. But cruise ships, with their international crew and foreign registration, present a unique situation. There are only a few cases where cruise ship workers have attempted collective action and in none have they been successful.

In 1981, 240 Central American workers went on strike aboard a Carnival Cruise Lines ship in Miami to protest the firing of two co-workers. The strike ended quickly when the company called the U.S. Immigration and Naturalization Service, declared the strikers illegal immigrants, bussed them to the airport and flew them home (Reynolds and Weikel 2000: T-5). Similarly, in January 1986 Norwegian Cruise Line solved a sudden labour dispute aboard *Norway* by loading fifty-five South Korean, Jamaican and Haitian room stewards on buses at the Port of Miami and sent them back to their home countries. Workers quickly come to learn, "on cruise ships, supervisors often tell seafarers who complain, 'If you don't like it here, you can go home.' Since the seafarer already paid for the return trip, the threat is real and the seafarers know it will be carried out at their expense" (Chapman 1992: 56). The mediating effects of diversity combined with the threat of losing their job if they complain are effective mechanisms for maintaining social control and obedience.

Two Perspectives

Many who take a job on a cruise ship hope to earn a living and see the world. What they often experience is quite different. It isn't only that there is less money than expected—a situation that worsened with the devaluing U.S. dollar in 2007—but the hours are long and there isn't much chance to see the world. Most find they have limited time left after work and sleep. With contracts that run as long as ten or twelve months, it is understandable why some workers say cruise ship employment is like being in prison. They are living and working in an authoritarian institution that has control over their time and over the nature of their day. Each day is much the same as the day before and the day after. In the end a cruise ship is a job, workers do what they must to earn the income promised, and they don't think about time until their time before going home is short. The system is well stratified, with workers from many countries filling the full range of positions required to operate a cruise ship; many of the occupational roles require limited skills (i.e., galley workers, janitors, deck hands) and have low levels of remuneration.

Passengers see the international nature of the crew in positive terms, even though each passenger meets relatively few crewmembers in their time on the ship. For them the cruise ship is the chosen venue for their vacation, and crewmembers, like in other hospitality settings, are there to provide service. This is consistent with the marketing used by most cruise lines—passengers are enticed by promises of pampering and exemplary service. There is little thought about the plight of the workers who pamper and even less aware-ness that the ability to sell a cruise for prices that are relatively lower than most land-based options is based in large part on low labour costs afforded by the international crew. Workers in Alaska have a minimum wage of $7.15 an hour; in Canada minimum wage ranges from $7.25 to $8.37 an hour. Workers on foreign-flagged cruise ships operating in Alaska and Canada's Pacific and Atlantic waters pay some workers less than $1.50 an hour; many earn less than $3.00 an hour.

Chapter 7

Rethinking Cruise Vacations

Is a cruise the idyllic and perfect way to spend a vacation? The advertising promises unlimited food, lots of entertainment and activities and a price that is hard to beat when compared to analogous land-based vacation options. We are assured a cruise ship is safe, that it is environmentally clean and that it brings an economic boom to ports, which just love to welcome the ships and their passengers. And many are dazzled by a crew that is internationally diverse and which they are told will pamper them. From all appearances one would be a fool not to jump at an opportunity for a cruise vacation. That is certainly the appearance given by the cruise industry and research findings say more than fifty million Americans say they would like to take a cruise in the next three years (CLIA 2007). But does a cruise deliver all of the wonderful things promised? The foregoing chapters suggest that may not be the case.

Rethinking as a Passenger

A number of issues must be considered by those thinking about or planning a cruise vacation. Safety and security are high on the list. Passengers need to treat with caution the cruise industry's claim that it is the safest form of commercial transportation. Both sexual assault and sexual harassment are known problems that the industry continues (ineffectively it appears) to deal with. There have also been disappearances under mysterious circumstances from cruise ships. Sex-related incidents and disappearances are not commonplace but they are no longer uncommon; they are certainly more frequent than the industry's mantra of safety suggests.

Passengers need to take care for their own personal safety and that of their children. Children should be supervised by parents, and there should be great caution when leaving children in the care of others or on their own. Adults (especially women) need to take the same precautions onboard a ship as they would in any major city. Try to not wander around on your own, especially late at night, and avoid situations that appear risky. Passengers should resist over intoxication given this may increase vulnerability to crime. They should also not allow others access to their drink so as to avoid it being drugged. A cruise can be a fun time but passengers need to avoid being misled into a false sense of security.

Another area in which passengers need to be cautious is around health and medical care. Despite industry claims that passengers bring illness with them, passengers need to assume norovirus is present and take all reasonable methods of prevention possible, at least if they want to ensure remaining healthy. Much of this involves common sense such as frequent washing of hands, good personal hygiene, avoiding foods that are handled directly by servers or passengers, or that are improperly refrigerated or inadequately cooked and being cautious with foods that are uncooked. It may not be possible to totally avoid becoming ill. If that happens keep in mind that the main health risk from norovirus is dehydration. Remain hydrated as best you can and ride the virus out for a day or two.

There are also cautions if a passenger requires medical care. Keep in mind that the physician and onboard medical services are provided for a fee and are not guaranteed by the cruise line. As the cruise line would say, they are provided for the passenger's convenience. The cruise line accepts no liability or responsibility for services rendered. As such, passengers should always keep in mind alternative providers for a second opinion, when possible. This may involve making contact with a physician in a port or making a phone call to their physician back home. For minor ailments this is likely unnecessary, but it is probably a prudent idea for anything serious or that raises more concern to you than to the onboard medical care provider. Although a health problem is unlikely, it is always a good precaution to have travel health insurance just in case. Most of these policies have other coverage that may be useful, including transport home should a passenger miss the ship in a port of call or be evicted from the ship by the cruise line.

The economics of a cruise are another area for concern. Cruises are no longer all-inclusive, which means passengers need to be cautiously aware of their spending while on the ship. The ease of signing for beverages and services makes it tempting to spend more than they planned or even thought was possible. As well, there are the onboard revenue centres that are ready to take a passenger's money.

A cruise passenger should weigh carefully the advantages and disadvantages of shore excursions sold onboard. A few hours of research on the internet is likely to give a good sense of what there is to see in a port of call, how best to see it and how best to get to sites or the beach from the ship. It is possible in many ports to arrange private tours in advance or to plan a tour without a guide. The advantage over the ship's pre-planned tour is that you avoid the crowd mentality, which characterizes group tours, avoid stops at unwanted locations (including stores) and you are free to be on your own schedule, and it may cost less. There are side benefits—the satisfaction of finding your way around a place on your own and knowledge that money spent is staying in the local economy.

The cruise contract is a sobering document and raises areas for concern.

It is legally binding and defines the landscape of a cruise vacation. Most relevant is its list of areas where the cruise line repudiates responsibility and liability. Of particular significance are a cruise line's non-liability for the actions of concessionaires or their employees and its right to change an itinerary without notice. It is essential to read the cruise contract before embarking. It defines the limits of the cruise line's responsibility and lays out what must be done if something goes wrong. In your own interest, it is important to document anything that happens onboard that could later lead to a claim. The cruise contract specifies the methods for notifying problems to the cruise line and time limits on those notifications. Keep in mind that travelling on a cruise ship is like going on foreign territory; the ship is registered somewhere other than North America and the cruise line itself is foreign-registered.

There are also moral concerns about cruises. Issues around environmental practices and disregard for responsible stewardship of the ocean environment are high on this list. In contrast to claims of leadership and responsibility, a history of environmental violations and the volume of waste produced cause concern about the cruise industry. The issue comes down to how conscientious you believe the industry should be in its protection of the environment. It is easy to expect cruise ships to be highly conscientious based on the industry's rhetoric, but the words are quite different than industry practice and cruise ship behaviour. You must decide whether a cruise ship is a morally viable, environmentally responsible vacation mode.

In addition the cruise industry brings to attention a number of social justice concerns. Are workers being treated fairly and are they being paid a wage that is equitable? Similarly, are ports being treated fairly and is their share of cruise tourism equitable? These are questions that need to be confronted by cruise passengers as well as by ports: do you support an economic structure that has been appropriately referred to by some as a "sweatship." As regards labour, a cruise ship is very similar to sweatshops found on land, with their long hours of work, low levels of pay and authoritarian workplace. For ports, a cruise ship is a mixed blessing. It offloads large numbers of human cargo with open wallets, but it also brings a greedy corporate structure that collects a portion of the money spent. The moral question is whether we as passengers participate in supporting such an unjust and exploitative system. The answer is made difficult because passengers benefit from a less expensive vacation as a result of the socially unjust practices.

Rethinking as a Port

Ports have their own set of concerns when it comes to cruise tourism. One, as already mentioned, is the distribution of passenger spending ashore and onboard. Ports need to think more like businesses when it comes to the cruise industry. This means driving a harder bargain, such that a greater proportion of money spent in the location remains there. It also means charging port fees that are consistent with the cost of running a port. An obvious fear is that if one port does this then cruise ships will instead go to another port nearby. Given that likelihood it is imperative that ports work together and avoid being played off against one another for the benefit of the cruise industry. This is particularly important in places like the Caribbean, the inside passage of British Columbia and Atlantic Canada.

Another consideration for ports is that land-based tourism provides considerably more spending and income per person than cruise ship passengers. While cruise ships bring more people in a short period of time, land-based venues bring guests who sustain spending over a longer period of time. In Belize, for example, stayover visitors account for 90 percent of the employment in the tourism sector even though they represent only 25 percent of tourist arrivals. Ports need to make conscious decisions about which sector to grow (cruise versus stayover), with full information available to them. Many ports have found that passenger numbers can reach a point where they negatively impact the traditional stayover visitor.

This interaction is particularly important to consider when a port city is faced with large investments for cruise tourism. As most ports know the infrastructure needed for cruise tourism (piers, terminals, capability to accommodate a large number of people for a short period of time) is different than for stayover tourism. The latter depends on hotels and resorts, restaurants, recreational facilities (including beaches) and/or historical, cultural and other sights. Investments by a port in cruise tourism should be viewed in contrast to the benefit of a similar investment in other forms of tourism. In other words, which provides the best economic reward for the local economy and local employment—cruise tourism or stayover tourism? Ports also need to realize that they have some power and do as Port Everglades did when the cruise line called for improved facilities: negotiate a deal where the cruise line pays for it directly with increased passenger fees.

Admittedly it is realistic for cruise tourism to exist side-by-side traditional stayover tourism. The key is to find a balance between the two. The exact proportions and numbers will vary widely by destination size, infrastructure, economy and location. Seasonal destinations may have different tolerances than those that are year-round. Destinations that are large and spread out may comfortably accommodate a larger number of cruise passengers than destinations that consist of a historic centre or is a small geographic area. The answer is to be found in each individual community. But the community must first inoculate itself from being mesmerized by the cruise industry's promises of huge economic returns and by the grandeur and opulence of the ships that visit. Realism about the benefits and about the costs of cruise tourism is essential.

Ports must also be realistic about their attractiveness as a cruise destination. Some places by virtue of their location are assured business no matter what they do—the ports in British Columbia's inside passage are a good example given U.S. cabotage laws requiring a foreign port in cruises to Alaska. Others are in a geographic location that makes it difficult to attract cruise ships; St. John's, Newfoundland, for example, fits well in transatlantic itineraries but is too far east to include in most east coast itineraries. In locations like the Caribbean there are a variety of factors that make a port more or less attractive. Spending in St. Thomas has always been high because U.S. travellers have a higher duty-free limit there than elsewhere in the Caribbean and cruise ships stop there for that reason. Other islands have natural beauty and pristine beaches or have manufactured themselves as a cruise destination. In setting expectations for cruise tourism ports need to carefully consider the competition (i.e., other ports) and what they have to offer. As mentioned already, ports maximize their benefits if they work cooperatively with other ports, no matter whether they are a large popular port or a small burgeoning port.

Rethinking as a Crewmember

Employment on a cruise ship poses a serious quandary. Most workers are attracted by the income to be made. Even those in low paying jobs are likely earning significantly more than they would at home. It is an ideal setup. The cruise line gets cheap labour and most of the workers feel like they are being paid well, at least until they experience first-hand the work environment on a cruise ship. There are the hours and pace of work—working for as long as a year without a day off and with little time to themselves during that year. But there is also the absence from friends and family and, for many, not being home to experience their child's birth and childhood. Cruise ship workers often say they are sacrificing so that their children will have a better life and greater opportunity.

Incomes on cruise ships vary widely. Those in unskilled positions may be paid as little as $400 a month, in skilled positions as much as $1,200 or $1,500 and in service positions (such as waiters and room stewards) as much as $2,000 a month. Deduct from this the cost of uniforms and other expenses (especially the cost of telephone calls home), as well as expenses such as Holland America Line's $200 a month deployment costs or repayment of money advanced by a recruitment agent back home. Despite these costs, the income offered by a cruise line may still appear attractive. But there are other issues that need to be considered.

One issue is lifestyle. A cruise ship is a contained environment. Many workers have little or no contact with passengers. They work their twelve- or fourteen-hour days and otherwise hang out in the crew bar, recreation areas below deck or their room. By company policy, those who do have passenger contact have strict limitations on their access to passenger areas and on their freedom to engage in social chit chat with passengers. Though they have a better deal insofar as they see the light of day and may even get a breath of fresh air, they are still working fourteen hours a day and are left to spend their remaining time in crew-restricted areas. They spend their leisure time with other crewmembers or on their own. As any crewmember will tell there is a mini society among crew, the nature of which varies from ship to ship depending on ethnic and racial mixes and management style and practices. Women on all ships must be aware of the problem of sexual harassment and assault and in advance have strategies for how they plan to deal with it.

Another issue relates to rights. Cruise ship workers must accept that their options are limited when there is a dispute over work conditions, over remuneration or when they suffer an injury in the workplace. Traditionally these cases could be heard by U.S. courts for workers on ships operating out of U.S. ports, but things have changed. Increasingly these disputes must be referred to arbitration, a system that puts the worker at a disadvantage, given that they are unlikely to be able to afford representation by counsel and that the benefits awarded are predefined by the employment contract. This includes payment for injury or disability. Included in the standard employment contract for Filipino workers is a complete schedule of payments for every possible disabling injury. As mentioned earlier, the maximum payment for workers who died in the boiler blast on Norwegian Cruise Line's *Norway* in 2003 was $50,000.

None of this is meant to tell a person not to work on a cruise ship. Rather, it is important that those who choose to work on a cruise ship make their choice with full knowledge about what they are getting into. There are admittedly many who return for multiple contracts and who do relatively well. Some tell of using their income to put children through school; others talk about saving enough to open a business or restaurant at home. It is a hard work life but one that is manageable as long as they are prepared and know what to expect.

What the Future Holds

There is no reason to believe the cruise industry will change significantly in the near future. Their business model is sound and pays off. They keep costs low through their labour practices and their relationships with ports and suppliers and maintain an enviable profit level, which is buoyed further by innovations in generating onboard revenue. This is particularly the case with new ships being built, especially Royal Caribbean's Genesis-class, but also for large new ships being built by Carnival and Norwegian. Over the next decade we are likely to see many of the older and smaller cruise ships replaced by newer behemoths, with all the imaginable amenities and attractions. The ships have become a sea-based resort.

As new ships arrive in North America and Europe the older ships will be redeployed to markets that are emerging: Asia, South America (especially cruises marketed to South Americans), Spain, Australia, New Zealand and areas of the Mediterranean. Many ports and areas will see double-digit growth in cruise passenger numbers and will be faced with issues around managing cruise tourism and maximizing the benefits derived by the local economy and community. It is in the early stages of development that a port has the greatest chance of establishing a fair and equitable relationship with cruise corporations.

One issue for some may be cruise industry ownership of a local or regional port. This is likely to be the wave of the future, and it has serious financial implications for ports and port communities. From the cruise industry's perspective ownership and development of cruise terminals is good business, especially when ports are willing to give away as much as they are. A time is foreseeable when a cruise ship's itinerary could only be comprised of locations where the cruise line owns the port facilities and a stop at the cruise line's private island. The business model may be good for the cruise industry, but it is not necessarily in the best interest of passengers and ports.

Another issue is the industry's old tonnage. These are ships that often have not been upgraded with regard to environmental systems and practices. Thus, the same corporation that makes grand claims about its responsible environmental practices in Alaska or California may be discharging nasty effluents in others parts of the world, where environmental sensitivities or regulations may not be so great or may not be enforced. It is commendable that the industry has improved its environmental practices in areas of North America. Governments and consumers now need to ensure that the same practices are put in place industry-wide and that it be done sooner than later.

Some may say that the necessary changes will come in due time, that we should trust the industry to do the right thing. The problem is that we may not have as much time as the industry is likely to take. We've seen in the past with regard to environmental practices that behaviour is best influenced by legislation, along with monitoring and enforcement. The industry will attempt to get away with whatever it can, which means that governments (with consumer support) need to clearly define limits. Alaska took the first small step. It is time for other governments to follow suit with more comprehensive environmental regulations and enforcement schemes.

Governments also need to address the issue of onboard crime. The cruise industry has ineffectively dealt with sexual assaults onboard cruise ships even though this has been a problem for more then a decade. Instead of addressing and resolving the issue, the industry continued to claim the ships are safe and has largely ignored solutions. Given that passengers are at risk for crime and that the cruise industry has shirked its responsibility for dealing with it, it is incumbent upon governments to either take responsible for the security of their citizens or to at the very least clearly advise their nationals of the risks associated with cruise travel. We can be sure that a government's threat to make a public advisory that cruise travel is unsafe would be enough to kick the industry into immediate action that largely solves the problem. That would give them an economic motivation. But for now since crimes against Americans are rarely prosecuted, it is highly unlikely that crimes against other nationals will be pursued at all and all of this (though supposedly reported to the FBI) is kept outside the public's view. The cruise lines are fine with passengers not having a right to know the history of each cruise ship in order to assess the relative risk associated with one cruise ship versus another. It is about time for these things to change.

Appendix

Cruise Ship Calls, Victoria, British Columbia, 2007

A. Summary of Data

Dates / # Ships	Daytime vs Evening	# Hours of Call	Other Cdn ports	# of calls	# of Pax	Total Pax*
Before 18 May						
12 ships	79% daytime 21% evening	Average 9.1	Average 1.2	14	Average 2,093	29,298
18 May – 15 September						
8 ships	11% daytime 89% evening	Average 6.1	Average 0	123	Average 1,962	241,294
16 September – 3 November						
15 ships	74% daytime 26% evening	Average 8.5	Average .70	27	Average 1,962	52,964
Summary	27% daytime 73% evening	Average 6.8	Average .20	164	Average 1,973	323,556

B. Early Season (Before May 18)

Cruise Line • Ships	Time of Port Call	# Hours of Call	Other Cdn ports	# of calls	# of Pax	Total Pax
Celebrity						7,740
• Infinity	8:00–17:00	9	2	1	2,000	2,000
• Mercury	7:00–17:00	10	1	2	1,870	3,740
• Summit	8:00–17:00	9	1	1	2,000	2,000
Holland America						5,528
• Oosterdam	8:00–17:00	9	1	1	1,840	1,840
• Zuiderdam	8:00–23:59	16	1	1	1,848	1,848
• Oosterdam	18:00–23:59	6	1	1	1,840	1,840
Norwegian (NCL)						2,200
• Norwegian Pearl	7:00–16:00	9	1	1	2,200	2,200
Princess Cruises						7,220
• Diamond	8:00–17:00	9	1	1	2,670	2,670
• Golden	19:00–23:59	5	0	1	2,600	2,600
• Sun	17:00–23:59	7	0	1	1,950	1,950

Cruise Line • Ships	Time of Port Call	# Hours of Call	Other Cdn ports	# of calls	# of Pax	Total Pax
Royal Caribbean						6,610
• Radiance	7:30–17:00	9.5	1	1	2,500	2,500
• Serenade	7:00–18:00	11	2	1	2,110	2,110
• Vision	10:00–18:00	8	1	1	2,000	2,000
Summary: 12 ships	79% daytime 21% evening	Average 9.1	Average 1.2	Total 14	Average 2,093	Total 29,298

C. Mid Season (May 18–September 15)

Cruise Line • Ships	Time of Port Call	# Hours of Call	Other Cdn ports	# of calls	# of Pax	Total Pax
Holland America						94,324
• Amsterdam	18:00 – 23:59	6	0	18	1,380	24,840
• Noordam	18:00 – 23:59	6	0	18	1,918	34,524
• Oosterdam	18:00 – 23:59	6	0	19	1,840	34,960
Norwegian (NCL)						39,600
• Norwegian Pearl	18:00– 23:59	6	0	18	2,200	39,600
Princess Cruises						107,370
• Dawn	7:00 – 14:00	7	0	11	2,670	29,370
• Dawn	12:00 – 19:00	7	0	2	2,600	5,200
• Golden	19:00 – 23:59	5	0	18	1,950	35,100
• Sapphire	8:00 – 17:00	9	1	1	2,600	2,600
• Sun	17:00 – 23:59	7	0	18	1,950	35,100
Summary: 8 ships	11% daytime 89% evening	Average 6.1	Average 0	Total 123	Average 1,962	Total 241,294

D. Late Season (September 16 – November 3)

Cruise Line • Ships	Time of Port Call	# Hours of Call	Other Cdn ports	# of calls	# of Pax	Total Pax
Celebrity						22,700
• Infinity	7:00–16:00	9	2	1	2,000	2,000
• Mercury	7:00–17:00	10	1	9	1,870	16830
• Mercury	8:00–17:00	9	0	1	1,870	1,870
• Summit	8:00–16:00	8	1	1	2,000	2,000

Cruise Line • *Ships*	Time of Port Call	# Hours of Call	Other Cdn ports	# of calls	# of Pax	Total Pax
Holland America						12,054
• *Amsterdam*	18:00–23:59	6	0	1	1,840	1,840
• *Oosterdam*	18:00–23:59	6	0	1	1,848	1,848
• *Oosterdam*	8:00–23:59	16	1	1	1,840	1,840
• *Noordam*	18:00–23:59	6	0	2	1,918	3,836
• *Ryndam*	7:00–12:00	5	1	1	1,258	1,258
• *Zaanrdam*	8:00–17:00	9	1	1	1,432	1,432
Norwegian (NCL)						6,440
• *Norwegian Pearl*	18:00–23:59	6	0	1	2,200	2,200
• *Norwegian Star*	8:00–17:00	9	1	1	2,240	2,240
• *Norwegian Sun*	8:00–16:00	8	1	1	2,000	2,000
Princess Cruises						11,770
• *Dawn*	7:00–14:00	7	0	1	1,950	1,950
• *Diamond*	8:00–17:00	9	1	1	2,670	2,670
• *Golden*	1900–23:59	5	0	1	2,600	2,600
• *Golden*	8:00–17:00	9	1	1	2,600	2,600
• *Sun*	17:00–23:59	7	0	1	1,950	1,950
Summary: 15 ships	74% daytime 26% evening	Average 8.5	Average .70	Total 27	Average 1,962	Total 52,964

* number of passengers

References

ABC Radio News. 2006, June 26. Available at <www.abc.net.au/pm/content/2006/ s1672345.html>.

Adams, Margaret. 1990. "Rape Case Threatens Cruise Industry Image: Girl, 14, Says Crewman Assaulted Her." *Miami Herald* (Broward Edition), February 5.

Alaska DEC. 2004. *Assessment of Cruise Ship and Ferry Wastewater Impacts in Alaska.* Juneau: Alaska Department of Environmental Conservation.

Ando, T., J.S. Noel and R.L. Fankhauser. 2000. "Genetic Classification of Norwalk-like Viruses." *Journal of Infectious Disease* 181, Supp 2 (May).

Anglen, Robert. 2005. "Daughter Vanishes While on Alaskan Cruise." *Arizona Republic* November 10.

Archer, Jane. 2007. "Are Cruise Destinations Overcrowded?" *Daily Telegraph* November 19. Available at <www.telegraph.co.uk/travel/main.jhtml?xml=/ travel/2007/11/19/et-cruise-119.xml> (accessed November 19, 2007).

Ashworth, Jon. 2001. "A Ship That Thinks It's a Conference Centre." *London Times* July 14.

Associated Press. 2007. "Big Island Cruise Ship Visits to Drop, Eliminating Jobs." *Honolulu Advertiser* November 19. Available at <the.honoluluadvertiser.com/article/2007/Nov/19/br/br6219034785.html> (accessed November 19, 2007).

Babson, Jennifer. 2003. "As the Industry Booms, Key West Considers Limiting Some Cruises." *Miami Herald* January 5. Available at <www.maimi.com/mld/ miamiherald/4876455.htm> (accessed January 5, 2003).

Blake, Scott. 2003. "'Megaship' Set to Sail." *Florida Today* November 11. Available at <www.floridatoday.com> (accessed November 11, 2003).

Bluewater Network. 2002. "Luxury Cruise Lines Sued for Illegal Dumping: Lawsuit Aims to Halt Illegal Dumping of Ballast Water by Fun Ships in California Ports." Joint press release from Bluewater Network, Environmental Law Foundation, San Diego Baykeeper, and Surfrider Foundation, April 24. Available at <www. bluewaternetwork.org/press_releases/pr2002apr24_ss_ballastwater.pdf> (accessed April 25, 2002).

Bolt, Kristen Millares. 2007. "Cruise Line Sludge Could Go to County Waste Plant." *Seattle Post-Intelligencer* September 18. Available at <seatllepi.nwsource.com/ local/332246_port19.html> (accessed September 18, 2007).

Brannigan, Martha. 2008. "Who Uses Advanced Waste-Removal Technology?" *Miami Herald* February 3. Available at <www.miamiherald.com/1060/story/404319.html> (accessed February 4, 2008).

_____. 2007. "Widow Sues Carnival, Alleging Wrongful Death." *Miami Herald* October 26. Available at <www.miamiherald.com/business/story/284890. html> (accessed October 26, 2007).

Carter, Paul. 2006. "Nudity and Public Sex Out, Says P&O." *The Daily Telegraph* June 28. Available at <dailytelegraph.news.au/print/0,20285,19617407-1702,00.

html> (accessed June 28, 2006).

Carver, Kendall. 2007. "Crime Against Americans on Cruise Ships." Testimony Before the Committee on Transportation and Infrastructure, United States House of Representatives, Subcommittee on Coast Guard and Maritime Transportation, March 27. Available at <transportation.house.gov/Media/File/Coast%20Guard/20070327/Carver.pdf> (accessed March 30, 2007).

CATMAT. 2005. "Committee to Advise on Tropical Medicine and Travel: Statement on Cruise Ship Travel." *Canada Communicable Disease Report* 31, ACS 8 and 9 (October 15).

CDC. 2007. "Norovirus: Technical Fact Sheet." Atlanta: Centre for Disease Control. Available at <www.cdc.gov/ncidod/dvrd/revb/gastro/norovirus-factsheet.htm> (accessed November 12, 2007).

———. 2002. *Telebriefing Transcript: Outbreak of Gastrointestinal Illness Aboard Cruise Ships.* December 12. Available at <www.cdc.gov/od/oc/media/transcripts/t021212.htm> (accessed December 15, 2002).

Cerveny, Lee K. 2007. *Sociocultural Effects of Tourism in Hoonah, Alaska.* Portland, OR: U.S. Department of Agriculture (General Technical Report PNW-GTR-734).

CESD. 2007. *Cruise Tourism in Costa Rica & Honduras: Policy Recommendations for Decision Makers.* Washington, DC: Centre on Ecotourism and Sustainable Development.

———. 2006. *Cruise Tourism in Belize: Perceptions of Economic, Social and Environmental Impact.* Washington, DC: Centre of Ecotourism and Sustainable Development.

Chapman, Paul K. 1992. *Trouble On Board: The Plight of International Seafarers.* Ithaca, NY: ILR Press.

Chen, Stephanie. 2007. "Trouble at Sea: Free-Agent Doctors." *Wall Street Journal* October 24.

CINQ. 1998 "Who Said It." *Cruise Industry News Quarterly* (Winter).

CLIA. 2007. *Cruise Industry Overview: Marketing Edition—2006.* Available at <cruising.org/press/overview 2006/7.cfm> (accessed January 3, 2008).

CMC. 2007. "Beache Warns That Islands Need United Approach to Cruise Tourism." *CBC Barbados* October 23. Available at <www.cbc.bb/content/view/13018/45/> (accessed October 23, 2007).

CND. 1997. "Irreconcilable Differences and the Best Way to Make Money." *Cruise News Daily* September 2 (Issue 1060).

Constantineau, Bruce. 2007. *Vancouver Sun*, October 27. Available at <www.cananda.com> (accessed October 27, 2007).

Copeland, Claudia. 2007. *Cruise Ship Pollution: Background, Laws and Regulations, and Key Issues.* Washington, DC: Congressional Research Service.

Cramer, Elaine H., Curtis J. Blanton, George H. Vaughan, Cheryl A. Bopp and David L. Forney. 2006. "Epidemiology of Gastroenteritis on Cruise Ships, 2001–2004." *American Journal of Preventative Medicine* 30, 3 (April).

Cramer, Elaine H., David X. Gu and Randy E. Durbin. 2003. "Diarreal Disease on

Cruise Ships, 1990–2000." *American Journal of Preventive Medicine* 24, 3 (April).

Cramer, Kelly. 2006. "The Art of Piracy." *Broward–Palm Beach New Times* November 9. Available at <www.browardpalmbeach.com/2006-11-09/news/the-art-of-piracy/> (accessed November 9, 2006).

Dale, Terry. 2007. "Cruise Ship Security Practices and Procedures." Testimony Before the Committee on Transportation and Infrastructure, United States House of Representatives, Subcommittee on Coast Guard and Maritime Transportation, September 19. Available at <transportation.house.gov/Media/File/Coast Guard/20070919/Dale Testimony – follow up.pdf> (accessed October 20, 2007).

Davies. Lisa. 2006. "Police Seek Mystery Woman." News.com.au, June 14. Available at <www.news.com.au/story/print/0,10119,19461691.00.html> (accessed June 13, 2006).

Devine, Miranda. 2006. "Ship of Fools all at Sea After Throwing Decency Overboard." *The Sun-Herald* June 18.

Dishman, Laurie. 2007. "Laurie Dishman." International Cruise Victims Association website. Available at <www.internationalcruisevictims.org/LatestMemberStories/Laurie_Dishman.html> (accessed June 12, 2007).

Duncan, Philippa. 2007. "Sun Fails to Shine for Tourism Trade." *The Mercury* December 4. Available at <www.news.com.au/mercury/story/0,22884,22866932-5007221,00.html> (accessed December 4, 2007).

Dupont, Dale K. 2003. "Pollution Case Haunts Carnival." *Miami Herald* July 24. Available at <www.miamiherald.com> (accessed July 24, 2003).

Eagle, Nathan. 2008. "Cruise Ship Emission Restrictions Ahead." *The Garden Island* February 22. Available at <www.kauaiworld.com/articles/2008/02/22/news/news03.txt> (accessed February 22, 2008).

Elliot, Harvey. 2007. "Cruise Ships Threaten Seychelles." *The Times* October 18. Available at <travel.timesonline.co.uk/tol/life_and_style/travel/holiday_type/cruises/article2688149.ece> (accessed October 19, 2007).

EPA. 2007. *Draft Cruise Ship Discharge Assessment Report*. Washington, DC: U.S. Environmental Protection Agency (Report #EPA842-R-07-005).

Eriksen, Michael. 2006. "Love Boats on Troubled Waters." *Trial* 43, 3 (March).

Estes, John. 1993. *Testimony Before the Subcommittee on Labor Standards, Occupational Health, and Safety of the Committee on Education and Labor of the House of Representatives.* May 13. Washington, DC: GPO (Document # Y4 ED8/1 103-9).

Federal Trade Commission. 2002. *Statement of the Federal Trade Commission concerning Royal Caribbean Cruises Ltd/P&O Princess Cruises PLC and Carnival Corporation/P&O Princess Cruises plc, FTC File No. 021 0041, October 5, 2002.* Available at <www.ftc.gov/os/2002/10/cruisestatement.htm> (accessed October 5, 2002).

Fox. 2007. "Ship Pollution." Fox6 TV News, September 28. Available at <www.fox6.com/news/local/story.aspx?content_id=035d1bf9-7f1c-4071-b192-34d39846ae7a&rss=800> (accessed September 29, 2007).

Fox, James Alan. 2006. "Statement on Crime Aboard Cruise Ships." Testimony Before the Committee on Government Reform, United States House of Representatives, Subcommittee on National Security, Emerging Threats and International Relations. March 7.

Fox, Larry, and Barbara Radin Fox. 1995. "Anchored in the Docks." *Washington Post* October 8.

Frantz, Douglas. 1999a. "Gaps in Sea Laws Shield Pollution by Cruise Lines." *New York Times* January 3. Available at <www.nytimes.com/library/national/010399cruise-industry.html> (accessed January 31, 1999).

_____. 1999b. "Getting Sick on the High Seas: A Question of Accountability." *New York Times* October 31. Available at <www.nytimes.com/yr/mo/day/news/national/cruises-medical-care.html> (accessed October 31, 1999).

_____. 1999c. "Lawmakers Want I.R.S. Help on Cruise Ships and Tax Laws. *New York Times* March 15.

_____. 1998. "On Cruise Ships, Silence Shrouds Crimes." *New York Times* November 16. Available at <www.nytimes.com/library/national/111698cruise-ship-crime.html> (accessed July 14, 1999).

Gadher, Dipesh. 2001. "Cruise Liners Face Tougher Hygiene Tests." *Sunday Times* May 6. Available at <www.timesonline.co.uk/tol/global/> (accessed May 6, 2001).

GAO. 2004. *Maritime Law Exemption: Exemption Provides Limited Competitive Advantage, But Barriers to Further Entry under US Flag Remain.* Washington, DC: General Accounting Office (Doc # GAO-04-421).

Glass, Joel. 1996. "Compromise on US Cruise Tort." *Lloyd's List* October 1.

_____. 1993. "Two held for Cruise Death." *Lloyd's List* March 4.

Gorecki, Karen, and Bruce Wallace. 2003. *Ripple Effects: The Need to Assess the Impacts of Cruise Ships on Victoria B.C.* Victoria: Vancouver Public Interest Research Group.

Greenwood, Don. 1999. "Reducing Sexual Assaults on Cruise Ships: Risk Assessment and Recommendations." Unpublished consultant's report. June 7.

h.b. 2007. "Costa Calida Liners Leave Little in Cartagena." *Typically Spanish* May 10. Available at <www.typicallyspanish.com/news/publish/printer_10395.shtml> (accessed May 10, 2007).

Herz, Michael, and Joseph Davis. 2002. *Cruise Control: A Report on How Cruise Ships Affect the Marine Environment.* Washington, DC: The Ocean Conservancy.

Hilton, Spud. 2007. Cruise Briefing: Passengers Now Charged Fee Just to Leave the Ship." *San Francisco Chronicle* August 12. Available at <www.sfgate.com/cgi-bin/article.cgi?file=/c/a/2007/08/12/TR6GRA5QO.DTL&type=printable> (accessed August 12, 2007).

Hokstam, Marvin. 2002. "Cruise Ship with Sick Passengers Abandons Visit to St. Maarten." *Miami Herald* December 10. Available at <www.miami.com> (accessed December 15, 2002).

House of Representatives. 1994. *Coverage of Certain Federal Labour Laws to Foreign Documented Vessels.* (House Report #103-818). Washington, DC: GPO.

Hudson, Lynette. 2007. "Richard Liffridge." International Cruise Victims website. Available at <www.internationalcruisevictims.org/LatestMemberStories/Richard_Liffridge.html> (accessed September 2, 2007).

Hughes, Peter, and Bernice Davidson. 2005. "Will Big Ships Sink Small Islands?" *Daily Telegraph* May 21. Available at <www.telegraph.co.uk/travel/732845/Will-big-ships-sink-small-islands.html> (accessed May 21, 2005).

Huie, Nancy. 1995. "The Business of Shopping." *Cruise Industry News Quarterly* (Summer).

ICCL. 2002. "ICCL Medical Facilities Guidelines Policy Statement (updated January 1, 2002)." Available at <www.iccl.org/policies/medical2.htm> (accessed January 5, 2002).

_____. 1999. "ICCL Environmental Statement." Press release, July 27. <iccl.org/pressroom/press13.cfm> (accessed July 31, 1999).

Inside Edition. 2008. "Cruise Art Auctions: Great Bargain or Lousy Deal?" *Inside Edition* February 11. Available at <www.insideedition.com/news.aspx?storyID=1284> (accessed February 12, 2008).

ITF. 2000. "The Dark Side of the Cruise Industry." *Seafarers' Bulletin* 14.

Johnston, Jane, and Steve Gration. 2008. "Coastlines, CAGS and Communications." Media International Australia, in press. Available at <www.uq.edu.au/emsah/mia/>.

King County Wastewater Treatment Division. 2007. *Cruise Ship Wastewater Management Report.* Seattle: Department of Natural Resources and Parks.

King, David. 2006. "Plan to Throw Cruise Victim Overboard." *The Sunday Times* March 18. Available at <www.sundaytimes.news.com.au> (accessed March 18, 2006).

Kissel, Ted B. 2000. "The Deep Blue Greed." *Miami New Times* February 3–9, 2000. Available at <www.miaminewtimes.com/issues/2000-02-03/news/feature3.html> (accessed February 6, 2000).

Klein, Ross A. 2007a. "The Politics of Environmental Activism: A Case Study of the Cruise Industry and the Environmental Movement." *Sociological Research Online* 12, 2 (March). Available at <www.socresonline.org.uk/12/2/klein.html> (accessed May 5, 2007)

_____. 2007b. "Crime Against Americans on Cruise Ships." Testimony Before the Committee on Transportation and Infrastructure, United States House of Representatives, Subcommittee on Coast Guard and Maritime Transportation, March 27. Available at <transportation.house.gov/Media/File/CoastGuard/20070327/Klein.pdf> (accessed March 28, 2007).

_____. 2005a. *Cruise Ship Squeeze: The New Pirates of the Seven Seas.* Gabriola Island, BC: New Society Publishers.

_____. 2005b. *Playing Off the Ports: How BC Can Maximize Its Share of Cruise Tourism.*

Vancouver: Canadian Centre for Policy Alternatives. Available at <www.cruise-junkie.com/ccpa3.pdf> (accessed August 31, 2005).

_____. 2003a. *Cruising—Out of Control.* Ottawa: Canadian Centre for Policy Alternatives. Available at <www.cruisejunkie.com/ccpa2.pdf> (accessed August 31, 2005).

_____. 2003b. *Charting A Course: The Cruise Industry, the Government of Canada, and Purposeful Development.* Ottawa: Canadian Centre for Policy Alternatives. Available at <www.cruisejunkie.com/ccpa.pdf> (accessed August 31, 2005).

_____. 2002. *Cruise Ship Blues: The Underside of the Cruise Industry.* Gabriola Island, BC: New Society Publishers.

Klein, Ross A., and Kathleen M. Halley. 2001. "Jumping Ship." *Doctor's Review* 19: 4, (April).

Korten, Tristram. 2000. "Carnival? Try Criminal: What Happens When a Female Passenger is Assaulted on a Cruise Ship? Not Much." *Miami New Times* February 3–9. Available at <www.miaminewtimes.com/2000-02-03/news/carnival-try-criminal> (accessed February 5, 2000).

Krohne, Kay. 1999. Unpublished consultant's report examining current efforts of Royal Caribbean Cruises Ltd. in the area of preventing sexual harassment and assault. May 26, 1999.

LaMendola, Bob, and Tom Steighorst. 2002. "Cruise Line Blames Passengers for 3rd Viral Outbreak on Ship." *Sun-Sentinel* November 12. Available at <www.sun-sentinel.com/news/yahoo/sfl-rxship12nov12,0,6638757.story?coll=sfla percent2Dnewsaol percent2Dheadlines> (accessed November 12, 2002).

Liffridge, Victoria. 2007. "Richard Liffridge." International Cruise Victims Association. Available at <www.internationalcruisevictims.org/LatestMemberStories/Richard_Liffridge_2.html> (accessed June 15, 2007).

Lindesmith, Lisa, Christine Moe, Severine Marionneau, Nathalie Ruvoen, Xi Jiang, Lauren Lindblad, Paul Stewart, Jacques LePendu and Ralph Baric. 2003. "Human Susceptibility and Resistance to Norwalk Virus Infection." *Nature Medicine* 9, 5 (May).

Londner, Robin. 2003. "Oceana, Royal Caribbean Argue Over Sewage." *The South Florida Business Journal,* July 21, Available at <southflorida.bizjournals.com/southflorida/stories/2003/07/21/daily8.html> (accessed July 21, 2003).

MAIB. 2006. *Report on the Investigation of the Fire Onboard Star Princess off Jamaica 23 March 2006.* (Report No 28/2006). Southampton, UK: Marine Accident Investigation Branch.

Marusic, Zrinka, Sinisa Horak and Renata Tomljenovic. 2007. "The Socio-Economic Impacts of Cruise Tourism: A Case Study of Croatian Destinations." *Proceedings of the 5th International Coastal and Marine Tourism Congress: Balancing Marine Tourism Development and Sustainability* (ed. Michael Luck et al.). Auckland: AUT University.

Matsui, Doris. 2007. "House Resolution Aims to Decrease Crime Rates on Cruise

Ships: Americans to Be Safer At Sea." Press release, September 18. Available at <matsui.house.gov/Newsroom.asp?ARTICLE2939=9228&PG2939=3> (accessed October 18, 2007).

McAllister, Bill. 2000. "A Big Violation on Wastewater: Some Ship Readings 100,000 Times Allowed Amount." *The Juneau Empire* August 27. Available at <juneau-empire.com> (accessed August 27, 2000).

McCartney, Juan. 2007. "Measure to Improve Spend of Cruise Visitors." *The Bahama Journal* December 21. Available at <www.jonesbahamas.com/print. php?a=15240> (accessed December 21, 2007).

McClure, Robert. 2007. "Cruise Line's Dumping Fine Inflated—But It Pays It Anyway." *Seattle Post-Intelligencer* January 24. Available at <seattlepi.nwsource. com/local/300871_cruise24.html> (accessed January 24, 2007).

_____. 2006. "Celebrity Cruises Asks for Leniency in Fine." *Seattle Post-Intelligencer* December 20. Available at <seattlepi.nwsource.com/local/296572_cruise20. html> (accessed December 20, 2006).

_____. 2003. "Cruise Ships Not Using Low-Pollution Fuels After All." *Seattle Post-Intelligencer* September 11. Available at <seattlepi.nwsource.com/local/139108_ cruise11.html> (accessed September 12, 2003).

MMWR. 2002. "Outbreaks of Gastroenteritis Associated with Noroviruses on Cruise Ships—United States 2002." *Morbidity and Mortality Weekly Review* 51, 49 (December 13).

_____. 2001. "Norwalk-Like Viruses." *Morbidity and Mortality Weekly Report* 50, RR-9, (June 1).

Moewe, M.C. 2005. "Disappearances Leave Mystery." *Business Journal of Jacksonville* June 3. Available at <www.bizjournals.com/jacksonville/stories/2005/06/06/ story1.html> (accessed July 4, 2005).

Montgomery, Christina. 2007a. "Setting Out to Sea in an Eco-Friendly Ship." *The Province* May 31. Available at <www.canada.com/theprovince/news/money/ story.html?id=304a40a5-4fd8-4996-a0ee-a1d3bfdaa571> (accessed May 31, 2007).

_____. 2007b. "Cruise-ship Pollution Initiative Actually Contributes to Problem." *The Province* October 7. Available at <www.canada.com/theprovince/news/ story.html?id=438279ef-ec5e-42b0-a582-3cce6a54df75> (accessed October 15, 2007).

Morgan, Spencer. 2003. "Virus Gives Cruise a Sinking Feeling." *New York Daily News* September 1. Available at <www.nydailynews.com> (accessed September 2, 2003).

Murray, Thomas J. 2005. *The Impacts of the Cruise Ship Industry on the Quality of Life in Key West.* RFQ No: 04-001, City of Key West Naval Properties Local Redevelopment Authority.

National Research Council. 1995. *Clean Ships, Clean Ports, Clean Oceans: Controlling Garbage and Plastic Wastes at Sea.* Washington, DC: National Academy Press.

Nielsen, Kirk. 2000. "The Perfect Scam: For the Workers Life Is No Carnival, Believe It or Not." *Miami New Times* February 3–9.

NTSB. 2008. *Marine Accident Report: Heeling Accident on M/V Crown Princess, July 18, 2006.* Washington, DC: National Transportation Safety Board (Report #MAR-08-01). Available at <www.ntsb.gov.Publictn/2008/MAR0801.htm> (accessed January 11, 2008).

_____. 2007. *Marine Accident Brief: Boiler Rupture on Bahamian Cruise Ship S.S. Norway, Port of Miami, May 25, 2003.* Washington, DC: National Transportation Safety Board (Report #MAB-07/03). Available at <www.ntsb.gov/publictn/2007/MAB0703.htm> (accessed November 30, 2007).

_____. 1998. *Marine Accident Report: Fire on Board the Panamanian Passenger Ship Universe Explorer in the Lynn Canal Near Juneau, Alaska, July 27, 1996.* Washington, DC: National Transportation Safety Board. (Report #MAR-98/02)

OCTA. 2006. *Science Panel Recommendations to the International Council of Cruise Lines.* Washington, DC: Conservation International.

OECD. 2003. *Voluntary Approaches to Environmental Policy: Effectiveness, Efficiency, and Usage in Policy Mixes.* Paris: Organization for Economic Co-operation and Development.

O'Hara, Timothy. 2004. "Protesters Cruise Lower Duval." *Key West Citizen* March 12. Available at <keysnews.com/280021664867615.bsp.htm> (accessed March 12, 2004).

Oliphant, Jim. 1999. "When the Fun Stops." *Miami Daily Business Review* July 14. Available at <www.floridabiz.com> (accessed July 15, 1999).

Orlich, Angela. 2007. "Cruise Ship Security Practices and Procedures." Testimony Before the Committee on Transportation and Infrastructure, United States House of Representatives, Subcommittee on Coast Guard and Maritime Transportation, September 19, 2007. Available at <transportation.house.gov/Media/File/Coast Guard/20070919/orlich testimony – follow up.pdf> (accessed October 20, 2007).

Palarino, R. Nicholas, and Pat DeQuattro. 2005. *Hearing Memorandum: International Maritime Security, Subcommittee on National Security, Emerging Threats and International Relations, U.S. House of Representatives, December 8.*

Peisley, Tony. 2003. "Shore Excursions Make Impressive Profits." *Cruise Business Review* December 5.

Perez, Evan. 2003. "Carnival Fires Pollution Auditors Over False Compliance Reports." *Wall Street Journal* August 28.

Plunkett, Nagra. 2007. "Government of Jamaica Keen on Negril Cruise Ship Port." *Jamaica Gleaner* December 5. Available at <www.jamaica-gleaner.com/gleaner/20071205/news/mews1.html> (accessed December 5, 2007).

Prager, Joshua Harris. 1997. "For Cruise Workers, Life Is No 'Love Boat'." *Wall Street Journal* July 3

PWC. 2001. *Economic Contribution of the F-CCA Member Lines to the Caribbean and Florida.*

Price Waterhouse Coopers, July 27. Available at <http://f-cca.com/downloads/exsummary.pdf> (accessed March 5, 2003).

Reid, David. 2007. "Earth's Eighth Continent." *The Tyee* November 21. Available at <thetyee.ca/News/2007/11/21/PacificGarbagePatch/> (accessed November 21, 2007).

Reynolds, Christopher. 1995. "Into the Beckoning Arms of Paying Port Merchants." *Los Angeles Times* September 17.

Reynolds, Christopher, and Dan Weikel. 2000 "For Cruise Ship Workers, Voyages Are No Vacations." *Los Angeles Times* May 30.

Richards, Susan. 1991. "Pestered at Sea." *Los Angeles Times* December 1.

Rose, David. 2007. "Cruise Ship Sails into Storm over Whitening Botch." *The Times* November 23. Available at <www.timesonline.co.uk/tol/life_and_style/health/article2926268.ece> (accessed November 23, 2007).

Schmidt, Kira. 2000. *Cruising for Trouble: Stemming the Tide of Cruise Ship Pollution.* San Francisco: Bluewater Network. Available at <www.bluewaternetwork.org/reports/rep_ss_cruise_trouble.pdf> (accessed November 12, 2001).

Seatrade Insider. 2007. "Envisioning the Future of On-Board Revenue." Seatrade Insider News March 17. Available at <www.cruise-community.com/ShowStory.asp?ID=11447> (accessed March 18, 2007).

_____. 2006. "Cruise Victims 'Address' Security Hearing." Seatrade Insider News March 7, 2006. Available at <www.cruise-community.com/ShowStory.asp?ID=9125> (accessed March 7, 2006).

_____. 2004. "Changing Face of Lines' Investment in Ports." Seatrade Insider News June 7. Available at <www.cruise-community.com> (accessed June 7, 2004).

Senes, Yurji. 1999. "Cruise Line Settles Suit by Ex-Worker Citing Rape." *New York Times* December 5.

SF Gate News. 1998. "Former Employee Claims Luxury Liner Allowed Sexually Charged Working Environment." *SF Gate News* December 7. Available at <www.sfgate.com/archive/1998/12/07/state0125EST0098.DTL> (accessed December 24, 1998).

Shanghai Daily. 2007. "Ship Owners Fight Greek Fine." *Shanghai Daily* June 22. <www.shanghaidaily.com/article/2007/200706/20070622/article_320574.htm> (accessed July 2, 2007).

Shaw, Gillian. 2007. "Cruise Ships on Pollution Hot Seat." *Vancouver Sun* June 2. Available at <www.canada.com/vancouversun/news/business/story.html?id=061e69de-6406-4699-9f82-029ccb52b2f8> (accessed June 2, 2007).

Shipping Gazette. 2007. "HAL to Cancel all Norwegian Itineraries from 2009." *Shipping Gazette* June 19. Available at <shipgaz.com/news/index.php> (accessed June 19, 2007).

Singh, Alita. 2007. "First Pile Driven for New Mega Cruise Ship Pier." *The Daily Herald* December 28. Available at <www.thedailyherald.com/news/daily/k190/port190.html> (accessed December 28, 2007).

Sloan, Gene. 2007. "Cruise Smoking Bans Clouded by Complaints." *USA Today* September 6. Available at <www.usatoday.com/travel/news/2007-09-06-cruise-smoking-bans_N.htm?csp=34&POE=click-refer>.

Smart, G. 2004. "Stormy seas ahead." *MSNBC,* January 29. Available at <msnbc.msn.com/id/3860856/> (accessed February 1, 2004).

Starmer-Smith, Charles. 2008. "Flying Three Times Greener than Cruising." *Daily Telegraph* January 19. Available at <www.telegraph.co.uk/travel/main.jhtml?xml=/travel/2008/01/19/et-cruise-green-119.xml> (accessed January 20, 2008).

Sullivan, William M. 2007. "Cruise Ship Security Practices and Procedures." Testimony Before the Committee on Transportation and Infrastructure, United States House of Representatives, Subcommittee on Coast Guard and Maritime Transportation, September 19. Available at <transportation.house.gov/Media/File/Coast Guard/20070919/Sullivan follow up.pdf> (accessed October 20, 2007).

Supreme Court of Florida. 2007. *Carnival Corporation vs. Darce Carlisle, Case No. SC 04-393,* February 15.

Sys-con Media. 2005. "Princess Cruise Possible Sold Fake 'Picasso' and Fake 'Miro' at Sea Auctions." Available at <au.sys-con.com/read/101684_p.htm> (accessed June 20, 2005).

Tjaden, Tracy. 2002. "Cruise Lines Blasted: Tourism-industry Funded Oceans Blue in Hot Water Following Critical Report on Industry." *Business in Vancouver* (Issue 681), November 12–18. Available at <www.biv.com> (accessed November 13, 2002).

Topham, Gwyn. 2006. *Overboard: The Stories Cruise Lines Don't Want Told.* Sydney: Random House Australia.

U.S. Bureau of Transportation Statistics. 2002. "Summary of Cruise Ship Waste Streams." Available at <www.bts.gov/publications/maritime_trade_and_transportation/2002/html/environmental_issues_table_01.html> (accessed July 6, 2005).

Wagner, Dennis. 2007. "Gullible Travels: Art Sales at Sea." *Arizona Daily Star* April 9. Available at: <azstarnet.com/sn/printDS/177533> (accessed April 9, 2007).

Waymer, Kim. 2007. "Ships' Soot Deadly, Study Shows." *Florida Today*, November 17. Available at <www.floridatoday.com/apps/pbcs.dll/article?AID=/20071117/BUSINESS/711170345/1003> (accessed November 17, 2007).

Weiss, Ken. 2003. "Cruise Line Pollution Prompts Legislation." *Los Angeles Times*, August 18. Available at <www.latimes.com> (accessed August 18, 2003).

Widdowson M-A., A. Sulka, S.N. Bulens, R.S. Beard, S.S. Chaves, R. Hammond, et al. 2005. "Norovirus and Foodborne Disease, United States, 1991–2000." *Emerging Infectious Disease* 11, 1 (January). Available at <www.cdc.gov/ncidod/EID/vol11no01/04-0426.htm> (accessed November 3, 2007).

Wilson, Carla. 2008. "Tax Funded Cruise Ship Facilities in Shaky State." *Times Colonist*

February 19. Available at <www.canada.com/victoriatimescolonist/news/ business/story.html?id=66c609dc-7f9d-4b69-9c02-4280c4c5584d&k=94826> (accessed February 19, 2008).

_____. 2004. "Campbell River Sets Sights on Cruise Ship Visits." *Times Colonist* July 13. Available at <www.canada.com/victoria/timescolonist/index.html> (accessed July 13, 2004).

Yamanouchi, Kelly. 2003. "Cruise Lines Admit Pollution Violations." *Honolulu Advertiser*, December 12. Available at <the.honoluluadvertiser.com/article/2003/ Dec/12/bz/bz02a.html> (accessed December 12, 2003).

Yancey, Kitty Bean, 2001. "Cruise Lines Draw Profits from Selling Works of Art." *USA Today* February 9. Available at <www.usatoday.com/travel/ vacations/2001/2001-02-09-cruise-auctions.htm> (accessed February 10, 2001).

Yoshino, Kimi. 2007. "Cruise Industry's Dark Waters: What Happens at Sea Stays There as Crimes on Liners Go Unresolved." *Los Angeles Times* January 20. Available at <www.latimes.com/business/la-fi-cruise20jan20,1,6485727. story?track=crosspromo&coll=la-headlines-business&ctrack=1&cset=true> (accessed January 20, 2007).

Index